NATIONS OF THE MODERN WORLD

ENGLAND	W. R. Inge
SCOTLAND	Sir Robert Rait & George S. Pryde *Revised by* G. S. Pryde
AUSTRALIA	J. C. Horsfall
FRANCE	P. E. Charvet
ISRAEL	Norman Bentwich
ITALY	Gerardo Zampaglione
SA'UDI ARABIA	H. St. John Philby
SOUTH AFRICA	J. H. Hofmeyr *Revised by* J. P. Cope
THE SUDAN	Sir Harold MacMichael
TURKEY	G. L. Lewis

NATIONS OF THE MODERN WORLD

ITALY

ITALY

By

GERARDO ZAMPAGLIONE

LONDON
ERNEST BENN LIMITED

First Published 1956 by Ernest Benn Limited
Bouverie House · Fleet Street · London · EC4
Printed in Great Britain

Contents

MAP

Chapter 1

Italians and their Land

IT HAS been said that Italy is a geographical expression. Prince Metternich, the Austrian statesman, is responsible for this definition, which shows how little he knew of Italian affairs and how incapable he was of foreseeing the future of the country stretching south of the Hapsburg Empire. For, while many different features can be found in her, it is nevertheless a fact that Italy, geographically, is not an expression, but an extremely solid reality. This territory, in which centuries of history have been enacted, possesses a unique individuality. Perhaps only an island such as England could have a more clearly defined character. The ancients were obviously aware of this when they agreed that the peninsula, surrounded in the North by the Alps and on three sides by the Mediterranean Sea, formed one single unity known by the name of 'Italia'. This appears in ancient charts, such as Ptolemy's map and Peutinger's Tabula, both of which were drawn during the early centuries of the Christian era. The same idea was expressed poetically in those famous lines in which Italy is defined as the 'beautiful land which the Apennines part and the sea and the Alps surround'.

The most appealing feature for visitors coming from distant lands is the 'classic' environment in which people move, things are done, and the country progresses. This environment, composed of so many elements, can hardly be described. Undoubtedly there is something exciting in walking down a Roman road and looking at ruined buildings, where twenty centuries ago people were living, thinking, suffering, or rejoicing. The physical aspects of the land, the warm, clear atmosphere, the luminous and restful lines of the hills (which certainly inspired Roman architecture), the picturesque coastline, the nature and colour of trees and plants, such as the olive tree and the grapevine, are intimately related to a tradition which we usually call 'classic'. Such features are to be found especially in the South. There the elements of the past have not yet disappeared before the advance of the mechanical age; people live nearer to

Nature, according to a pattern similar to that found among the early inhabitants who gave birth to Roman culture and civilisation. Seldom has Nature so much influenced the people of a country, their ways of thinking and feeling, of worshipping and working. The Roman Empire, Catholicism, and the Renaissance, all of which originated in Italy, bore the mark of this environment.

Not far from Rome, on the Tyrrhenian coast, a short promontory stretches into the sea. This is the Circeius Mons. Legend has it that in the caves still to be found in its hills lived Circe, the sorceress, who turned Ulysses' companions into animals. Everyone for whom history and art have some appeal should visit the spot. There are no special ruins or monuments, but one can admire an unspoiled Mediterranean scene, where the sea, the sky, the rocks blend in a visual and spiritual ensemble. The visitor's interest will also be stirred by the thought that recent excavations have revealed human remains as ancient as those of Neanderthal Man. The district is indeed one of the cradles of mankind. Probably the main attraction of such resorts as Capri, Amalfi, Sorrento near Naples, or Portofino and Rapallo near Genoa lies in this 'classic' appeal and in the special mood it evokes. How otherwise could one explain the love for Italy felt by gifted men like Byron and Shelley, Axel Munthe and Ezra Pound, and the effects which the environment had on them and their literary production?

Equally appealing are the memories of early Christianity. It is difficult not to sense the moral impact of a religious tradition nearly 2,000 years old, to which our civilisation is in so many ways indebted. It is impossible not to feel some emotion upon viewing the Roman catacombs, when one realises that it was in their caves that the Christian faith developed and grew, despite persecution. It has been said that Catholicism is a Mediterranean religion in the sense that much of its ritual and liturgy reflects the sentiments and the ways of Mediterranean people. This may or may not be true, but certainly in Italy, more than in any other country, one may receive a complete and most impressive vision of the pageantry and ritual which mean so much to the Catholic mind. If the traveller is seeking religion, he will certainly find it in Italy. For prayer and meditation he should go to the mountain recesses of Umbria and Tuscany, where everything speaks of the tradition of St. Francis of Assisi and his preaching of gentleness and love; if it is the testimony of earlier times, when faith and martyrdom often went hand in hand, he will find it in the early basilicas, in the silent chapels, and the long corridors of the catacombs. If, finally, he is searching for exaltation of the Lord through the perfection of art, then Rome, Florence, Venice, Milan, and practically every town, large and small, will show him their unsurpassed artistic treasures, accumulated over the centuries by a people which has always worshipped God in terms of beauty.

For the visitor of a more practical mind, to whom art and literature appeal less than technical progress, Italy may also speak an impressive language. For the age of research and science would not have come into being had it not been for the cultural movement which spread from Italy to the rest of Europe and is known as the Renaissance. As this name clearly indicates, it was a rebirth, not only of the arts, but in every field of thought, practical and spiritual, religious and scientific. Leonardo da Vinci (1452–1519) was the prototype of a man of that epoch and there was no field of knowledge to which he did not direct his speculation. The same can be said of so many other Italians. The testimony to their lifelong studies and works is to be found in the buildings they erected, in the books they wrote, in their conception of life, contrasting so much with those of previous eras. The business-minded visitor may think that the Italian approach to business is not the one he deems best, possibly because it is one to which he is not accustomed, but can he forget, while visiting the ancient trading cities of Lombardy, Tuscany, or Liguria, that it was here that such modern institutions as banking, insurance, and commercial law originated?

The main difficulty in trying to give an outline of Italy's way of thinking is to reveal clearly the contrasting aspects of the country's and the people's life, different facets of the same reality, in which the natural versatility of the race is reflected. Some of these contradictions may be exemplified here. Milan is proverbially one of the most up-and-doing cities, yet it is also one of the most artistically minded and the place where the best art exhibitions are held. Rome is a city of art and history where one would think that people would be content to live in indolent adoration of the past; on the contrary, it is a place where industry has developed, and it has become one of the busiest spots in the country. The South, where industry is relatively undeveloped, might give the impression that people are not interested in mechanical progress; yet when they have the right opportunity of dealing with modern methods they become excellent mechanics and skilled workers. Love, wine, and song are certainly associated with and appreciated by Italians, but these are not their principal interest. The merchants and industrialists hate to be conventional or superficial, but are eager to get busy and do things. Achievement is their keyword. Among the working classes one may find refinement, at times reaching a degree of sophistication. The Italians are considered optimists and to be people who like easy living; nonetheless they tend to represent depressing aspects of daily life. This is proved by the themes chosen for their films, which have won worldwide recognition. They are considered egotists, always trying to have their say and to impose their way of thinking; yet their minds are open to moral and intellectual influences from abroad. Some are slow-moving, while others are constantly searching out new ways of life, new kinds of employment, and seem to be the incarnation of restlessness. Some would never leave their villages, yet others make excellent sailors and emigrants, and there is practically no large city in the world in which an Italian community may not be found. They are generally considered devoted to their families, and the great majority are profound believers, yet their attitude towards religion induced Erasmus to say that they are all atheists. The Church enjoys an extensive influence, yet Italy has the strongest Communist party outside the Iron Curtain. Even compromise between Communism and religion, although condemned by the Church, is, nevertheless, justified in many a community, where the Communist-elected mayor takes part officially in the processions organised by the Catholic hierarchy. So it is with political inclination. Everybody seems interested in politics, and electioneering may be a colourful affair with everybody taking part in the game, yet the people feel suspicion for anyone who runs for Parliament or is making a career of politics. The Italian is generally humorous, but may become the victim of solitude and easily lose his cheerfulness. These and more contradictions are to be found in the Italian character, but many common features remain, and all of them bear the signs of ingenuity, honesty, self-respect, and humanity.

Spreading south from the Alps into the Mediterranean, Italy is at once in contact with Central Europe and yet remote from it. She is regarded as a southern European country, but if one considers the Mediterranean and the North African continent as a single unity with the rest of Europe, then her position is more central. In ancient times, when the Mediterranean was the most important region of the known world, this position was of even greater significance than now and Italy was looked on as the land from which any movement towards material or moral expansion was bound to get its impulse. Unlike the Greeks or the Phoenicians, who became mainly trading and maritime peoples, the Romans at first took but slight advantage of the sea. Their origins were rural, their way of life that of a peasantry, tied to the soil, but capable of using weapons of war whenever it was necessary. Thus, Roman expansion took place by land, and naval battles, such as those against Carthage, were episodes in wars bound to be decided on some continental battle-ground. As late as the time of Augustus, when they had achieved a position without precedent in the world, forming an empire which is still an inspiring example of statesmanship, the Romans knew that all they had achieved had been possible because of their rural qualities, which made of them sound soldiers and capable builders. They would not have succeeded in governing so many countries, and their movements would not have been so quick and unpredictable, if they had not enjoyed the special freedom of centrality. Troops could in fact be moved from one region of the Empire to another, without endangering its over-all security. The strategical move that Roman troops performed so ably, by which a unit of soldiers could be switched from one battle-front to another, was probably inspired by the position of their land.

It is no mere coincidence that Christianity, although born in the Near East, eventually ended by centralising its organisation in Rome. At the beginning of the Christian Era Rome was not only the principal administrative city of the Empire, but it also possessed lines of communication with every part of the known world. In a highly centralised State such as this the spiritual conquest of its capital was a guarantee of world-wide success.

It should, however, be pointed out that while the central geographic position of the country has been advantageous, it has also caused much harm. When Italy lacked political unity and was split into many small States, European armies fought their battles on her plains for continental supremacy. The Po Valley provided France and Austria with a suitable arena in which to practise the principles of the art of war. Later, during Napoleonic times, it was the stage on which the Corsican General won his first battles; again, during World Wars I and II extensive fighting took place in this same area. For this reason, all major Powers, from the downfall of the Roman Empire to the last century, have tried to establish a firm foothold in it. Political unification was therefore long retarded because European statesmen feared that the formation of a centralised State in the South could reverse these centuries-old policies. Only when the balance of power changed was it possible to unify the country through the leadership of Piedmont, the little northern monarchy, which, on account of its position, was called 'the doorkeeper of the Alps'. This was the fate of the northern plains in Italy, the ones which are most intimately linked to the rest of continental Europe.

Of no less importance is the peninsular region spreading south in the Mediterranean Sea. If continental Italy has been connected with wars for European supremacy, the rest of the peninsula proper, together with the islands of Sicily and Sardinia, has played a decisive role in Mediterranean equilibrium. For centuries this famed sea has been the main artery for the peoples of the earth. Across its blue waters innumerable migrations and conquests have taken place, sometimes westwards, sometimes eastwards. Peninsular Italy has always been there, cutting the sea into two basins approximately equal in size. The port of Messina in Sicily is equidistant from Gibraltar, Suez, and Odessa.

The strategic importance of easy access to the sea and to Africa was understood all through medieval times, for it was frequently from Italian ports and harbours that the Crusaders embarked for the Orient. After the cutting of the Isthmus of Suez in 1869, the Mediterranean became a short route to India and other Asiatic countries. In 1870, with the achievement of political unity, Italy found herself immediately at the centre of disputes for Mediterranean supremacy. England understood this from the beginning and made it a point of her diplomacy to be on friendly terms with the newly formed State. Italy reciprocated this friendliness towards the greatest naval Power of the times, realising that, by holding the keys of Gibraltar and Suez, England was in a position to close the sea in which she was contained. During World War I the consequences of this policy were evident. Complete supremacy in the Mediterranean was achieved due to Anglo-Italian co-operation, and the Austrian navy was compelled to seek refuge in recesses of the eastern Adriatic coast.

Except during ancient times, when the Mediterranean was considered a Roman lake, and during the medieval period, when maritime republics such as Venice, Genoa, Pisa, and Amalfi flourished and spread widely their commercial connections, Italy, although a sea-minded Power, has never enjoyed complete maritime freedom, because the Mediterranean is a closed basin. From the discovery of America in 1492 to the present era, the Italians have deeply felt this sense of containment.

The Alps dominate the north of Italy, their highest peak being Mont Blanc, the 'Monarch of the mountains', as it was called by Lord Byron (15,782 feet). Their watershed forms the dividing line between Italy on one side and France, Switzerland, and Austria on the other. Towards Yugoslavia this natural boundary is not so sharply marked. Therefore, since 1918, when this country came into being, fixing a border has always been a difficult task.

Despite their height, it is easier to cross the Alps than other chains, such as the Rocky Mountains of British Columbia, for their high valleys form several accessible roads leading to Central Europe. One of the best known is the Brenner Pass, starting approximately from the ancient city of Verona, stretching north-east through Trento, Bolzano, and Innsbruck, and forming a vital link between Italy and Germany. These valleys have decreased, from a military standpoint, the importance of the Alps as an obstacle to invasion. The population is widely spread throughout the highest altitudes, where agriculture is carried on to an extent that would be considered unprofitable in most countries. Water from glaciers and mountain streams provides hydro-electric power. One of the chief sources of income is the tourist trade, for here the scenery has a majestic grandeur, with its many peaceful slopes, the deep colours of its lakes, and the transparency of its skies. The north-eastern section of the chain is particularly beautiful, on account of the presence of dolomite (magnesian limestone), a pinkish rock, which in the evening sunset produces a gorgeous colouring. The Prealps are lower mountains, stretching to the base of the Alps proper. They contain the larger and better-known lakes (Lakes Como, Maggiore, Garda, and Iseo).

Below the Prealps we find a wide plain, formed by the basin of the River Po, its tributaries, and other rivers. This area covers about 15 per cent of the country's territory and is the principal agricultural region. At the beginning of the present geological era a large part of it was a sea gulf, later filled in by erosion materials brought down by rivers. The delta of the Po expands yearly and so does the Adriatic coast around Venice, where various lagoons have been formed. Ravenna, once a harbour and a political centre of the Roman Empire, is now eleven miles from the sea, while Adria, formerly an important Etruscan port which gave its name to the Adriatic Sea, is now thirteen miles from it. The plain is divided into two sections, known as the high and the low altitudes. In the former the cultivation of cereals, mulberry trees, and grape-vines is carried on; the latter produces rice and fodder for cattle-raising. The marshes, where the rice is grown, have become world famous through the film *Bitter Rice*. The eastern side of the plain ends with the region of Friuli. Here the Alps come to a termination, and an opening is left into the Balkan peninsula. The language of some of the people is peculiar, and among modern languages is the nearest approach to ancient Latin. Towards Yugoslavia the Carso region is famous for its limestone mountains and the subterranean drainage of rainfall, with the consequent formation of underground streams and lakes. Hence the name of Karstic soil (from the German name *Karst*, which stands for Carso) given to all lands where such phenomena prevail.

The rest of the peninsula is covered by the Apennines, another range which starts in the north at the Col di Tenda near the French border and runs south to Sicily. These peaks are not so high as those of the Alps (the highest being the Gran Sasso, 9,560 feet). The scenery is also less impressive, because the range is mainly formed of calcareous materials and most easily subject to erosion. The uncontrolled cutting of timber through the centuries has accentuated this condition, and the soil has often remained starved of humus, with the result that farming is carried out with difficulty. On the Ligurian coast the Apennines dip into the sea. Here the inhabitants by ingenuity and hard work have succeeded in building a series of terraces on the mountain slopes, where flowers are cultivated abundantly. This is the Italian Riviera. With its mild climate, beautiful landscape, it competes very favourably with the French Côte d'Azur. The delightful ports of Santa Margherita, Portofino,

Rapallo, and San Remo are perfect tourist attractions. Genoa, the chief industrial city and once an independent republic, has a fine harbour and important shipyards.

Farther south, the Apennines, running in an irregular, longitudinal line, divide the country into two regions, the Tyrrhenian on the west and the Adriatic on the east, respectively named from the seas which wash their shores. On the Adriatic the land slopes towards the coast, forming various parallel valleys. The water supply is quite irregular, and dependent on mountain torrents. During the summer there are periods of severe drought. In winter, on the contrary, flood conditions are common. On the Tyrrhenian side some of the valleys run north to south, others east to west. However, the water supply is more constant, due to several rivers, among them the Tiber. In the lower regions, near the Tyrrhenian Sea, there are various plains, including the Maremma in Tuscany, where land reform is now being carried out. South of Rome we find the Pontine plain, once covered by marshes, where land has been extensively reclaimed and the malaria pest eliminated. At Naples the land is of volcanic origin and of great fertility. The Gulf of Naples is guarded by two islands: Capri and Ischia, year-round resorts especially dear to tourists.

The peninsula ends in the shape of a boot. The toe is formed by Calabria and the heel by Apulia. The slow expansion of industry in these areas was caused by lack of resources and by the unco-operative attitude of past governments. But the southerners are now engaged in a programme of industrialisation and land reform which, in the opinion of its planners, should bring their region to the same level as the others, where industry and modern ways of life are already an established fact. Later we shall examine what is being done, but here we should stress the efforts made to improve the less-developed part of the country. It has been said that if enough work and capital were put into the South it could become like California. There is, of course, much exaggeration in this, but local conditions of life will undoubtedly improve. The South was in ancient times one of the lands of gracious living, prosperity, and sophisticated culture. For centuries before Roman conquest it was a Greek colony, noted for its economic splendour. Even to-day, when we speak of a sybarite as a person devoted to luxury and pleasure we do not always remember that this word refers to an inhabitant of the ancient Greek city of Sybaris, some ruins of which are still to be seen on the shores of the Ionian Sea in a most impressive part of Calabria.

The South is surrounded by three seas—the Adriatic on the east, the Tyrrhenian on the west, and the Ionian on the south. The features of the country accentuate those of northern and central regions. The Apennines massively occupy it, limiting the soil which can be tilled and made to produce. If we exclude the plains of Apulia, the widest of which is the Tavoliere, the South is eminently mountainous, with an irregular and insufficient water supply. Even Apulia does not reach a high fertility, because of lack of water. Drought is mainly caused by African winds, known even to the Romans, that sometimes blow with most destructive effect just at harvest time.

The rivers are more like torrents and the preservation of their embankments is one of the most urgent problems. Among the mountains of Calabria the groups of the Sila and Aspromonte should be mentioned. They are covered with thick woods, although heavy felling was done by the Allied armies during the last war. The coasts, being uniform and lacking natural gulfs, are not well adapted to the building of harbours.

The three major islands of the Mediterranean—Sicily, Sardinia, and Corsica—are Italian geographically, although only the two former are part of the Italian Republic, while the latter has belonged to France since 1768. The mountains of Sicily are a continuation of the Apennines, from which they are separated by the Strait of Messina, a narrow waterway dreaded by ancient navigators because in those waters the rock of Scylla and the whirlpool of Charybdis were the cause of the loss of many a ship. The plain of Catania, spreading at the feet of Mount Aetna, a volcano which often passes through a period of eruption, is extremely fertile. Sicily has had a long and troubled history. Because of her central position in the Mediterranean, many civilisations and people have met on her shores. In ancient times she belonged to the Phoenicians, the Greeks, and the Romans; later to Byzantium and the Arabs, until the Normans conquered her at about the same time as the Battle of Hastings. The existence of this Norman kingdom in the extreme south of Europe is not well known to the English people. Its political influence was not limited to Sicily, but extended to other regions. Being capable men and ruthless conquerors, the Normans set up an efficient State which, although it did not last long, left a distinctive mark on the island's life. They were patrons of the arts and erected monuments in which they combined Norman styles with Byzantine and Islamic forms, thus producing masterpieces of architectural perfection, such as the Cappella Palatina in Palermo and the cathedrals of Cefalu' and Monreale. Although the island later became a French and Spanish dependency, it always retained the memories and some institutions of the Norman period. In particular, the parliament formed by the holders of fiefs closely resembled the English House of Lords.

Even Sardinia resembles the Continent. This region is crossed by a range of metalliferous mountains, similar to those of Tuscany, the region across the Tyrrhenian Sea. The scenery is rough and rocky. The islanders, having lived for centuries without much contact with other countries, have developed their own ways and habits founded on ancient traditions. An interesting feature is the ruins of buildings called 'Nuraghi', 6,000 of which have been counted. Many theories have been put forward as to the period during which they were erected. According to some scholars, they were tombs, or watchtowers, or fortresses, the testimony of a very ancient civilisation which flourished before the foundation of Rome, probably related to similar monuments discovered in other parts of the Mediterranean—namely, in the island of Crete.

Mount Vesuvius, near Naples, was made famous by many volcanic eruptions during the course of history. That which occurred on August 24 A.D. 79 and which destroyed the cities of Pompeii, Herculaneum, and Stabiae, was witnessed by the scientist and writer, Pliny the Elder, then a praefect of the Roman navy, who lost his life in it. The excavations in Pompeii have brought to life unknown and intimate aspects of ancient life.

Besides Vesuvius, other volcanoes are Mount Aetna in Sicily and Stromboli on the island bearing the same name, off the north Sicilian coast. Other minor volcanic areas are to be found in Tuscany, around Naples, and in Sicily. Some of the lakes near Rome have been formed by ancient craters. It is probably because of her volcanic structure that Italy has been troubled by earthquakes from remote times up to the present day. No region is exempt from seismic danger, although it is more serious in certain areas. Sardinia and Corsica, generally considered aseismic, are a definite exception.

The climate is, of course, linked to geography. Because of the peninsular shape, sea influence is greatly felt. The Mediterranean forms in winter a reservoir of heat, while in summer it has a cooling effect. This influence is progressively less felt the farther one gets from the coast. It is, therefore, very small in the Po Valley, the most continental among Italian regions. The weather is also influenced by the high mountain ranges. The Alps provide protection from northern winds. Where there is no such protection—namely, on the border with Yugoslavia—the country is hit by a north wind called the *bora*. African winds influence conditions in the South. Rainfall varies according to latitude and altitude. Generally speaking, the North gets more rain and is cooler than the South, while the warmest regions are the islands.

Not all territories that are geographically part of the peninsula belong to the Italian Republic. Corsica is a French dependency. Malta, belonging to England, gives her, together with Gibraltar, Suez, and Cyprus, an excellent command of the Mediterranean seaways. The Peace Treaty between Italy and the Allies granted Yugoslavia several territories on the eastern border and some islands in the Adriatic Sea, and allowed France to occupy the cantons of Briga and Tenda in the Alps, thus improving her strategical position towards the Po Valley.

Two independent States exist within Italian territory. One is the republic of San Marino in the Apennines, with a population of 13,000. This is an historic curiosity and the last to survive of the free communes that flourished politically and economically from the Middle Ages up to the beginning of the modern era. San Marino has survived much political turmoil without losing an independence that was also recognised by Napoleon and Metternich. During the last war, despite her neutrality, she suffered heavy raids and destruction, which caused a diplomatic controversy with Great Britain concerning the reparation of the damage. The little republic is governed by appointed administrators (the so-called regents) and by a parliament of sixty members. Strangely enough, in post-war elections a parliamentary majority was won by the extreme left parties, so that San Marino is the first State outside the Iron Curtain with a Communist administration.

Of greater interest is the Vatican City, an independent State inside the city of Rome, formed by St. Peter's Basilica and the Apostolic Palaces. Its status is based on the concordat between

Italy and the Holy See signed in 1929. The Pope is the head of the Catholic religion and the sovereign of a State, consisting before 1870 of the greater part of central Italy, while it is now limited to less than a square mile and has a population of nearly 1,000 persons. This dual position has created some confusion as to the status of the diplomatic corps accredited to his court. It is a recognised international principle that the Pope enjoys the right of appointing and receiving diplomatic representatives, despite the fact that he may not have any territorial possessions. The envoys to the Vatican, such as the Minister of the United Kingdom, are accredited to the Chief of the Catholic Church, not to a temporal sovereign. Such representation also existed, in fact, during the years between 1870 and 1929, when the Pope enjoyed no sovereignty of his own. It might be added that in most Catholic countries the papal Nuncio is, by right, the recognised Dean of the Diplomatic Corps.

From a racial point of view, one generally thinks of Italians as short individuals, with dark hair and eyes and a marked tendency towards brachycephalism. This is a superficial judgment, just as thinking that the type with blond hair, blue eyes, and a tall stature, commonly called northern, is the only one existing in Germany. It is, in fact, difficult to determine the racial prototype of any European country, and there is no definite Italian type. The colour of the hair and eyes, as well as the height, may differ from region to region. The inhabitants of the Alps have characteristics similar to those of the people living in the mountains of Savoy, Switzerland, and Austria, and are generally tall and blond. People of the Po Valley have dark hair and eyes, whereas those of the northern Apennines along the eastern Adriatic coast down to the region of Abruzzi have a tendency towards a lighter colour. Darker features prevail along the Tyrrhenian coast and gradually increase farther south, reaching their peak in Calabria, Sicily, and Sardinia. But even here the population is far from homogeneous. Blond types with blue eyes are not at all uncommon in some predominantly dark regions. Equal differences exist as regards the shape of the skull. Generally speaking, dolichocephalism prevails among the fairer types, and brachycephalism among the darker. Historical events can be traced in this great variety. The darker Italian of the Po Valley and of the central regions is probably a descendant of races living in the peninsula before the Roman conquest and belonging to a Mediterranean stock. Racial traits in the South and in the islands were influenced by Greek and Phoenician colonisation and later by Byzantine and Moorish conquest. Sicily, for example, was a Saracen possession between the ninth and the eleventh centuries, and this caused some immigration from the Near East and Northern Africa. The fair type prevailing in some regions can be explained by the penetration of northern races, such as the Lombards and the Normans. It should not be forgotten that these people occupied the South of Italy in different epochs and established independent States, such as the Lombard principalities of Salerno, Capua, and Benevento and the Norman kingdom of Sicily. Their racial influence has survived. Ethnical changes have also been caused in later times by intermarriage between people of the North and the South.

The number of inhabitants has increased during the last century and a half, rising from about 19 million in Napoleon's time to the present 48 million. This figure, of course, does not take into account the many millions who left the country in the recent decades. Despite her mountainous nature, Italy is densely populated, considering how small is her total area (116,228 square miles). The birth rate has always been high, especially in the South, although there are now indications that it is decreasing. The rate of increase in 1951 was 7·8 per thousand, while during the years between 1922 and 1926 it amounted to 12 per thousand. Tentative estimates suggest that the birth rate will further decrease in subsequent years and that the population will stabilise at 50 millions. The excess of births over deaths was 365,333 in 1953, as compared to the average yearly figure of 460,323 during the period between 1922 and 1926. The death rate has dropped as a result of improved economic, medical, and social conditions. A great deal has been done to fight infectious diseases, outstanding results having been achieved against malaria, a disease which has practically been rooted out. Life expectancy increased from 61·85 years in 1943 to 66·66 in 1950.

Because of irregular distribution of natural resources and of several other factors, North and South developed differently. The North has a prosperous agriculture, a strong industry, and an efficient working class, quite modern and progressive. The South, having lived for centuries in depressed conditions, has been ruled up to recent times by the country gentry. Before World War I landownership placed a man in a select category enjoying not only privileges deriving from wealth, but also political and administrative influence. Sometimes the ruling class won the elections by using its social standing and also the services of bully-boys (the so-called *mazzieri* in Apulia), whose task it was to frighten the electors into voting for certain candidates. To-day the situation has changed. Titles of nobility were abolished by the constitution of 1948. Possession of property no longer guarantees any special privilege or political authority.

In northern Italy farmers live on the land they till, while in the South they have a tendency to live in large communities. Historical events are, as usual, responsible for this. The long coastline, with few harbours and low shores, was in the past vulnerable from the sea. Moorish invasion and pirates' raids were not infrequent. The inhabitants were compelled to unite in strongholds and be ready for defence when the necessity for it arose. Hence the building of fortresses and towers along the coast and the tendency of the people to congregate in the hills or in easily defended spots. Farther from the sea, where invasion was not to be feared, the assembling of people in groups was necessary for protection against bandits and feudal lords, who waged constant war against each other, thus keeping the country in a permanent state of unrest and greatly weakening its resistance to foreign aggression. Settling on the land was dangerous because of endemic diseases, such as malaria, often raging in the plains at the foot of the mountains. It thus happens that living on the farm does not appeal to the southerner, who after a day's work prefers to go back to his village. Some thickly populated centres of the South still bear a rural aspect because the great majority of the people go farming during the day. Much smaller centres in the North look more like cities. The southerners do not lose such habits even when they emigrate to new countries. In the United States of America, for example, few Italians have settled on the land, the majority preferring to remain in the cities. This urban concentration in the predominantly rural provinces of the South is to-day an obstacle to land reform, the aim of which is that large estates should be split into smaller ones and allotted to poor peasants prepared to live on them with their families.

Many dialects are used in Italy, which often differ even in neighbouring localities. Their formation and survival are due to the existence of various ancient stocks, to which, by imposing the use of Latin, Rome gave linguistic unity, just as England did in India, where English has replaced various native tongues. Despite unification, the local people never forgot their original languages, to the use of which they probably returned after the fall of the Roman Empire and the political anarchy that followed. Even to-day many modes of pronunciation and words used in certain parts of the country can be traced back to pre-Roman times. The Tuscans pronounce the letter C in the same peculiar way as the Etruscans, a highly developed population of unknown origin, living in Tuscany and later conquered by the Romans.

During medieval times various centres of culture developed all over the country, each of which gave birth to a language of its own, basically founded on Latin, but with variations determined by local tongues. One such centre, formed in Sicily as early as the thirteenth century, was favoured by the political stability imposed by the Norman Conquest, and the Sicilian dialect was used. Troubadours and poets of the North used a tongue based on the Lombard dialect. However, among all idioms, Tuscan prevailed. Its national recognition was brought about by great writers, by its literary and phonetic beauty, and by its relative simplicity. Although it soon became the recognised national language, it unfortunately did not overcome native dialects used by the lower classes.

Some minorities speak languages other than Italian. The more important group is formed by the Germans living on the borders of Austria. They have been granted the right to use their own idiom while transacting official business and to have schools in which both Italian and German are taught. A special statute has been issued for their region. Some communities on the border of Yugoslavia speak Slovenian, others on the western border a French patois. Linguistic groups also exist in the South, probably formed by the descendants of refugees who escaped from the Balkans during Turkish invasion, and who use Greek or Albanian. A small community of people in Sardinia speaks Catalan.

Italians are Roman Catholics. Occasionally they seem to consider religion as their spiritual property and not as a universal faith belonging to mankind, because the history of Italy during nearly 2,000 years has been intimately related to the Church of Rome. During the Middle Ages, mainly through Italian effort, Christianity, its thought and ethics, were saved from bar-

baric pressure in the North and Mohammedan advance in the South. Later, when Christianity was more settled in Europe, Rome challenged all forces endangering papal supremacy, and although the temporal power of the Pope was often opposed, he himself was always recognised as the successor of Peter, the Vicar of Christ, supreme over all persons and States, upon which he could cast the weapon of anathema and excommunication. This meant that Rome could exert great influences over Christendom. It was an Italian, St. Thomas Aquinas, who gave us a complete philosophical picture of the Revelation and of the essence of man and universe. Later Dante Alighieri blended in the *Divine Comedy* the Catholic conception of creation with a human approach to life, reflecting the Italian need to find in the universal truths many answers to human problems. Furthermore, Italian jurists, who possessed an instinctive capacity to formulate and define, greatly contributed to the erection of that monument of logic known as Canon Law. When the tide of Reformation in northern and central Europe almost demolished papal authority, it was in Italy that the movement for resistance originated and from which it spread to other countries. This was achieved by strengthening the Inquisition and by calling the Council of Trento (1545–63), at which theological principles and legislation governing the life of the Church were set down in a more definite manner. Following the Industrial Revolution, which brought about unrest between the managing and working class, an Italian, Pope Leo XIII, gave the final Catholic answer to social problems, putting the influence of the Church on the side of the working man.

The links between Catholicism and the nation have been so intimate that we should not be astonished that Italians consider the Church to be their spiritual domain.

Anti-clericalism has often appeared in Italy in the form of religious or political movements, but it has always been looked upon with suspicion and contempt. Even Communists, although believing that religion is the opium of the people, never oppose Catholicism as such, but generally attack the clergy, on the grounds that the Church does not express or follow the evangelical teaching. For propaganda reasons, their action appears inspired by excess of zeal, not by lack of faith.

An example of this approach to religion is the way the Communist members of the Constituent Assembly voted in 1947, when the problem of relations between Church and State came under examination. Previously these relations were regulated by the Lateran Treaty of 1929 between Fascist Italy and the Holy See. The provisions were fair to both contracting parties and followed the principle that each should be independent of the other. Since the constitution was then being drafted, Catholic members of the Constituent Assembly wanted these provisions to be introduced unchanged. Some left-wing parties were opposed to this plan, but the Communists gave further proof of their Machiavellian tactics by voting in favour of the Lateran Treaty, lest the Catholics alone might appear, in the opinion of the people, to be defending religion.

Italians consider Catholicism a reason for national pride and prestige, for through the Church a way of thinking close to their own has reached distant people. This influence changed as it met different racial temperaments, local traditions and situations, but the basic idea whence Catholicism sprang was largely determined and guided from Italy. Catholics all over the world look to Rome for leadership and indoctrination. Every twenty-five years, and sometimes more often, they are called to Rome to attend the ceremonies of the Holy Year. Millions of foreigners have therefore come as humble pilgrims since the earliest times, and this has, of course, developed in the Romans and the Italians in general a sense of pride.

It has been noticed that Catholicism, having been influenced by the Italian mentality, has reciprocated this influence by moulding the Italian character. This is fundamentally true, since any religion, being intimately related with the life of a people, must in the end contribute to the formation or modification of its nature. So has Protestantism modified the Swedes and Hinduism the Indians. But Catholicism, although taken for granted by the majority, is none the less an object of meditation and active research. The Italians' love of logic and their legal approach strengthen religious sentiment.

Although Catholicism prevails in many a field that elsewhere would be regarded as belonging to the secular and not to the religious aspect of life, Italians feel no intolerance towards other denominations. The Jews are perfectly amalgamated with the rest of the population. They are considered simply as citizens belonging to another religion, and no stress whatever is laid on their racial origin. No doctrine of racial superiority was ever held by the people, and only by force could the Fascist Government enact its anti-Jewish measures. During the German occupation (1943–45) many Jews were protected from persecution and deportation by the people and the clergy. This wide tolerance is proved by the fact that Italy had a Jewish Premier from 1910 to 1911, in the person of Luigi Luzzatti. A similar sentiment is shown towards Protestants. Italy's constitution guarantees complete religious freedom, and this right is not only sanctioned by the law, but is also deeply felt by the nation. There was also a Premier of Jewish origin and Protestant faith in the person of Sidney Sonnino, who was in power in 1906 and again from 1909 to 1910.

National sentiment is deeply rooted. It is a silent feeling, which at times can explode very noisily. These outbursts may perhaps originate from the Latin temperament and its swift reactions, which can be especially violent when national rights are trodden on or some injustice is perpetrated against the community.

Though Italians are attached to their country, they are not imperialists. They have been inspired by the teachings of Giuseppe Mazzini (1805–72), the great patriot who fought for independence and spent part of his life in exile in England. He believed in a national home for the Italians because he knew that all people should have their independence. The urge for colonial expansion was, therefore, never much felt in Italy, where material advantages deriving from the possession of colonies had little, if any, appeal to the people, who thought it intolerable that a country which had suffered so much from foreign occupation should move to the conquest of other nations. All colonial expansion after 1870 was mainly the responsibility of three Prime Ministers, Francesco Crispi, Giovanni Giolitti, and Benito Mussolini, who deemed it a great error that Italy should refrain from conquests at a time when all other major European Powers were expanding.

A political trend wholeheartedly supported by the people is that for international unity. Italians feel a natural inclination towards other lands and people. In recent times they have favoured all programmes that aim at advancing European integration in the economic, political, and military fields (Council of Europe, European Coal and Steel Community, European Defence Community). The policy followed by Alcide De Gasperi, who headed the Government between 1945 and 1953, although dictated by his strong personality, was approved of by the majority. The Premier never found difficulty in convincing his countrymen that continental unity was more important than anything else and that any sacrifice that advanced it even a little was worth while.

It is common opinion that Italians are individualists and are intolerant of discipline. Although this statement contains much exaggeration, it is true that the Italians have a strong personality which does not allow them to accept any outsider's point of view without knowing where they stand, what their rights are, and what is expected of them. This individualism increased during the long foreign domination, when the Government was not an authority representing the people, but the expression of a Power encamped on Italian soil. Resisting this authority was considered meritorious. Some of this individualistic mentality survived even after 1870, and traces of it are still to be found.

A remarkable feature is the attachment to the family group. This is also the consequence of times when persons could get no guarantee from the law and turned instead to their own kin. Their sense of mutual aid is especially aroused when some member of the family has been victimised by the injustice of an outsider. Here again appears the ancestral spirit of family assistance. This sentiment may astonish a foreign visitor, who, upon entering an Italian home, is immediately questioned as to his family ties. These questions do not originate from mischievous curiosity, but rather from a genuinely human approach. Family affection goes hand in hand with economy. Italians save money even when it would seem almost impossible to do so. This is especially true of emigrants, who send home quite large sums.

Great is the Italians' inborn sense of art. Many of them are capable of creating things of beauty, and all of them feel the impact of their artistic heritage. This is the consequence of the environment and of the passionate nature of a people keen to manifest their feelings, whose emotional and mental processes are influenced by external conditions. Their creative capacity reaches a high degree of refinement and elegance. Exhibitions always arouse the interest of connoisseurs and of the public, for tradition is alive in the works of contemporary Italian artists. Violence of feeling and action, a sense of colour and proportion, a somewhat troubled nature, an intense religiosity found in the works of the great masters are present in the most recent exponents of a tradition that cannot die. Italian handicraft is known throughout the world and is, of course, outstanding. Renowned is their love of music. In the province of Parma, for instance, where Giuseppe Verdi and Arturo Toscanini were born, the people have a highly developed musical ability, and this tendency makes them a difficult audience to please. Neapolitans are naturally given to singing and are famed for the light and harmonic voices of their tenors.

Italian literature is little known in England. A few authors, such as Dante Alighieri and Giovanni Boccaccio, are sometimes quoted, but seldom read. Unfortunately the Italian language, at one time frequently spoken in Europe among educated people and diplomats, is little spoken to-day. Yet the influence exerted on foreign literature by Italy has always been great. Shakespeare, Byron, and other English poets drew much of their poetical inspiration from Italian life and ways, and writers of Italian blood, such as Dante Gabriel Rossetti and Christina Rossetti, achieved an outstanding place in English literature. An artistic approach is also to be found in the Italians' love for politics. This is seldom understood in the right spirit by people from abroad, for the interest is caused not by a desire to indulge in a display of frivolity, as if politics were a game, but by the conviction that each participant is genuinely contributing to a worthwhile cause. Besides, the Italian mind enjoys examining life from a universal point of view. Sometimes, because of this approach, more immediate interests are temporarily lost sight of and problems are considered from too wide an angle.

This brief picture of Italy, her geographical features and major characteristics, is far from complete. But could it be otherwise, when so many influences blended together to produce the remarkable past of a country where Western civilisation had its cradle? Italy has given so much to the world in the fields of philosophy, ethics, discovery, and achievement, and her contributions have entered the domain of humanity to such a degree, that it is practically impossible to analyse these separately and give her credit for each of them. Her history has been one of progress in all fields. Her people have been creative and inspiring, and their response to life emotional, intellectual, and practical. Unfortunately, she has received little in return and her aspirations have often been denied. Her independence and unity date back little more than eighty years, and only lately has the country been in a position to fence in her own interest. Yet it is the author's opinion that a most inspiring future is ahead, that the evils and experiences of the past will provide a new impulse, already to be perceived in the domain of spiritual leadership and practical achievement.

Chapter 2

Birth of a State (1815–70)

THE ITALIAN term 'Risorgimento' needs explanation, since it is sometimes misinterpreted as 'Renaissance'. Although both words imply a moral and cultural resurrection, each relates to a different period of history. Risorgimento, as stated in Funk and Wagnall's *New Dictionary of the English Language*, means, 'Originally the uprising of the Italian people against Austrian domination in the nineteenth century; now used to cover all the events culminating in the unification of Italy in 1870'. According to Webster's *New International Dictionary*, Risorgimento is 'the movement for political unity in Italy in the nineteenth century'. These definitions, much alike in substance and form, are correct, but do not stress the profoundly moral, social, religious, and political impact of the movement. Indeed, the Risorgimento, before being a succession of events, uprisings, revolutions, and wars that led to the Italians' unification under one government, was a new trend of thought and an important milestone in the development of humanity. This was fully understood by Swinburne, who dedicated to the Risorgimento some of his more inspired verses.

The French Revolution and Napoleon's epoch had contributed much towards awakening Europe's sleeping people. The eighteenth century, through the works and actions of philosophers and of certain enlightened rulers, had been one of preparation for human progress. Yet little had been done to awaken the conscience of the people. Philosophers, no matter how brilliant their speculation, speak to a minority which rarely has any spiritual contact with the majority of toilers forming the backbone of a nation. To these instead nothing is more appealing than the sound of warfare, especially when it is backed by the promise of great changes and achievements.

The movement, which started in France in the year 1789, and Napoleon's victories, had demolished the barrier that for so long had prevented the lower classes from forging their destiny. The people felt they were no longer the objects, but the subjects of history. Even during the darkest moments of the French Revolution, when events were dominated by the mob (against which Edmund Burke launched his anathema in the House of Commons), it was generally felt that behind the uprising of the populace there was something more than a simple request for bread or a natural antipathy for the Austrian-born Queen. There was an inspired, even if ill-expressed, desire for liberty, equality, and fraternity. These were terms new to the common man.

The stirring events which took place between 1789 and 1815 were profoundly felt in Italy, where for centuries the people had languished under foreign domination, administrative misrule, and feudal abuses. Yet European statesmen did not understand this profound change. When, after Napoleon's downfall, they met in Vienna, their aim was to restore the old order upon the Continent. They thought they were dealing with the same countries they had known and governed twenty-five years before. But war had opened the eyes of many, and the principle that men are born alike was now inspiring the actions and desires of a new society. Napoleon, although quick in doing away with many of the liberties proclaimed by the revolution, never denied the basic principle of equality. The abolition of fiefs, of medieval taxation, of the rights of birth, of corporations, had given the individual the feeling that he was equal to anyone else and could freely climb the ladder of society. If differences still existed, the moral principle had won recognition. Yet the statesmen meeting in Vienna firmly believed that all this could be abolished. It was said of them that they had learned nothing and forgotten nothing. The phrase sums up effectively their belief that, by ignoring what had taken place during the previous twenty-five years, history could begin again where it had left off in 1789.

The Italian set-up after the Congress of Vienna (1815) reflected the idea that authority should be enforced through monarchs, who were entitled to govern by divine grace. Such an autocratic concept of power was certainly inspired by Prince Metternich, Chancellor of the Hapsburg Empire, and by Czar Alexander I of Russia, whose actions were strangely dominated by the belief that he was guided by God. Before the French Revolution four republics had existed in Italy—namely, Venice, Genoa, Lucca, and San Marino. The governments of these four

States had been influenced by a small oligarchy that the French had swiftly eliminated from power. Since the word 'republic' smacked too much of revolutionary events, only San Marino was restored to its previous form; as it was purely an historical curiosity. Venice and Genoa were annexed to other States and Lucca was given to a ruler.

The political map was as follows: the Savoy family was re-established in Piedmont, the buffer zone between France and the Austrian possessions in the Po Valley. The domains of this monarchy, destined to play such a great part in the unification of the peninsula, included the island of Sardinia, the city of Nice, and the Savoy region, and had increased through the annexation of the Ligurian coast with the port of Genoa, heretofore independent. The acquisition of this important outlet to the sea by a country which over the centuries had been mainly rural was destined to change the people's mentality and urge them to commercial and maritime expansion. Austria got back Lombardy. That this region should return to its former Austrian owners after Napoleon's defeat was, in a certain sense, comprehensible. Not so, however, the annexation of Venice and the surrounding region of Venetia, an independent republic for more than a thousand years. Venetia had been annexed by Austria in 1799, with Napoleon's blessing. Later it had been incorporated in the so-called Kingdom of Italy, of which Napoleon himself was the sovereign, but which in reality was nothing more than a dependency of the French Empire. After the fall of the latter, Austria influenced the Congress to obtain the confirmation of the previous annexation.

Austria's influence extended beyond the regions she directly governed to other States of the peninsula. These came under her either through connections between royal families or by means of intervention in their internal affairs. The Duchy of Modena in the Po Valley was given to Francis IV, a relative of the Hapsburgs and a descendant of the D'Este dynasty. Parma and Piacenza were given to Marie Louise, daughter of the Austrian Emperor, and Napoleon's wife, who was completely under the influence of the Court of Vienna. Marie Louise governed the State with the provision that on her death it should be returned to the Bourbons of Parma, who, for the time being, were ruling the city of Lucca, transformed from a republic into a duchy. Tuscany was given to Ferdinand III, an Austrian prince of the Hapsburg–Lorraine branch. The temporal possessions of the Pope in central Italy were returned to Pius VII, with almost the same boundaries as before the French Revolution.

The Bourbons, who had escaped during the Napoleonic wars, returned to Naples, where Ferdinand I was proclaimed King of the Two Sicilies, thus uniting the kingdoms of Sicily and Naples, which had previously been under his rule as separate States. In 1812, under the influence of the British commander-in-chief, Lord William Bentinck, Ferdinand had granted the Sicilians a constitution based on that of England, by which political franchises were recognised and a legislative body created, similar to the House of Lords. Even this mild reform, which might eventually have led to the formation of a democratic mentality in regions oppressed for centuries by moral, political, and religious coercion, seemed too much to the Bourbon King. In 1815 he was quick to abolish the charter he had sworn to defend only a few years before. Among Sicilians the longing for the constitution of 1812 remained as one of many reasons for unrest.

This was the map of Italy as drawn by the Congress of Vienna, impregnated with the idea that nations should remain under the rule of their sovereigns, who, obviously, would not indulge the people's aspirations for liberty and independence. Austria, Russia, and Prussia, the three big continental victors, pledged themselves with the Holy Alliance to intervene in the domestic affairs of other States if the *status quo* was endangered by revolution.

The ideal of an Italian resurrection, a 'Risorgimento', made headway during this period of reaction. The most enlightened people began to realise that there was a great need of equality, of eliminating social discrimination, of personal liberty, and of the rights and franchises that go with it. Although these benefits had been enjoyed for only a short period, they had spread the idea that only along the paths of liberty would progress be ultimately achieved. Constitutional representation was considered the only way by which these needs could be given legal expression. Thus, the word 'constitution' acquired a magical meaning, as if by granting it monarchs would be giving the people a key to unlock their future. Many believed that if political liberty was achieved, economic and social problems would gradually be adjusted. It was also hoped that the different States would merge and become one single unit occupying the whole peninsula, completely independent of foreign Powers. This, naturally, meant eliminating from Italian territory the

Austrian Empire, so firmly entrenched upon it. The difficulties were great and the Italians had to overcome them without arms, money, or organisation against most powerful enemies.

The destiny of nations is often shaped by a few idealists who sense that the time for changes is imminent. This frequently happens while the majority, less capable of foreseeing the future or of determining the course of events, is preoccupied with everyday affairs. The Risorgimento is an example of this. A small minority believed that the dream of poets, historians, and philosophers could at last be realised.

Among the professional and educated classes which had sprung up during the previous two decades, many were discontented with existing conditions. Discontent, being a purely negative attitude, is rarely the source of action when personal and national fortunes are at stake. But in this case it helped to forge a national spirit. Officers who had been dismissed from Napoleon's armies, officials who had served in previous administrations, intellectuals and students formed this minority. They began to realise that their country, spreading south of the Alps into the Mediterranean, was ready for political unity.

During previous centuries Italian political maturity had been at a low ebb, since the land had constantly been occupied by foreign States interested only in exploitation. During the wars between France and Spain in the sixteenth and seventeenth centuries a popular slogan stated that it mattered little who won these conflicts, the important thing being for the people to carry on and to eat. Things had now changed. No longer was there a cynical approach to national problems, but an intelligent interest in the country's future. It was unfortunate that at the beginning of the nineteenth century no political writer of the calibre of the English Burke, or the German Fichte, gave expression to the changes taking place in the minds and hearts of the people. It was not until the next generation, thirty years later, that the fundamental works of the Risorgimento were finally written and the new ideas critically examined and discussed. For the present, however, much inspiration was derived from poets such as Vittorio Alfieri (1747–1803) and Ugo Foscolo (1778–1827). Their works were widely read and memorised. Encouragement was also drawn from foreign authors, such as Madame de Staël. These writings were warmly welcomed in the reading-rooms of the peninsula and provided an impulse towards the achievement of the newly discovered aims.

One idea was gradually taking shape in the minds of patriots. They now believed that the newly revived monarchies and the all-powerful Austrian Empire could be ousted by conspiracy. Through the formation of illegal secret societies they hoped to exert sufficient pressure upon the various governments to achieve political solutions more consistent with their ideals. Men of action and of thought deemed that if dynasties could unite in the Holy Alliance to defend their privileges, the people should also unite for the purpose of challenging those privileges and of setting in their place the right of the citizens to govern themselves. Their first aim was to enlist the support of people who shared their hopes. Although it was not practical and caused many unsuccessful uprisings, this programme helped to merge the widely different mentalities of people from various regions.

Patriots began to organise secret societies for the purpose of stirring the feeling of rebellion and encouraging revolts. The most important—and one that quickly spread over the country—was the *carboneria*. Its origin is unknown, but it probably derived from Freemasonry, since masonic ceremonies and symbols were used. People affiliated were called *carbonari* or charcoal vendors, and their ritual signified that they were nothing more than workers without any political aims. Soon, however, everyone was aware of their existence, and the word *carbonari* came to mean revolutionaries and rebels. These men were idealists and poets who knew little of politics and were chiefly moved by emotional impulses. They spoke of liberty and unification without knowing exactly what these words meant.

This was the time of romanticism, and writers all over Europe were making great efforts to restore sentiment in literature and art. The same imaginative disposition was penetrating other fields. Lord Byron's death at Missolonghi in Greece had given youths a stirring example of how one could sacrifice one's life for a nation's independence, even though it was not one's own. A famous patriot, Santorre di Santarosa (1783–1825), seeing he could do little to free his own land, preferred fighting elsewhere for the cause in which he believed, and like Byron died in the Greek struggle for liberation.

Since many parts of Europe were subjugated by despotic governments, Italy was not the only country aspiring to independence. Poland, Hungary, and the countries under Turkish rule were fighting to break their chains. It was natural that the most ardent champions of freedom should be attracted to one another, for although belonging to different nations and speaking different languages, they were linked by a common cause. During those years Italians fought in nearly all European revolutions, and men of other nationalities took part in Italy's uprisings and wars of independence. While European monarchs had allied themselves to stamp out the seed of revolt, the people were also uniting in a most valid and far-reaching alliance, which was soon to blossom and bring forth fruit.

Many who believed in uniting the peninsula pointed out that political union was meaningless unless it went hand in hand with spiritual and social unification. Among the people most convinced of this was the poet Ugo Foscolo, who wrote, in his *Discourses on Italian Servitude* (*Discorsi della servitù d'Italia*):

> 'A sect is a permanent state of division caused and maintained by a certain number of men. These men, by separating themselves from the rest of the community, profess, publicly or privately, religious, moral, or political opinions. They do so in order to back secret interests and defend them by means of actions which are contrary to the good of the community.'

It was unfortunate that Foscolo, essentially right, was not capable of suggesting an alternative course of action. The immediate aims of patriots who liked calling themselves *cospiratori* (conspirators) varied from region to region. The *carbonari* of Lombardo–Venetia were asking for independence from Austria and looking towards Piedmont for guidance and military assistance; those of the papal States aspired to a government freed from the influences of the Catholic clergy; those of Naples were asking for a constitution similar to that granted by the King of Spain; while those of Sicily wanted independence from the Bourbon monarchy or a constitution similar to that of 1812.

The frame of mind of the South should be examined, for that was the region where the first open revolt broke out. In Naples, many discontented people were members of the *carboneria*. They were chiefly officers of the army of Murat, Napoleon's brother-in-law, whom the Emperor had placed on the throne of Naples. In 1820 these officers, tired of the general situation and of the treatment they had received, rebelled against King Ferdinand and compelled him to grant a constitution. The following year another rebellion broke out in Turin, against the King of

Piedmont. Even the heir-apparent to the throne, the future King Carlo Alberto, had a part in it. In both cases the revolutions, while successful at first, quickly failed. The constitutions were promptly nullified and those who had taken part in the uprisings prosecuted. Overcome by fear and disillusion, many emigrated to other countries.

For ten years the peninsula remained comparatively calm, until 1831, when a new uprising broke out in central Italy, starting in the city of Modena. This time patriots endeavoured to be more practical. They reasoned that, since Austria dominated the peninsula, nothing could be done without the assistance of some Power having interests opposed to those of the Hapsburgs. This help could perhaps be found in France, where the revolution of 1830 had brought Louis Philippe to the throne and put in power men of more liberal outlook. Among the first acts of the French Government there had been a declaration of non-intervention in the domestic affairs of other countries. In our day the underlining of such a principle would not bear any special significance, but in the atmosphere of the time this simple proclamation filled the Italians with confidence and hope, for although it contained no implication that France would aid a revolt, they believed it did.

Patriots thought that the people were now in a position to bargain with, at least, the minor monarchs, and that some agreement could be reached between them. The liberal leader Ciro Menotti contacted the Duke of Modena for the purpose of ensuring his assistance. His programme was outlined in a letter to a friend who had advised him to be cautious and in which he wrote:

> 'What do we care if the Duke of Modena is wicked? He has treasures and strength, and we will make the best of them. We will give him a crown, and he will give us independence and liberty. And if he should try to deceive us or evade us, we could easily remove him from the throne, once we became our own masters!'

While trying to appear practical, Ciro Menotti was the victim of his imagination and was gambling on hope. The uprising was badly organised; it lacked material strength and received no support from France or the Duke. The outcome was that the poorly armed troops were easily defeated by Austrian units and the organisers either exiled or sent to the scaffold. Yet the revolt was important because, although failing in its immediate aims, it made of Italy's problem a European issue, which no statesman on the Continent could ignore.

A clear statement of the nation's aims was needed. Giuseppe Mazzini (1805–72), who possessed the active mind of a thinker and the humanity of a writer, was the proper man to provide much-needed guidance for this new fervour. In 1831 he founded 'La Giovine Italia' (Young Italy), a secret society destined to become famous all over Europe. The basic aims of this organisation were: popular sovereignty, direct action by the people, independence, unity, republican institutions, and the principle of nationality. Mazzini's ideals were expressed in a letter he wrote to a German patriot:

> 'I admire my fatherland, because I adore all fatherlands; our liberty because I believe in liberty; our rights because I believe in rights. Natural sentiment belongs to all for the progress of all. A nation must be to humanity what the family is, or should be, to the fatherland. If it acts harmfully, if it oppresses, if it becomes the vehicle of injustice and sponsors and supports temporary interests, it loses the right to existence and digs its grave. This is my secret doctrine concerning nationality.'

Mazzini believed that God was the people's best friend and that in Him they would find salvation from moral and material ills. Hence the implication that an alliance was necessary between the people and God, and that European Powers were guilty of blasphemy when trying to justify despotic power and contempt of popular opinion by stating that their actions were inspired by the Christian doctrine. His slogan, *Dio e Popolo* (God and the people), was the standard of national independence around which the nation was to unite. Mazzini believed the republican form of government to be the ideal one. Monarchies, large or small, appeared to him all one with despotism and corruption. Although unsuccessful in obtaining concrete results, he gave determination to his disciples, inspiration to his followers, and caused grave concern to Austria and the Italian States. Nearly all the uprisings after 1831 were inspired by him, but ended in disaster. He was therefore compelled to find refuge in England, where he lived for several years. One of the most romantic and adventurous among these uprisings was organised by the brothers Attilio and Emilio Bandiera, who in

1844 landed on the coast of Calabria, hoping to raise the populace against the Bourbons. Unfortunately they were soon captured and executed. Mazzini created a trend of thought that lasted through the Risorgimento up to our time, and laid the foundation of the present Italian republic.

Vincenzo Gioberti (1801–52), in his work, *Del primato morale e civile degli Italiani* (The Moral and Civil Primacy of the Italians), published in 1843, advanced a political theory in which more emphasis was placed on Catholicism and its influence. According to this author, the essence of Italian life and history was to be found in religion. Hence his enthusiasm for everything pertaining to tradition, his constant attempt to find analogies between Italy's past and Catholicism, and his opposition to foreign patterns. He felt that his countrymen should free themselves from the burden of ideas derived from the French Revolution and solve their problems within the doctrine of the Church. This theory was extremely successful, although it was interpreted in foreign countries as an expression of nationalism. Non-Catholics felt that it was not justified by history, while its allegations were considered unconvincing by a generation that had learned from Immanuel Kant the art of judging and analysing critically.

Gioberti proposed a federation of Italian States placed under the protection of the Church with military strength provided by Piedmont. Thus Italy would achieve unity and regain her place in the world, and the respect to which she was entitled. This doctrine was, of course, absurd. History has often proved that when basic issues are at stake during a nation's critical moments it is impossible to harmonise contrasting forces and interests. Monarchies, such as the Bourbons of Naples and the Savoys of Turin, were so different in background, purposes, and methods, that nothing could make them co-operate under a federative government. The Bourbons were insistent upon despotic policies, while the Savoys were gradually acknowledging the necessity of keeping up with the times and of granting constitutional liberties. Austria held a great part of northern Italy and would not be likely to withdraw. The Pope, as the pastor of the Catholic Church and the chief of a State, both of which often had conflicting interests, was in a difficult position destined to become more so if he agreed to be sovereign of a federation. Pope Pius IX, who had been impressed by Gioberti's work, was soon to understand how impractical the theory was, for in 1848, during the war between Piedmont and Austria, he was compelled to give priority to his religious duties, rather than to his national inclinations. On that occasion he declared he would take no part in a war against Austria, a Catholic Power.

Gioberti's moderate ideas convinced many who were not keen to follow Mazzini, and who, as good Catholics, did not wish to oppose the Pope, that it was possible to reconcile religion with independence and achieve unity without excessively altering the *status quo*.

In Italy the events of 1848 and 1849 were largely influenced by the works of Mazzini and Gioberti. Revolutions broke out at first in France, Germany, Austria, and Hungary. This helped to arouse the people of Italy, who had already shown signs of unrest the previous year when Austria, trying to intimidate Pope Pius IX, whom she considered guilty of fostering liberal opinions, occupied the northern part of the Papal States. In 1848 revolutions broke out all over the peninsula. The monarchs of Naples, Piedmont, and Tuscany, and the Pope himself, were compelled by popular pressure to grant constitutional governments. The greatest and most heroic revolts were those of Milan and Venice against Austria.

In this atmosphere of enthusiasm for the national cause King Carlo Alberto of Piedmont decided to back the popular uprising and to realise the centuries-old dream of unifying northern Italy under his dynasty. Although he lacked sufficient military preparation, he waged war against Austria. After two campaigns, separated by a short armistice, he was finally defeated at the Battle of Novara in 1849 and compelled to abdicate in favour of his son, Victor Emmanuel II.

Other events of great significance took place. Tuscany rebelled and her ruler was obliged to deliver his powers into the hands of a constitutional government. Rome also revolted and the Pope was compelled to find refuge in the Kingdom of the Two Sicilies. A republic, headed by Giuseppe Mazzini, was proclaimed on February 9, 1849. Its military defence was entrusted to Giuseppe Garibaldi (1807–82), whose courageous accomplishments were to stir the whole world. However, the new republic did not last long, because France soon decided to restore the Pope and sent an expeditionary force against it. Resistance was hopeless against such overwhelmingly powerful enemy forces, and defeat soon followed, despite incredible acts of gallantry. Among those who lost their lives was Goffredo

Mameli, a twenty-one-year-old poet, who wrote Italy's national anthem.

In the North, Austria crushed the revolts of Brescia and Venice. The latter city fell in August, 1849, after a most impressive resistance against blockade by land and sea. Only famine and disease succeeded in overcoming the determined and courageous Venetians. The Austrian Empire, having strengthened its position by defeating Piedmont and by crushing the uprisings, restored to the peninsula the political order of 1815.

Outwardly Austria was the victor, but in reality these two fateful years moulded Italian unity. The groundwork had been laid for further decisive events. The kingdom of Piedmont, by refraining from abolishing the constitution of 1848, as other States had done, showed the Italians how much it believed in their cause, and became the centre of the movement for national independence. Patriots flocked to its borders from all regions where they had been victims of persecution. Thus began the gradual conversion of many from republican to monarchic sentiments. Daniele Manin (1804–57), leader of the ill-fated Venetian revolution, wrote, from exile, to the King of Piedmont offering his services if he would lead the national movement for liberation. Even Mazzini, despite his republican faith, was ready to help if Piedmont would provide the necessary military leadership. Garibaldi, who had escaped after the fall of the Roman Republic, also offered to come to the aid of the common cause.

Piedmont gave Italy an example of good administration with the premiership of Camillo Benso di Cavour (1810–61). This statesman combined complete devotion to the national cause with experience and ability in public affairs. A student of political science and economy, he helped his country by developing agriculture, building railways, and encouraging industry. He placed great emphasis on military preparation, and no money was spared to make the army an efficient instrument of war. He helped maritime trade, and Genoa again became one of the busiest harbours in the Mediterranean. His efforts in other directions were also successful. In 1850 Parliament passed special legislation (the so-called Siccardi laws) by which ecclesiastical immunities and privileges were abolished. Other reforms were enacted in the field of public education. Cavour, realising that Piedmont, in her feud against Hapsburg domination, needed a powerful ally on whom to rely, did not repeat Carlo Alberto's error of starting a war without the necessary diplomatic and military backing. Since France and England were sympathetically inclined towards the Italian cause, he carefully cultivated their friendship, and when war broke out between Russia on one side, and England, France, and Turkey on the other, he allied Piedmont to the latter. An expeditionary corps was sent to the Crimea, where it fought with particular gallantry in the Battle of the Chernaya (August 16, 1855). Cavour was reproached for this policy and he was accused of betraying the national cause to gain personal prestige. Events, however, were soon to prove him right. In 1856 the Congress of Paris was convoked and Piedmont was admitted on an equal footing with the other Powers. Thus the Italian problem, regarded since 1815 as an internal affair of a few States, and chiefly an Austrian concern, at last came to the attention of the major Powers. Count Walewski, the French Foreign Minister, put the Italian question before the Assembly of Paris.

While no immediate results were achieved, Cavour took advantage of the situation by making personal contact with Napoleon III, the newly-elected Emperor of the French, a man who was fully acquainted with the Italian problem, having taken part in the uprisings of 1831. Cavour impressed him, as well as Lord Clarendon, who represented the English Government, very favourably. The outcome of this diplomatic manœuvring was the signing in 1859 of the Treaty of Plombières between Piedmont and France. The two countries agreed to form a kingdom in northern Italy by merging Piedmont with the Italian domains of Austria. France committed herself to give Piedmont military assistance, in return for which she would receive Nice and the Savoy region. War broke out in April the same year following an Austrian ultimatum. The combined forces of France and Piedmont marched east into Lombardy, winning many victories, among them the battles of Solferino and San Martino. When they entered Venetia and began the siege of the fortress of Peschiera, it was thought that the Austrians would soon withdraw. But, unexpectedly, and for reasons still unknown, the Emperors of Austria and France signed an armistice at Villafranca. Deeply embittered by Napoleon's breach of promise, Cavour promptly resigned as Premier of Piedmont. Of the Austrian possessions only Lombardy was annexed to Piedmont, while Venetia remained in Austrian hands. Nevertheless the final stage of Italy's unification had been reached, for the people of the duchies of Parma, Modena, Tuscany, and the northern papal States rebelled against their governments and asked for annexation to Piedmont. France, although worried lest the new State should rapidly become stronger than originally foreseen, made no official objection because of England's sympathy for Piedmont, and because she was receiving Nice and the Savoy region, in spite of the fact that she had forfeited these territories by signing the armistice of Villafranca.

In January, 1860, Cavour, who had been recalled as Premier, perceived that the moment had arrived to complete the programme begun in previous years. Sicilian patriots had asked Garibaldi to land an armed force on their island and rout the Bourbon dynasty from it. Despite the risks involved, Cavour decided to back the venture which appealed to Garibaldi's romantic personality. If successful, the expedition would make the annexation of the southern provinces possible; if it failed, the responsibility would not be placed officially on the Government of Piedmont. On May 5, 1860, with the knowledge and assistance of Cavour, Garibaldi and his thousand volunteers embarked on two ships near Genoa. A few days later an army known as the 'Mille' (the thousand) landed at Marsala on the west coast of Sicily. Under Garibaldi's blows, the forces of the King of Naples crumbled to pieces, and the cities, one by one, opened their gates to the long-awaited deliverer. After Garibaldi's initial successes, volunteers enlisted under his banners from every part of the country, and when he entered the city of Naples, his march became a triumph. The King fled with his best troops to the fortified port of Gaeta. The last battle was fought on the Volturno River.

In central Italy the situation was more critical, for papal and French troops were trying to subdue the rebellious inhabitants. In the hope of stirring the population and of bringing Garibaldi, who was showing republican tendencies, under the influence of the dynasty of Piedmont, Cavour organised a military enterprise, personally commanded by King Victor Emmanuel II. Occupying the regions of Marche and Umbria, in the papal States, the expedition met little resistance from the Pope's forces. The King of Piedmont and his army continued their march, advancing south into the kingdom of Naples. Cavour's fears that Garibaldi might turn republican were unwarranted, for, when he met the King, he placed himself at his disposal, thus emphasising that he did not intend to retain control of the territories he had conquered. Indeed, a few days later he gave up the command of his troops and retired to the small island of Caprera, in the Tyrrhenian Sea. The former Bourbon King held the fortress of Gaeta until the beginning of 1861, when the city fell after an attack from land and sea.

On March 14, 1861, the unity of the peninsula was sanctioned legally and constitutionally when Parliament met in Turin. Members representing the newly annexed regions attended, and Victor Emmanuel II was officially proclaimed first King of Italy. Thus in less than two years the peninsula, with the exception of Rome and Venice, was at last under one sovereign and one government.

The new State, with over 21 million inhabitants, brought a great change to the map of Europe and to diplomatic relations between the major Powers. Heretofore Italy had been considered a divided country lacking unity and strength. Now instead she became a decisive factor in the continental balance of power. The English Foreign Minister, Lord Russell, showed immediate appreciation of the events that had taken place, and in a note written to his representative in Turin he rejoiced that the Bourbons had been expelled from Naples. Drawing a parallel between this event and the English Revolution of 1688 when the Stuarts were overthrown, he praised the way the people had revolted against their governments and unanimously accepted the principle of constitutional monarchy. In March 1861 England recognised the new State, an example which was followed a month later by Switzerland and the United States of America. Unfortunately for Italy, Cavour died a few months afterwards.

Many problems were still unsolved. The Bourbons, who had escaped to Rome, still had powerful friends in the southern provinces on whom they could rely. From his Roman refuge the former King of Naples began his intrigues, and guerrilla warfare started in which both partisans and brigands took part. The Italian Government was not lenient to these domestic enemies, and, when caught, many of them were put to death.

Rome and Venice continued to be thorny issues. Rome and the surrounding region of Latium, the only territories still held by the Pope after the annexation of central Italy, were intimately related to the life of the Church and their future was of direct concern to the whole Catholic world, yet Italian leaders were moved by the desire to complete the task of unifying the peninsula. Cavour, before his death, had insisted that Rome should become Italy's capital. In a famous speech delivered on March 25, 1861, before the Chamber of Deputies, he had said: 'The choice of a capital is determined by great moral considerations. It is the people's duty to determine the questions related to it. Now all historical, intellectual, and moral factors which must determine the features of a capital of a great state are to be found in Rome. Rome is the only Italian city that does not bear solely municipal memories. The history of Rome from the time of the Caesars to the present day is the history of a city, the importance of which surpasses by far its territory. This is, therefore, the city destined to be the capital of a great State!' Cavour thought that the problem of relations between Church and State could be solved by making the two bodies independent of one another. This concept he summarised in the words: 'A free Church in a free State.' This idea, so obvious and logical, was loudly heralded as a new constitutional principle, bound to satisfy the two parties and provide them with the means of accomplishing their functions.

Cavour's successors (Ricasoli, Rattazzi, Farini, Minghetti, La Marmora, Lanza) had to cope with innumerable difficulties. Garibaldi, for instance, caused the Government much trouble in the summer of 1862. With 2,500 volunteers, he left the Sicilian coast and landed in Calabria, intending to march on Rome. This expedition was patterned on the one that had brought about the annexation of the kingdom of Naples. But it was fraught with danger for the newly formed State, for Rome was defended by French troops and its occupation at that moment was bound to have large repercussions on the whole Catholic world. The Government therefore had to step in before any international complications arose. Troops were sent to meet the invaders and a battle ensued in which Garibaldi was wounded. In the years that followed Garibaldi continued to create turmoil and confusion by engaging in adventures that excited the imagination of simple-minded people who thought action, instead of diplomacy, was most needed. The opposite, however, was true. After an agreement with Napoleon III, by which Italy committed herself not to occupy Rome (1864), the capital was transferred from Turin to Florence.

The problem of Venice, on the other hand, was ripe for a

solution. Recent events had brought Italy and Prussia closer together, for both had a common foe in the Austrian Empire. In 1866 an alliance was signed between the two States, and it was not long before war broke out against Austria. This third war of independence is considered by Italians a sad event, although the Austrians, after having been defeated by the Prussians at Sadowa, agreed to renounce Venice and the surrounding region, which after a plebiscite were annexed by Italy. Despite this favourable result two lost battles, Custoza (by land) and Lissa (by sea), left bitter memories and detracted somewhat from the joy of achievement. Strategically, the annexation of Venice left Italy in an unfavourable position. Two territories to which Italy felt herself entitled for geographic and historical reasons—Alto Adige in the Alps, with the cities of Trento and Bolzano, and the region of Istria with Trieste—remained in Austrian hands. The new borders left the Po Valley defenceless and practically at the mercy of the Hapsburg Empire.

As to Rome, the problem of the 'eternal city' was linked to that of relations between Church and State, and these were far from good. It seemed as if the Government lost no occasion to make them more difficult and tense. Legislation was introduced invalidating religious marriages, abolishing several religious bodies, and confiscating the estates of the Church. Unrest spread throughout the papal domains. Garibaldi moved around the peninsula organising volunteers. By late summer 1867 these preparations had reached alarming proportions. As Napoleon III threatened to intervene in favour of the Pope, Garibaldi was arrested and expelled to the island of Caprera. Although his troops were ordered to disband, some of them, led by the Cairoli brothers, entered the papal States and almost reached the outskirts of Rome. Here they were routed by the Pope's troops. Meanwhile, Garibaldi succeeded in escaping from Caprera. Reaching Florence, he inflamed the people in favour of war. He then took command of the armed rebels and entered the papal territory. Napoleon III took immediate action. French troops met Garibaldi's men at Mentana near Rome, where they proved to be far superior in number and equipped with better weapons. Garibaldi was defeated and escaped. He was soon arrested and again confined at Caprera.

With France hostile, the Roman problem could not be solved. Nor for the moment did it seem as if the situation was likely to alter. French Catholics were, in fact, extremely strong and were determined to use their influence on the Emperor in defence of the Pope's last domains. But events took a different turn with the outbreak of the Franco-Prussian War in 1870. France was quickly at the mercy of the well-organised Prussian army, and the Italian Government considered itself released from the treaty by which it was committed not to occupy Rome. King Victor Emmanuel II wrote to the Pope asking him to put an end to the nation's troubles by allowing his state to be annexed. The Pope answered that he would give in only to force. Military action was therefore decided upon, and on September 20, 1870, Italian troops entered the city of Rome. Thus the Pope demonstrated to the world that he did not consent to renounce his power but was only yielding to violence. He therefore confined himself in the Vatican as if he were a prisoner of Italy's Government. In a plebiscite on October 7, 1870, the Roman people voted in favour of annexation to Italy. At last unity had been achieved which only a few years before had been considered impossible, and the nation could now strive for social and economic improvement. Italy, with nearly 27 million inhabitants, was now a major European Power and had entered the family of nations. The final goal of the Risorgimento had been realised.

Chapter 3

The Heritage of the Risorgimento (1871–1915)

NO EUROPEAN nation, with the exception of those under Turkish rule, had languished for so long under a foreign Power. It is small wonder, therefore, that Italy, at last independent, did not immediately determine a policy for the future. Theodore Mommsen, the German historian, once inquired of Italy's statesman, Quintino Sella: 'What do you intend doing in Rome? We are all worried, for it is impossible to stay in Rome without universal aims or purposes!' Sella, who was thus offered a chance to explain why Italy wished to complete her unity, and who might have spoken of the Roman heritage, of Christianity, of the Renaissance, all of which were sufficiently universal ideals to justify the city's annexation, answered that science was what the Italians were looking for in Rome. As if the patriots who had died on Austrian scaffolds and by the Bourbons' bullets had been solely interested in the advancement of knowledge! No answer could be more alien to the dreams of those Italians who had gallantly fought in order that a nation, proudly conscious of its past, might arise from the small States of the peninsula and assume its place among European Powers.

Fascist historiography has alleged that after Cavour's death statesmen were incapable of providing the country with the leadership it needed. As a consequence, the years between the achievement of unity in 1870 and the declaration of war on Austria in 1915 were looked upon with contempt. On the contrary, these years were of outstanding importance in forming the structure of the nation. People had to abandon the heroic mentality of the Risorgimento years and become interested in more practical matters. The time had passed when a group of ardent but inexperienced patriots could conquer a kingdom. Uncontrolled actions were outdated. Diplomacy in European affairs and a new type of administration were needed to give the nation stability. Any disappointment felt by people of the earlier generation, or any criticism of Government activities after 1870, was due to the contrast between the heroic past and the necessities of ordinary life. It was a time of transition: Italy now had to balance her budget, find new sources of income, stamp out illiteracy, and plan a national programme of public works. Wars and revolutions may satisfy the adventurous inclinations of people, but they do not improve their welfare.

A great deal had been written and spoken about liberty, Parliament, the constitution, and individual rights, but few people had any clear idea of the real significance of such terms. Liberty, to some, meant keeping the country in a state of turmoil. Democracy, to some, was the equivalent of a parliamentary system; by others it was interpreted as rule by direct action—that is, by the mob. Few understood that democracy is an empirical concept with no limitations. The English never defined it because definitions can easily bring about most contradictory consequences (in our time a 'progressive' democracy has come to mean a form of unprecedented tyranny!). It was natural that such different conceptions should influence parliamentary life. Discontent arose among citizens who felt the nation was not living up to their idealistic expectation. This was not true. The people, dominated by the memory of Cavour's strong personality, did not appreciate that elections after 1870 brought to Parliament men of value who found many occasions to display their capacities. Unfortunately for the popularity of these men, the problems with which they had to deal were not of the type that appeals to the populace, always more impressed by the rattling of arms than by the silent logic of figures. As the right to vote was limited in Italy to few categories of taxpayers, only 2 per cent of the population was represented. Parliament was therefore the expression of the wealthy classes, especially the owners of landed property.

Relations between Church and State remained strained, making life difficult for both. After the annexation of Rome an Act was passed by Parliament known as the 'Legge delle Guarentigie' (Law of the Guarantees). It recognised the Pope's position and granted him the prerogatives and honours of a sovereign. He was left the palaces of the Vatican and the Lateran, exempted from taxation, and a yearly sum was allotted to him in the State budget. He was also granted the right of freely receiving diplomatic missions from foreign States and of sending his own envoys abroad. The Law of the Guarantees was an example of good statesmanship that enabled Italy to master the strong opposition encountered in dealings with Catholic countries. Friction and animosity lasted for several years, but in many ways the Church was freer than she had ever been in the past, when, for example, Italian States had restricted her powers, especially in the appointment of bishops. Such limitations no longer existed. Pope Pius IX died in 1878, and Leo XIII was elected to succeed him. This famous Pontiff, who was to occupy a special place in history because of his stand on social questions embodied in the encyclical *Rerum Novarum*, followed the example of his predecessor and again protested against the occupation of the papal States.

Fiscal and economic questions had been shelved during the years of the Risorgimento, and it now became the unpleasant but necessary task of the Finance Minister, Quintino Sella (1827–84), to balance the country's budget. His financial policy of 'economy to the bone' drew criticism, for additional taxation has never made a man or a government popular. Taxpayers, especially in the South, fondly recalled the time when the Government required less money, and a phrase began to circulate: 'One was better off when things were worse!' It was not, however, a fair judgment, for modern experience has proved that the most heavily taxed countries are often the most progressive. After 1870 Italy was in fact animated by a great desire to do things and get on her feet. A programme of industrialisation was embarked on, especially in the North, where geographical conditions, communications, and supplies were more favourable. Soon Italian industries were competing with those of countries such as England, France, and Germany, and were taking part in many international exhibitions.

A national scheme of railway construction was launched in order to bring the various regions closer together. In 1871 the Mont Cenis tunnel, connecting Italy with France, was opened. Ten years later the St. Gotthard tunnel, linking Italy with Switzerland, was completed. A large programme of public works was initiated, and private enterprise was stimulated. Cities developed rapidly as new factories were established to meet the demands of an increasing population. Between 1864 and 1871 new residential districts were built in Florence, and Rome, after it became the capital, underwent a similar development. Turin regained power in the financial and industrial field and became, after Milan, the country's chief production centre. The harbours of Genoa and Naples showed revived activity through increased trade and the emigration movement. Despite widespread criticism, Italy's position was improving, and so was the general standard of living. Gradually the generation that had contributed so much to the making of the nation passed away. Mazzini died in 1872, and Garibaldi, who devoted his last years to literary work and lived in voluntary seclusion on the island of Caprera, died ten years later. King Victor Emmanuel II was succeeded on his death in 1878 by his son, Humbert I.

The year 1876 was a crucial one. Parliament was divided between right and left. The former, to which Cavour had belonged and which had been in power throughout the years of the Risorgimento, was defeated. A new majority was formed, led by the former leftist opposition. Since both parties were represented in a parliament elected by a minority of people holding property and paying taxes, there was nothing revolutionary in the change. The left, however, followed more advanced ideas by advocating reforms, such as granting political suffrage to wider classes of people, compulsory and free education for all, and reduction of the unpopular tax on flour. The policy of the left is often known by the name of *Trasformismo* (*transformism*). The term generally refers to the scientific doctrine according to which one species develops from another, but in its political meaning it expressed the idea that statesmen belonging to the left had no clear platform, but adapted their programme to general circumstances and conditions. The right, being out of office, should have formed a parliamentary opposition, but, since there was little difference between the two parties, members of the right voted on many issues for the Cabinet. As a reward, they were granted political favours, while Government offices would give special consideration to the problems and needs of their constituencies. *Trasformismo* thus became a word of contempt; it was thought the system was corrupting parliamentary life by confounding issues and sponsoring local interests.

In this censure there was much exaggeration and some truth, since in all democratic States the party in power can bestow a certain amount of patronage. Citizens whose idealistic concept of government was offended criticised the left, and their accusations of misgovernment were specifically directed against Agostino

Depretis (1813–87), who, although not always holding the premiership, led public affairs up to 1887. While it may be true that Depretis and his friends lacked the daring, courage, and ability of Cavour, it must be said that they were profoundly interested in consolidating what had already been accomplished. Citizens who felt that the country should follow a more vigorous policy in foreign affairs were not impressed by local and practical achievements. Their sentiments were violently expressed by Giosuè Carducci, the national poet, who through his writings was deeply influencing public opinion.

The Government's cautious approach in foreign policy was called *La politica delle mani nette* (the clean-hands policy). While Italy was acting with restraint, other Powers were displaying their imperialistic tendencies. So at the Congress of Berlin in 1878, when Austria and Great Britain were granted territories belonging to the Turkish Empire, Italy remained with clean, but empty hands. The Government found it also difficult to improve the condition of Italians living in Austrian territory. It was hoped that Austria would gradually adopt a more liberal attitude. These hopes unfortunately did not materialise, for Vienna began favouring the Slav and German elements living in Italian regions, thus complicating the population problem.

Italy had always shown great interest in acquiring Tunisia, to which many of her citizens had emigrated and which was only ninety miles from the Sicilian coast. Had she been able to acquire this territory, her position in the Mediterranean would have been considerably improved. Public opinion was therefore very embittered when France annexed that territory in 1881. As a consequence many citizens began thinking that an alliance should be made with Austria and Germany in order to re-establish the balance of power. No affection could be felt for Austria, whose actions had retarded the Risorgimento and who still held more than a million Italians within her borders. But the principle that nations cannot select their allies but must accept those offered by circumstances was then as true as ever. However, no feud existed with Germany, Italy's ally in the war of 1866. Bismarck himself, although considering the new State *une jeune et inquiète nation*, felt that he needed it in order to strengthen his hand towards Russia. The outcome was the signing of an alliance between the three Powers. Unfortunately, the Government of Rome, resentful towards France because of

Tunisia, was in a hurry to conclude a treaty. Impatience has always been the enemy of good diplomacy. Although Count di Robilant, the Italian ambassador in Vienna, suggested that the initiative should be left to the other two partners, his advice was not followed, and the treaty known as the Triple Alliance was quickly drafted and signed in Berlin in 1882. It was periodically extended up to the outbreak of World War I. In 1887, when it was renewed for the first time, Count di Robilant was Italy's Foreign Minister. He allowed Germany to take the initiative on the question of renewal and was able to obtain new and better conditions, which included protection of Italian interests in the Turkish Empire and the assurance that no occupation of the Balkans would take place without mutual consultation. That same year a treaty was signed with England for naval co-operation in the Mediterranean.

The strengthening of Italy's international position by means of treaties was chiefly aimed at facilitating her expansion in the African continent. This was a necessity imposed by her geographical and strategic position, which had become more precarious after the French annexation of Tunisia. Africa had been divided into spheres of influence by the major Powers, and Italy felt she was justified in expanding in the territories to which, as yet, no European sovereignty had been extended. This, it was believed, could be the solution to the problem of surplus population migrating to other countries.

Her first move in Africa was directed towards the coasts of the Red Sea, which, following the opening of the Suez Canal, had become an extension of the Mediterranean and the most important shipping route to the Indies. The Rubattino Steamship Company had already purchased from native rulers the Bay of Assab on the African coast of the Red Sea, for the purpose of establishing there a coal refuelling station for merchant ships. From that moment explorers and travellers, such as Antinori, Gessi, Cecchi, Giulietti, Bianchi, and Cardinal Massaia, risked their lives in daring expeditions. Geographical and colonial societies were founded to encourage exploration, trade, and, ultimately, annexation. In 1881 the Government bought the Bay of Assab from the Rubattino Company, and a year later enlarged its possessions by annexing neighbouring territories. In 1885 the port of Massawa, farther north, was acquired. English and Italian interests in this area should have aimed at the partition of the Sudan, but this design failed when English expansion came to a standstill, following General Gordon's death and the occupation of Khartoum by the Dervishes. Italian expansion was consequently directed toward the South-west, against Abyssinia, the native State spreading on the high plateau of East Africa.

Italy's colonial wars had many phases. In 1887, when influence was being spread more by political means than by warfare, an Abyssinian chieftain surprised at Dogali a column of 500 Italian soldiers, who, after fighting bravely, were overcome and massacred. A few months later Premier Depretis, who headed the left, died and was succeeded by Francesco Crispi (1819–1901), a gifted statesman who had assisted Garibaldi in the conquest of Sicily. He served two terms as Premier, the first one between 1887 and 1891, the second between 1893 and 1896. Crispi immediately impressed upon the country's African policy the mark of his strong personality. He in fact consolidated the new colonial possessions, and amalgamated them into one single colony bearing the name of Eritrea. Territories were also obtained from the British East Africa Company and, by welding them together, the new colony of Italian Somaliland was formed on the coast of the Indian Ocean.

In 1889 the Negus of Abyssinia died and a struggle began among minor chieftains for his succession. Menelek, King of Shoa, was the winner. The following year an agreement was signed between him and Italy known as the Treaty of Uccialli. This was the cause of much trouble. Two copies of it—one in Italian, the other in Amharic, the official Ethiopian language—had been signed, and each of them was to be considered authentic. Eventually a discrepancy between the two texts was discovered which related to Abyssinia's foreign policy. The Italian copy, published in Rome, stated clearly in Article 17 that Abyssinia was to conduct her foreign affairs through the Italian Government. This meant the recognition of a protectorate. The Amharic copy, on the other hand, read that the Negus 'could make use of the Government of the King of Italy for the dealing of all questions concerning other Powers and governments'. The consequence of these different wordings was that Abyssinia would not be compelled by the treaty to pass through Italian diplomatic channels, and therefore was not under any protectorate. Menelek denounced the treaty and prepared for war.

For some time the situation remained static until Italy started her expansion again and penetrated into Abyssinian territory, which, following an agreement with Great Britain, had been recognised as within her sphere of influence. The situation became critical when the Abyssinians in reply attacked the small Italian outposts. In the autumn of 1895 the fortress of Amba Alagi, held by 2,000 men, succumbed to overwhelming enemy pressure. A few months later the fort of Makallè was captured. The final battle that determined the war took place at Adowa, where an Italian army of 20,000 men (largely composed of natives) was defeated by 100,000 Abyssinians. Back in Rome, Crispi did not wait for his opponents to attack him in Parliament, but promptly resigned. A new government, again headed by a Sicilian, Di Rudini, signed an armistice, renouncing Italy's claim on Abyssinia as a protectorate, but retaining possession of Eritrea. Public opinion exaggerated the importance of this event. All great Powers have suffered setbacks during their colonial expansion, and Adowa should have been considered merely an episode. The Italians did not appreciate the importance of their territorial gains, chiefly because the moral issues of unity and independence, for which they had so recently fought during the Risorgimento, were still uppermost in their minds. It seemed to them unethical to deprive a country of its independence even if it was far from civilised and still tolerated slavery.

The Government's position was delicate as much on account of domestic events as of defeat abroad. A financial scandal had shocked the public in 1893, three years prior to the Battle of Adowa. Following a parliamentary inquiry, it was discovered that the Banca Romana, one of the country's most important banks, was open to the charge of grave mismanagement. Several politicians had borrowed money from the bank, but, unfortunately, the loans had the appearance of bribes. The truth concerning the affair will probably never be known, for all evidence about the case was destroyed. There was, however, much exaggeration in the charges of corruption. Felice Cavallotti, an extremely violent member of parliament, later killed in a duel, led the opposition. At the time of the scandal he had hopes of becoming Premier, and seized the opportunity to press his charges with great zeal. Discontent also spread among the lower classes. Revolts broke out in Sicily and in Lunigiana (a part of northern Tuscany) because of the people's poverty. Rebellion began even in the North, where a new social class, formed of industrial workers, was gradually coming into being. In 1898 a violent uprising broke out in Milan and profoundly impressed Government circles. Although it was quelled by military force, it showed that organised labour had entered the political picture.

Handicapped by lack of raw materials, Italy had arrived late on the production front. She had, nevertheless, succeeded in building up important industries that were successfully competing in many international markets. This had brought into being an industrial working-class concentrated in a few centres. The pattern of its growth was the same as that of other European countries. Trade unions were soon established and the movement rapidly acquired strength and importance. The workers struck for higher wages, shorter hours, and better working conditions. Politically, they had no definite programme because for the moment they were faced with too many economic problems to be interested in such political issues as electing their representatives to Parliament. Their immaturity had, in fact, caused insurrections in Sicily and Milan, the chief defect of which had been the lack of a clear programme. In 1898, during a wave of reactionary feeling on the part of the leading class, the Government, headed by General Pelloux, attempted to enact measures limiting the right of union and the liberty of the Press, but the Bill met with great opposition in the Chamber of Deputies, and thus focused the public's attention on the problems of the working class. New elections, held in 1900, resulted in the election of thirty-three Socialists, as against the previous sixteen. These were significant results, because political franchise was still limited to a small group of electors belonging for the most part to the richer classes, who were not inclined to follow revolutionary doctrines.

At the turn of the century King Humbert I was murdered by an anarchist in the park of the city of Monza, near Milan. This event shook public opinion. The King had been a constitutional monarch, in the English sense of the word, and had always respected the will of Parliament, unlike his father, who had been faithful to the letter but not always to the spirit of the constitution, and had often wanted to impose his will against the advice of his responsible ministers.

Humbert I was succeeded by his son, Victor Emmanuel III, scarcely thirty years of age. After the accession of the new King, the Government, headed by Giuseppe Saracco (1821–1907), was in office less than a year. It fell, unexpectedly, in 1901, giving Giovanni Giolitti the opportunity of returning to power. Giolitti had last been Premier eight years before, during the financial scandal of the Banca Romana. After the fall of Saracco he was ready for the succession and became the most influential member of a transitional Cabinet headed by Zanardelli (1826–1903). When this statesman resigned in 1903, Giolitti became Premier, and remained in power until 1914, either at the head of the Cabinet, or using figureheads such as Fortis and Luzzatti, who faithfully followed his policies. Giolitti's personality was controversial. His adversaries, during and after his lifetime, contended that he was solely an opportunist with an ability to attract men to his cause and manipulate elections to his advantage. According to this view, he copied Depretis and the *trasformismo* methods. Although he was never a declared enemy of Fascism, Fascist historiography was largely responsible for this trend of thought. Others—and this group included no less a man than the philosopher Benedetto Croce—believed his leadership was beneficial to the country's moral and material progress. His policies were fundamentally cautious and his temperament quite different from Crispi's. His ability in dealing with public affairs without giving in to temperamental moods contributed towards restoring Italy's international position.

Giolitti realised that an agreement with France was necessary. Relations between the two countries had been strained since the annexation of Tunisia and the signing of the Triple Alliance. Crispi had followed a policy of friendship towards Germany that could hardly be regarded with favour by France, where the memory of the recent German occupation was still very much alive. Crispi's visits to Bismarck had been publicised in a manner that did not ease relations. Furthermore, a serious incident had taken place in 1893 at Aigues-Mortes, where a number of Italians had been massacred by French workers. France had also waged an economic war by refusing to renew the trade treaty, thus limiting imports and causing grave concern to Italian farmers. This tariff war was brought to an end by a new commercial treaty, but under Giolitti's influence relations improved even more. Visits were exchanged between the sovereigns of Italy and President Loubet of France. Notes were exchanged, stating that Italy was not interested in the future of Morocco, while France made a similar declaration regarding Libya. This was an endorsement by each country of the other's colonial policies. Another declaration followed, on the part of Italy, concerning her neutrality in the event of France being attacked by a third Power.

Visits were also paid by the King and Queen to the Emperors of Russia and Germany, and to the King of England. The royal family did not, however, visit Francis Joseph, the Emperor of Austria, since he had never returned the call paid him by King Humbert I. The German Chancellor, Von Bülow, reluctantly accepted these independent policies, but was quoted as saying that he did not mind if his southern ally occasionally 'danced a waltz' with another partner. Although remaining faithful to the Triple Alliance, renewed in 1902, Italy's relations with Austria were strained. The greatest obstacle to a sincere friendship between the two countries was the position of Italians living within the Austrian borders. The *irredenti* (the unredeemed), as they were generally called, had been discriminated against by the Government of Vienna, and the request by the inhabitants of Trieste for an Italian university had been consistently rejected. Anti-Italian demonstrations had also taken place in Trieste with little if any intervention on the part of the Austrian authorities.

Italy's foreign policy, as expressed by her Foreign Minister, Tommaso Tittoni (1855–1931), was nonetheless faithful to the Triple Alliance, though displaying moderate friendship towards England and France. In 1906, during the conference of Algeciras at which the fate of Morocco was determined, Italy sided with France. In 1908 Austria annexed the regions of Bosnia and Herzegovina, formerly belonging to the Turkish Empire, which she had administered since the Congress of Berlin in 1878. This was a breach of existing agreements, according to which no territorial change could take place in the Balkans without previous consultations. Following this event, a widespread anti-Austrian feeling swept Italy. It was at this juncture that the moral foundation of the Triple Alliance collapsed. Vienna gave some formal satisfaction to Rome by granting minor concessions to her Italian minority. Their effect was eventually nullified by a rumour, which turned out to be true, that after the severe earthquake which shook Messina and Reggio Calabria in 1908, General Conrad, Chief of the Austrian General Staff, had suggested that the opportunity should be seized for a military occupation of the peninsula. The earthquake caused widespread tragedy and damage: 150,000 persons were killed and the number of injured was beyond count.

The first decade after the turn of the century was one of economic progress and achievement. After the first uncertain step the country had greatly advanced and there had been uninterrupted industrial expansion. Private enterprise began to abandon the old investments in landed property and to venture into new fields of industry and trade, bringing higher profits, creating more employment, and increasing State revenues. This happier state of the public budget enabled the Government to reduce the interest rate of the public debt from 4 per cent to $3\frac{3}{4}$ per cent, and later to $3\frac{1}{2}$ per cent. Treasury Minister Luigi Luzzatti (1841–1927), an able financier, who was also Premier for a short time, accomplished this reduction in 1910 and received much praise for his ability. Although no heavier taxation was introduced, more money was available for the welfare of the people, education, and public works. The moneys allotted for the budgets of the ministries concerned doubled between 1900 and 1907. The South, which previously had been abandoned, and to which the Government, even when headed by southerners, paid scant attention, became the object of important measures aimed at improving living conditions. The greatest feat accomplished in this area was the construction of the aqueduct of Apulia, which supplied sufficient water to a region known since Roman times as 'thirsty Apulia'. The improvement of production affected every branch of industry. Between 1890 and 1907 the index of foreign trade increased by 118 per cent. New methods of agriculture were introduced, especially in the Po Valley, where soil conditions and a more progressive attitude on the part of farmers favoured such innovations. The value of the yearly agricultural production advanced from five billion to seven billion lire between 1895 and 1910. Although trade agreements had favoured industry at the expense of farming interests, every effort was made to improve production in quality and quantity, as domestic consumption was increasing. During this period King Victor Emmanuel III founded the International Institute of Agriculture in Rome and financed it out of his personal income.

Under Fascism much objection was raised to Giolitti's liberal policy. He was criticized for lack of action, and was said to have given way to the revolutionary working class. Giolitti's seeming inability to settle strikes and quell labour unrest was, however, due to his firm belief that through trade unionism the conditions of the working man would improve.

For the first time, agrarian strikes took place in the North, where the organisation of trade unions had been easier and where farming had developed on a more industrial basis. In the South, on the other hand, the peasant class still clung to ancient traditions that were difficult to break. Such strikes seemed dramatic in those times, when public opinion was not used to labour unrest. In reality they were only a struggle for economic advancement. Giolitti might easily have repeated the mistake other statesmen had made in 1898, when popular demands had been violently rejected. Fortunately, he knew that the most responsible leaders of the working class would soon realise that the best way to increase salaries and improve general conditions was not to revolt but to strengthen the bargaining power of trade unionism. He fully understood that an economic demand which may seem a revolutionary issue during the course of a strike becomes nothing more than a matter of debate and of legislative action when brought before Parliament. In 1913 he widened political suffrage. This move was severely criticised by Conservatives, who thought that by so doing he was bestowing a political favour on a large section of the population that had not asked for it. Some people resentfully believed that the measure was motivated by his wish to influence the electorate more than by genuine trust in the people. These criticisms lack any foundation, because contingent reasons for adopting a policy, or introducing a reform, do not change the value and the consequences of the policy or reform. As Benedetto Croce has rightly pointed out, the duty of a statesman is to anticipate, and, if necessary, create, the needs of the people, not only to interpret them.

Up to this moment Parliament had been most unrepresentative of the country. The electorate had been limited to a small section of the citizens, and Catholics, complying with the papal order to abstain from the polls, had refrained from voting. After the death of Pope Leo XIII in 1903 the Conclave for his successor's election was highly dramatic. The majority of the Sacred College of Cardinals favoured the election of Cardinal Rampolla, who in the first scrutinies had been given the highest number of votes. His election seemed certain, when it was vetoed by the Archbishop of Cracow, acting on behalf of Francis Joseph, the Austrian Emperor, who was thus making use of an ancient privilege of his dynasty. Rampolla protested against this interference of temporal power in the affairs of the Church, but the Emperor's move was sufficient to alienate some of the votes essential for the two-thirds majority which was necessary for the election of the Pontiff. The Patriarch of Venice, Cardinal Sarto, was eventually elected, and assumed the name of Pius X. He was a peasant's son and a man of great humility who has recently been proclaimed a Saint. In order to counteract Socialist influence, he annulled the order that Catholics should abstain from voting at elections.

In this atmosphere of improved economic conditions, with a rising standard of living, Italy started and successfully concluded a new colonial period. A few years after Adowa, the nation's approach underwent a change. The population now numbered 34 million, and the need for territorial outlets was widely felt. Much had been done in the two East African colonies to improve local conditions and increase trade. For ten years Ferdinando Martini (1841–1928), a member of parliament and a writer, was governor of Eritrea, which under his able administration had made great strides. Up to 1905, when the State took over and new agreements were signed with the Sultan of Zanzibar, Somaliland was administered by private companies. The boundaries of the colony were fixed between the Juba River in the south and British Somaliland in the north. On the east the colony was bounded by the Indian Ocean, while on the west the frontiers of Abyssinia remained somewhat vague. These undetermined borders were one of the causes of war in 1935. A treaty was signed in 1906 between Italy, France, and England, by which each contracting party extended its influence in a different zone of Abyssinia.

Yet, Italy's colonial policy was chiefly influenced by her position in the Mediterranean, where her banking and trading companies had spread to many ports and cities, successfully competing with local and foreign enterprise. For centuries, indeed, Italian communities had existed in Mediterranean countries. Some could trace their origins back to the Venetians, while others had emigrated in later times. All had preserved the language, religion, and customs of their forefathers.

Other Powers had also strengthened their position in the Mediterranean. The Congress of Berlin had in fact given the island of Cyprus to England, already in occupation of Egypt and in control of the Suez Canal, while France dominated the western Mediterranean. Italy's expansion could take place only in Libya, which belonged to Turkey and was the last remaining North African territory free from European domination. Giolitti prepared for this colonial enterprise with rare ability, for all contacts and agreements from the turn of the century were made with the understanding that, sooner or later, Italy would annex that part of the African coast. After the crisis of 1911, when France and Germany had been on the verge of war over Morocco and had finally reached an agreement whereby that country was to be annexed by France while Germany would get territorial compensations in other parts of Africa, Giolitti realised that the time had come to begin the campaign for which he had been preparing for years. As a result Italy declared war on Turkey on September 29, 1911.

For a long time Turkey had been the 'sick man of Europe' and the object of much European intrigue. Her policies, external and domestic, had been determined by a combination of governmental weakness, Court corruption, and oriental shrewdness. Enmities and conflicting interests between great Powers had helped to keep the Ottoman Empire together. Its different nationalities were despotically dominated and its immense territories spread across Europe, Asia, and Africa. Since Libya was Turkey's last African territory, its defence became a matter of prestige, especially as the Government at Constantinople was now influenced by the Young Turks Party with its violently nationalistic outlook. Resistance to Italian occupation led by Enver Pasha, an able officer who had been educated at the German staff college, was stronger than anticipated. Troops on both sides displayed gallantry and military skill, but the Italians were superior in forces and controlled sea communications. The Turks could, however, rely on the co-operation of the Arabs, for they were united in a holy war against a Christian enemy.

The war was not limited to African soil. A naval battle was fought off the shores of Albania at the entrance to the Adriatic Sea. In April, 1912, the islands of the Dodecanese and Rhodes, in close proximity to the south-west Turkish coast, were occupied by landing forces. During the month of July, Italian light ships forced the Dardanelles. On the African battle-front operations were carried out with determination and success. Turkish resistance soon collapsed, and a peace treaty was signed at Ouchy, Switzerland, on October 15, 1912. Turkey renounced in favour of Italy her sovereignty over Libya, which included the provinces of Tripolitania and Cyrenaica. Rhodes and the Dodecanese were to remain in Italian hands until Turkish forces abandoned Cyrenaica. This evacuation proceeded slowly and the islands remained under Italian administration up to the outbreak of World War I. Since the two countries found themselves again at war, no restitution was ever made and they were eventually annexed.

The war was Giolitti's personal success. It crowned other outstanding achievements in the cultural and economic fields. In 1911 the fiftieth anniversary of the proclamation of the kingdom of Italy was celebrated. Three exhibitions paid public testimony to the many changes that had taken place in half a century. An industrial exhibition was held in Turin, an archaeological and artistic one in Rome, and another artistic one in Florence. Thus the three cities which had been capitals of the new State, and to which the people had looked for guidance and inspiration, were united in a successful effort to publicise the nation's achievements.

The country's influence on European affairs increased after the annexation of Libya. Unrest spread quickly to the Balkans, where ancient antagonism between the Christian nations of Serbia, Montenegro, Greece, and Bulgaria on one side, and Turkey on the other, broke out in the first Balkan War, soon followed by a second one. Events in the Balkans were of the greatest importance to Italy and Austria, because both Powers had interests in that area and were tied by agreements concerning it. In 1912 Germany, Austria, and Italy felt that a show of strength on their part might be appropriate. This could be done by confirming the Triple Alliance. The treaty was therefore extended, although it was not due to expire for a further year and a half. Things did not change very much, for while relations between Germany and Italy remained cordial, they were somewhat strained between Italy and Austria. There was, indeed, a profound difference of opinion in the interpretation of the aims of the alliance. Austria and Germany believed it was a way of strengthening their position and of backing their imperialistic policies. To Italy it meant nothing more than a defensive agreement against unprovoked aggression, as expressed in its wording.

Internally, the nation was passing through important changes. Electoral reform had not produced the results Giolitti had hoped for. New masses of voters, having received the franchise from a liberal government, did not support it at the polls to the extent that had been anticipated, and the elections of October, 1913, were a disappointment to Giolitti's followers. An agreement reached between Liberals and Catholics, favouring common candidates, was not sufficient to check the increase of Socialist deputies, seventy-four of whom were elected. At the same time two ministers resigned from the Cabinet. So precarious was his majority that Giolitti deemed it opportune to resign without even asking for a vote of confidence. Succession went to Antonio Salandra (1853–1931), whose premiership was troubled by social unrest and by the outbreak of World War I.

Chapter 4

Ideologies and Political Parties (1890–1915)

PHILOSOPHICALLY speaking, the Risorgimento was a direct result of doctrines which taught the primacy of the spirit. Italian philosophers in fact, such as Romagnosi, Rosmini, and Cattaneo, whose works inspired the nation's uprising, never departed from the idea that the world does not resolve itself in the changing forms of material forces.

Yet after unity was achieved new foreign philosophies began to spread throughout the country, and the Italian tradition was endangered by materialistic and positivistic schools. Herbert Spencer and Auguste Comte, with their disciples, maintained that man can have no knowledge of anything but phenomena, that this knowledge is relative, and that every inquiry into the origin of the universe is futile. These doctrines were in a sense the by-products of the industrial and mechanical age, for they claimed that nothing exists nor can be discovered beyond physical facts. Industrially developed States, such as Germany, France, and England, were turning their material achievements into philosophic principles. New scientific theories, such as Darwin's on the evolution of the species, seemed to encourage their impulse, giving it scientific justification. Italy, with different conditions and background from northern Europe, was virgin soil where seeds could germinate faster than elsewhere. The new materialistic ideas were therefore accepted with exaggerated enthusiasm. Positivism was soon presented by some Italians as the quintessence of speculation, while, more truly, it was a parody of philosophy, especially when it tried to explain the universe by stating that it could not be explained.

Such great Italians as St. Thomas Aquinas, Dante Alighieri, Tommaso Campanella, and Giovanni Battista Vico had drawn their inspiration from an absolute belief in the existence and superiority of the Spirit. Now, in the land which had given them birth, the prevailing doctrine based everything on phenomena and *prima facie* evidence. Speculation was regarded as a useless device invented by people who could not direct their intelligence to more practical activities; philosophy, as a science, was ridiculed as a waste of energy and time. The term 'science', in fact, was chiefly attributed to chemistry, physics, and natural history, inasmuch as they studied phenomena and things that one could see or touch. Other sciences, usually known as moral, such as art, history, and ethics, were considered minor activities, of extremely limited importance. Italians such as Roberto Ardigò accepted the new theories and contributed to their development.

The prevailing materialism in philosophy and evolutionism in natural science was bound to affect politics. For indeed, Italy, like other Latin countries, believed politics to be not only the art of public administration, but also a way of putting into practice ideals and principles relating to the realm of speculation. The ground was therefore ready to receive and accept new political doctrines such as Marxist Socialism, which towards 1890 made its first appearance in the peninsula, spreading among the working classes and some elements of the *bourgeoisie*.

The uprisings of Sicily and Milan resulted in reactionary policies on the part of the Government, but also aroused greater interest in the welfare of the masses. Factory workers of the North, in strong contrast to the unorganised southern populations, had, in fact, formed a new social class, especially aware of its interests and rights, now effectively defended by trade unions.

It was soon felt that since labour organisations had increased in strength they, too, should be given a political philosophy. This was provided by the theories of Karl Marx formulated in the *Communist Manifesto* and later in *Das Kapital*. The theory that capital is the consequence of a theft of the workers' produce made an immediate appeal to wage-earners, who in daily life were seeing the realisation of Marx's theory that the development of capitalism was accompanied by the impoverishment of the working masses.

Socialism, as a utopian ideal, was not a novelty in Europe. Thinkers like Owen, Lassalle, Saint-Simon, and Fourier had already propagated their ideas on the improvement of working conditions for mankind. Marxist Socialism, however, was quite different; nor was it the gospel of a gentle-minded man. It purported to give a scientific explanation of the evils of the modern world, and to offer an equally scientific solution. Marx believed that existing society would be overthrown by the rising forces of labour as soon as they acquired full consciousness of their strength. The workmen who revolted in Milan in 1898 were aware of the social changes and their implications and possessed a new class consciousness. They revolted not only for cheaper bread and better working conditions, but also for the fulfilment of a programme. Socialism, in the modern sense of the word, had hit Italy. The exponents of the Risorgimento, concerned with unification and independence, had only vaguely understood the working-man's problems, although the humanitarian approach was to be found in Mazzini's works and in the movement he inspired. Carlo Pisacane, a Neapolitan patriot who in 1857 had landed with a group of followers on the coast of Calabria in an attempt to foment an uprising of the peasants, had also been a Socialist, but his case had been an isolated one. After 1870 the workers' movement had been influenced by Mikhail Bakunin (1814–76), a Russian anarchist who had lived in exile in Europe and had made contacts with the rising Italian unions.

German Socialists were responsible for introducing Marxism into Italy, where it fitted into the already existing schemes of the working class. Italians like formulas and have a tendency to be doctrinaire. They constantly attempt to generalise and search for universal implications of events. The Marxist explanation of social problems, even if not always exact, was bound to be given an enthusiastic reception. A practical trade unionism, similar to that of the northern European countries, where it was mainly concerned with the economic struggle and supported political parties chiefly to strengthen its bargaining power, could not satisfy the Italian mind. Politics were, as usual, of first importance, and Marxist teachings were regarded as a sort of gospel. From 1890 onwards they were the object of study and meditation on a large scale. The *Communist Manifesto* and *Das Kapital* were translated and avidly read. Circles and clubs of social culture sprang up in several cities. The Socialist Party was set up in 1892 and Marxist doctrines immediately permeated its programme. In the congresses held at Genoa that same year and at Reggio Emilia in 1893 they received full support and became the party's official ideology, completely supplanting the original anarchist influences.

The first years of Socialism were filled with tumult. Anarchists, although expelled from the party, were in a position to influence its decisions when strikes or matters of policy were determined. They were certainly behind the crisis of 1898. The leaders of the movement, who were then arrested or exiled, realised the necessity of abandoning their uncompromising approach and of strengthening their influence by running for Parliament. While uprisings still took place in the following years, the working class in Italy, as in other countries, gradually abandoned its extreme revolutionary tendencies. After the original infatuation that persuaded the masses to believe a classless era was just round the corner, a reconciliation with practical life was reached. Trade unions strengthened their position as bargaining agencies and their leaders were no longer looked upon as political agitators, but rather as men who had an important task to accomplish in the new economic world.

Socialists showed their parliamentary strength in 1899, when they formed a coalition with republicans and radicals to prevent Parliament from approving new laws which they believed would limit public liberties.

For over a year there was violence in the Chamber of Deputies, filibustering, obstructionism, and at one time the ballot-boxes were broken.

Marxist ideas were being examined critically. An important circle was formed in Milan around the periodical *Critica Sociale* headed by Filippo Turati and Anna Kuliscioff, a Russian woman, exiled from her native country, who had come to Italy, where she contributed to the forming of Socialist thought. This review, which soon took a prominent place in the nation's life, proved that the working-man's rights could also be defended in the cultural field, which until then had been considered the exclusive domain of the upper classes.

From the year 1900 up to the outbreak of World War I, Socialism was also influenced by Giovanni Giolitti, who, although belonging to the middle class, possessed a special understanding of social problems and seemed to want to do the utmost for the emancipation of the working-man. Fascist historians considered that he displayed weakness towards a party whose ultimate aim was the destruction of the State. Giolitti, however, realising that the growing power of labour could be repressed only at the risk of civil strife, believed it more practical to control the new force and induce it to co-operate with the rest of society. A liberal in thought and action, Giolitti felt that there was nothing in social justice that conflicted with the ideal of liberty. On the contrary, the two concepts were merely different facets of the same reality. If the working classes were held down politically, through lack of representation, and economically, through lack of decent wages, they would seek a solution of their problems in revolutionary practices. Giolitti also knew that within Socialism several leaders favoured a policy of co-operation with the State, provided the basic points of their programme were not opposed. This trend was called *riformismo*. Its name emphasised that its exponents advocated a programme of reforms to be gradually achieved through legislation and not by means of violence. Socialist deputy Camillo Prampolini made this clear in a speech he delivered in the Chamber of Deputies in 1902, when he said: 'Essentially we are a reformist party. Our revolution is inherent in the final results of the reforms we favour, not in the means we employ to achieve these reforms.' Speaking of the workers, he added: 'Do not insult them by regarding them as incapable of liberty. . . . It would be cruelly unjust to attempt to suffocate with violence the instinctive aspiration that spurs these poor people towards a more advanced form of social life.'

Giolitti felt that he could co-operate with people who spoke in these terms, even if they sometimes followed turbulent moods that were more the consequences of national temperament than of political ideals. He also believed that all Italians should participate in the life of the State. As things stood, only a few could do so because of limited suffrage and because Catholics would not vote or run as candidates due to papal prohibition. Since no democratic government can really claim to enjoy the people's support if it is the expression of a minority, Giolitti's action aimed at the widening of the electorate so as to bring the greatest number of people into relation with the State. As to economic unrest, he believed the workers had a right to protest against existing conditions, and that strikes would ultimately result in an improvement in the general standard of living. Consequently, he seldom intervened on the side of management, for he felt that there was much in favour of the workers' requests. His policy of appeasement brought good results, for there was a great betterment in the country's economic and social life.

During the years 1903 and 1904 strikes and uprisings took

place all over Italy. Ultimately these agitations proved to be useful to Giolitti, who wanted Catholic voters to take part in public affairs. In fact in the year 1904 Pope Pius X allowed Catholics to take part in elections when it appeared that their participation in certain constituencies would determine a victory for an anti-Socialist. Because of this and the reaction of public opinion to extremist policies, Socialists lost ground in the Chamber of Deputies elected that year.

Giolitti was satisfied with these results, for he believed that the more conservative character of Parliament would teach the Socialists to be less violent in their methods and requests. The lesson was probably useful to reformism, for the more moderate element became stronger, and finally won a majority within the party at the Congress of Florence in 1908. Reformism was assisted in its rise by the General Confederation of Labour set up in Milan for the purpose of leading and organising trade unions. It advocated reforms without violence and soon gained considerable influence. Organised labour, busy with the struggle for better working conditions, was independent of the Socialist Party, although it co-operated with it whenever necessary. The leaders of labour were more practical in their approach to problems, for they were in constant touch with Government and management. Party men, on the contrary, whose contact was mainly with their electors, lacked this common-sense approach and displayed doctrinaire tendencies. The Florence congress was a victory for the labour organisations and the more moderate section of the party. Among the men who believed in gradualism, the most outstanding was Leonida Bissolati, a lawyer, who had greatly influenced the party with his non-extremist propaganda. This new attitude gave Giolitti much satisfaction because it was the fulfilment of his liberal policy towards labour. He said, in a famous speech, that Socialism had moderated its programme and relegated Karl Marx 'to the attic'.

Unfortunately, this was not the whole story. Changes in the ideology of a party can take place suddenly, especially if a certain number of determined and revolutionarily minded people are within its ranks. In the later congresses, held at Modena in 1911 and at Reggio Emilia in 1912, extremist elements came to the fore again, gaining control of the executive positions of the party. At Reggio Emilia the two antithetical conceptions of Socialism clashed. Bissolati and others had visited the King to congratulate him on having escaped an attack on his life. This was regarded as a contemptible display of servility. A young man—called Benito Mussolini—soon to make himself widely known, delivered on this occasion a most violent speech asking for their expulsion from the party.

The following years witnessed the strengthening of the extremist tendency in the Socialist Party, while the moderates, who had been expelled, formed a new party. Although conservative public opinion joyfully proclaimed that as a result of the split in the movement Socialism was dead, this was far from true. Extremism had a great appeal for the electorate, and in 1913, after Giolitti had granted universal suffrage, more Socialist members than ever before were elected to Parliament. Labour unrest became more intense and the weapon of the general strike was frequently employed. The so-called 'Red Week' of Ancona in the year 1914, when strikers performed several acts of violence, showed the consequences of extremist leadership. That same violence, accentuated and dramatised by war and nationalistic passions, was soon to bring forth fruits of wrath and to cause the rise of Fascism.

Political events follow given laws much as physical forces do. An action may easily bring about an equal, but opposite, reaction. The birth and development of Socialism on a national scale were accompanied by the appearance on the political stage of Catholicism. Since the birth of parliamentarianism, the Church, by exercising her influence in favour of certain candidates and parties, had considerably affected the political life of Europe's Catholic countries. Even the growth of a new class of wage-earners—the proletariat—had not weakened her influence, for experience had shown that one could be a socially minded workman and also a good Catholic. Both the clergy and the laity felt that by influencing in a religious way the rising forces of labour, the Church was putting into practice the evangelical teachings. This had been foreseen by Catholic sociologists of the nineteenth century. Although some had abandoned the path of orthodoxy, all had clearly anticipated the social trend of Catholicism. The names of men like Lamennais, Lacordaire, Montalembert, and Dupanloup come to one's mind. They performed the preparatory work which enabled Pope Leo XIII in 1891 to announce the social doctrine of the Church.

During the greater part of the nineteenth century Italian

Catholics had been chiefly concerned with political problems of unification and independence, and had not been particularly interested in the social aspect of modern life. After 1870 the tension between Church and State kept them away from public life. Pope Pius IX had officially prohibited them from taking part in politics. This attitude was summarised in the slogan 'Neither elected nor electors', which signified that Catholics would abstain from voting in national elections. This attitude helped to bring about a state of affairs in which liberal and anti-clerical politicians controlled the country. After the death of Pius IX the situation did not improve, for Leo XIII confirmed his predecessor's opposition and urged Catholics to insist on their resistance. These were years of bitter conflicts. Relations between the temporal and the ecclesiastical power were strained in several countries. France, the 'beloved daughter of the Church', was governed by radicals and extremists. The German Empire, where Catholics were numerous, was waging war against the Papacy by opposing its cultural and political influence. This action, known by the name of *Kulturkampf* and personally directed by Prince Otto Bismarck, was to make relations between the two Powers extremely tense.

The Church was also troubled by internal controversies known under the name of 'modernism', a philosophy which endeavoured to reconcile Catholicism to modern science, interpret the Scriptures according to these new views, and foster a reform of the hierarchy. The feud between the Church and her reformers was to end in 1907, when Pius X condemned modernism on the grounds that it was an alliance 'between faith and a false philosophy'.

At the moment of his election to papal dignity in 1903, Pius X again protested, as his predecessors had done, against the occupation of Rome. When a visit to the King of Italy in Rome by President Loubet of France was announced, the Vatican's Secretary of State, Cardinal Merry del Val, forwarded a note to the Catholic Powers in which he opposed such a visit, on the grounds that any head of a Catholic nation brought grave offence to the Holy Father by coming to pay homage in Rome 'to him who against all rights was retaining his civil sovereignty'.

Yet it was felt that these protests were essentially formal. More than thirty years had elapsed since the occupation of Rome, and experience had shown that, despite official feuds, the Church in Italy had been free to carry out her mission, in sharp contrast with the persecution she had suffered in other countries. Cavour's policy of a free Church in a free State, which inspired the Law of the Guarantees, had worked out a *modus vivendi* that suited both parties.

Although deprived of temporal power, the Church was free to exercise her apostolic mission throughout the peninsula, whereas before the Risorgimento she had had to cope with various States and comply with their requests in matters of policy and in the designation of bishops. Nor had Italy obstructed relations between the Holy See and other States. During the long reign of Leo XIII many Catholic voices had urged the Church and the State to reach an agreement, the necessity of which was advocated alike by Liberals and by more far-seeing Catholics, who felt that national unity would never be achieved until consciences had been appeased.

While Catholics were prohibited from taking part in political activity, the order did not include local and municipal elections, where the weight of their votes had always been felt. Catholics also began to spread Christ's message among the workers. Catholic unions were created in some regions, notably Lombardy and Venetia, where clergy and laity were both extremely efficient and capable.

The social implications of Catholicism became the object of study, as they had in other countries, where the Industrial Revolution had taken place earlier. The ground was thoroughly prepared for a change in the attitude towards political activities. An occasion for the Pope to issue new provisions presented itself in 1904, when the first general strike was proclaimed throughout the peninsula.

Church and State were completely unprepared for this unprecedented event, and while the strike did not bring the dire consequences foreseen at the time, it succeeded in shocking the nation. A group of citizens from Bergamo, an important stronghold of Catholic organisations, visited the Pope and reported their fears that the coming elections might result in the return of a candidate with radical and anti-clerical tendencies in their constituency. They asked the Pope to withdraw the prohibition and allow Catholics to vote for a liberal candidate who, if elected, would respect the Church's rights. On that occasion Pius X lifted the ban indirectly, by telling them to 'act according to their conscience'. As a result, for the first time in history two Catholics, from industrial regions in the North, were elected to Parliament. The following year the encyclical *Il fermo proposito* gave official recognition to the papal decision, and opened the way to the participation of Catholics in the nation's public life.

A political and social movement known as 'Democrazia Cristiana' (Christian Democracy) was founded in 1906 by Romolo Murri, a priest with a profound social feeling. The name of the movement shows that it was based on democracy and Christianity. Murri in fact advocated a programme of reforms to be introduced by the Church. Mazzini's influence could be seen in his thought, according to which democracy should be inspired by religion, otherwise it should not exist. This first political organisation was, unfortunately, too independent and outspoken. By ignoring and often criticising the hierarchy, it displeased the Church. The dissolution of the movement and the unfrocking of Murri followed. Although his work created a crisis within their ranks, Murri contributed to developing the political conscience in people who had been inactive for thirty-five years. If the Catholic party is now the keynote of contemporary Italy, credit must be given to Murri and his followers for their courageous, even if somewhat erroneous, attempt. Various symptoms showed that Italian life was prepared for this participation in public life. Everything pointed to the fact that anti-clericalism was on the decline. The Government had not taken sides in the fight between the Church and modernism, thus showing that it intended to safeguard everybody's liberty of conscience and that it did not want to be involved in theological problems. Nor had it supported the priests who had left the ranks of the Church, or the political and religious movements they had organised.

Giolitti made his programme clear in a speech delivered to Parliament in 1904, when he said that Church and State should be two parallels that never meet. He thus confirmed Cavour's policy of a free Church within a free State. The weakness of anti-clericalism was apparent when, after the turn of the century, a bill legalising divorce was turned down.

The Church was taking direct measures to solve some of the national problems. A constant stream of emigrants was leaving the country each year, many of them in a state of great poverty and moral destitution. Spiritual as well as material assistance was needed to help these people during the first years of residence in foreign countries and to counteract the influence of revolutionary ideas. It was well known that many Italians in the United States had been swayed by anarchism. King Humbert's assassin, for instance, had been inspired and assisted by the anarchist groups in Patterson, New Jersey. The necessity for Catholic guidance was therefore most urgently felt. Bishop Scalabrini of Piacenza created the 'Istituto dei Missionari' (Institute of Missionaries), and Bishop Bonomelli of Cremona the 'Opera di Assistenza degli Emigranti' (Agency for the Assistance of Emigrants). Both had in their programme the sending of priests to foreign countries where they could form parishes and assist newcomers. Soon the priest became, to the lonely, penniless Italians abroad, a beacon, a man on whom they could rely, who could speak their language, and above all, who well understood their problems.

There was great Catholic activity in the field of culture. One result of modernism was that it brought a revival of study. A well-organised Press spread the Catholic point of view in religion, ethics, and politics. This general approach, although strictly orthodox, was progressive and destined to attain concrete results. In 1908 Parliament debated extensively whether religious instruction in schools should be discontinued. The Socialist Leonida Bissolati had introduced a motion for its abolition. The question was of the greatest importance, for it would test the strength of the Church as a religious body, and also as a force that could influence elections. After much discussion Giolitti wound up the debate by saying that one should follow the road wanted by the majority of the people. This, evidently, was the road of adherence to Catholic tradition, for when a vote was taken Bissolati's motion was rejected by a large majority.

The time was ripe for a wider participation in public affairs. In 1907, Ernesto Nathan, the candidate of a coalition of anticlerical and leftist parties, had been elected mayor of Rome. This was a serious setback because it had taken place in the very centre of Christianity. A better organisation of the Catholic electorate was essential if full advantage was to be taken of the papal permission to take part in politics. It was therefore encouraging that in 1909 twenty-one Catholic members were elected to the Chamber of Deputies.

In 1913 Catholic influence was more strongly felt because electoral tactics were skilfully laid down. Giolitti and Count

Gentiloni reached an agreement—generally known as the Gentiloni Pact—on a common policy. The result was that thirty-three Catholics won seats and nearly all the deputies belonging to the Government's majority were re-elected. These results caused great excitement among the leftists, who felt that they had been beaten by Giolitti's superior ability. The Premier was always accused of influencing elections. This time, it was said, he had called upon the Church for assistance, and had received it. The leftists strongly protested against this alliance, although there was nothing immoral or unfair in it. Electoral agreements are a way of carrying on internal affairs in a democracy, as military alliances are the foundation of international affairs. Socialist animosity was clearly expressed by the following definition of the Gentiloni Pact: 'The Almighty placed at the service of the *prefetture* [governmental authorities in the provinces] the use of spiritual threats by parish priests. Crucifixes were given to voters to kiss as sacred commitments to cast their vote in favour of the liberal candidate, of the Jew, of the Freemason, nay of the very devil himself, were he a candidate sponsored by the government.'

Speaking of the doctrines prevailing before World War I, we must mention Gabriele D'Annunzio (1863–1938), who had a great moral influence on his generation. His sensual poetry was the source of patriotic and nationalistic inspiration and created a line of thought destined to achieve great importance in the country's life.

The birth of nationalism can be traced back to Dante, Machiavelli, Guicciardini, and all writers and thinkers who expressed the hope that a unified Italian nation would realise that she was destined by a noble heritage and constant dedication to spiritual ideals to occupy an important place on the world stage. While these ideas might have seemed utopian when Italy was still divided and dominated by foreign nations, they were no longer so when unity was achieved. Italians began to think of their future in terms of expansion and of power. This approach, at times naïve and provincial, was certainly not contemptible, especially when other countries were setting an example of national expansion. England was then in the full swing of an imperial policy three centuries old. Russia was expanding in Asia. Germany was annexing territory in different parts of the world. France, having recovered from the 1870 defeat, had seriously harmed Italy's strategic interests by the annexation of Tunisia.

Among all nations, why should Italy be the only pacifist one, when she needed land so badly for her increasing population? Nationalism, until the turn of the century, had not been a party, or an organisation, or even an idea. It had merely been the sentiment of a few people, at times boastful and arrogant, nearly always tactless, but, nevertheless, genuine. The first attempt to provide the public with a political orientation in a nationalistic sense was made by Alfredo Oriani (1852–1909). In his book *Fino a Dogali* (Up to Dogali), he stressed the importance of colonial expansion, but his words were completely submerged by the reaction that followed the Battle of Adowa. He was to achieve greater success with the book *La Rivolta Ideale* (The Ideal Revolt), in which he emphasised the destructive influence of Socialism on the minds of working-men, by causing them to think that patriotism had become an obsolete sentiment.

But even Socialists were realising that the people's welfare would be easier to achieve in a powerful country. The Socialist author Arturo Labriola, for instance, had hailed the Libyan War as a venture that would increase the wealth of the *bourgeoisie*, but also give the working-man a chance to improve his standard of living. While this turned out to be false, because Libya was a country in need of assistance and could give no help to Italy's economy, it nevertheless showed a new approach. Reformism had penetrated the trade unions, and the Socialist Party had somehow been influenced by the notion that the fatherland must not be ignored. Strangely enough, even the more violent current within Socialism, led by Benito Mussolini, which had made a stand against reformism leading to the expulsion from the party of its most representative men, often allowed a vague nationalist sentiment to make its appearance beneath the orthodox assertions of universal brotherhood. Catholics were also feeling the impact of patriotism in a way which would have been unbelievable a few decades before, when the controversy between Church and State had reached its peak. Although they stood for a doctrine that was universal in name and fact, the nation had become a reality that could not be ignored.

In this atmosphere, D'Annunzio's success was an easy one. His fictional reconstruction of ancient glories and his constant appeal to greatness and power stirred the public's imagination. He reiterated this particular theme for more than twenty years down to the outbreak of World War I. It seemed that in a country troubled by political contrasts only an artist could change the natural humanitarian trend of mind, by spreading new and more impressive ideals. Public opinion was sensitive to a voice coming not from a politician or a sociologist, but from a poet. D'Annunzio was highly critical of existing conditions and of the men he believed to be responsible for them, especially Giovanni Giolitti. His strictures and those of other nationalists, however, were not justified: Italy's economy was improving; industry and trade were expanding; and internationally the nation had become stronger than ever before. Yet this did not appeal to the irrational mood of people who believed parliamentarianism to be a waste of time, or, as they put it, 'a useless battle of words', and who thought Giolitti's cautious and practical policies were corrupting the nation. There was much rhetoric and little common sense in this approach. The ideal of a greater fatherland was therefore tarnished by the nationalists' arrogance and tactlessness. They also lacked a practical programme, for, while speaking loudly of greatness, destiny, conquest, and war, whenever asked how, against whom, and by what means these ends should be reached, they became vague and indefinite.

Nationalism, as a movement, started in Florence, after the turn of the century, around two periodicals, *Leonardo* and *Il Regno* (The Kingdom). New voices began to give concrete shape to what so far had been the mere anticipations of a poet and the feelings of a minority. Yet, the new writers, such as Enrico Corradini, Giovanni Papini, and Giuseppe Prezzolini, still displayed a certain *naïveté* in their articles when attempting to formulate a programme. The words 'monarchy', 'army', and 'fatherland' were constantly used, but not always with much purpose. These authors seemed to think that a theory could become real if only they could hammer it into the people's heads with sufficient vigour. The intrinsic weakness of this approach was soon felt by Papini and Prezzolini, who ceased contributing to *Il Regno*, and in 1908 founded *La Voce* (The Voice). This magazine dealt with nationalistic theory in a more practical manner, expressing the view that Italy's expansion would be possible only if it were preceded by a spiritual and economic development. The immediate programme, as put forward by its contributors, among whom was Benedetto Croce, included material progress, cultural improvement, and the solution of the country's structural problems.

Nationalists met in Florence in 1910, and agreed to found a party and establish a daily paper, *L'Idea Nazionale* (The National Idea), to be printed in Rome. The Libyan War seemed to be the testing ground of the movement. D'Annunzio published in the fourth volume of the Lauds a poetical celebration of the event. The noisy enthusiasm of nationalists broke out as if the success of the Libyan campaign had been due to their efforts. When, later, Libya was annexed, and Italian influence spread to the eastern Mediterranean, through the occupation of Rhodes and of the Dodecanese, their pride knew no bounds. They failed to realise that Libya would certainly have remained a Turkish possession had its conquest depended on their contribution. Despite the bombastic satisfaction displayed in speeches and articles, the public knew that the Libyan War was Giolitti's success. *La Voce* declared that Giolitti 'had changed the course of Italian life, robbing the nationalists of their thunder'. This was true. The Piedmontese statesman, the man who had overcome his opponents by winning them over to his side, the unappealing bureaucrat who could judge men and events with such coolness, had won an important victory over youthful intemperance.

The picture of Italy's political thought would not be complete without mention of a movement which developed after the turn of the century and influenced various sections of the country's intelligentsia. It was not an organisation of any kind, but simply a trend of thought centred round a person and his literary works. It was not political, but had practical consequences more far-reaching than anticipated by its founder, Benedetto Croce (1866–1952). Although it is said that philosophers live among abstractions and generalisations that prevent them from seeing the actualities of life, this is often not true, for their speculative mind gives them the ability to judge events, and even of directing them. The examples of Aristotle, St. Thomas Aquinas, Francis Bacon, and Fichte are proof of this. Croce's case is no exception. From the early years of the century up to his death he influenced, either directly or indirectly, the way of thinking of three generations. He lived intensely, studying and writing up to the last day.

Croce's activity began in Naples, a city with a centuries-old tradition of speculative research, where he campaigned against positivism and materialism that had been distorting the native idealistic trend of Italian thought. His philosophy, while in line with that of his older contemporary Francesco De Sanctis and in the tradition of the eighteenth-century thinker Vico, was strongly influenced by Hegel and the German school. The starting point of his system was the unity of the spirit, which was, for him, the beginning of all reality. In this unity he determined the ideal forms necessary to the comprehension of the outside world, in which the whole of spiritual life resolves itself. The first form, intuition, causes sentiment and lyricism in art. The second, reflection, transforms intuition into experience and knowledge of facts. The third, economics, directs the spirit towards concrete activities. The fourth is moral. Croce believed that these forms are not distinct categories, but simple variations of the spirit, the basic character of which is unity. A theory of this kind, directly linked to what the author called 'classic idealism', was bound to stir emotions and provoke unending controversy, especially as Croce was uncompromising in his belief that positivism was more improbable than any theory or religion with which it contended. Croce despised the closed circles the positivists had formed, which limited research and dwarfed the possibilities of the human spirit. He felt the purpose of philosophy was to support inquiry and find solutions to the problems that history and experience are constantly putting forward. These were in need of systematic interpretation which could be provided only if the mind was dissatisfied with what had already been achieved. He opposed pragmatism and intuition because he believed that the interpretation of facts could be kept on a strictly logical basis, and he rejected all systems that seemed illogical and intuitive. These were completely alien to his spiritual and liberal approach. He also fought determinism, and this caused him to criticise D'Annunzio's poetry as being artificial, irrational, and inclined to praise illiberal aspects of history.

In 1902 Croce founded a new periodical called *La Critica* (Criticism), in which he set out the results of his inquiries. It soon became the most important publication in its field, attracting the interest of Italian and European scholars, especially those of the younger generation. For nearly fifty years *La Critica* was a centre of inspiration and enlightenment. Bitterly opposed by nationalists and Marxists, it was a champion of liberty, and later, during the years of Fascist absolutism, it succeeded in keeping consciences awake.

A constant contributor to *La Critica* was Giovanni Gentile

(1875–1944), a Sicilian philosopher, nine years younger than Croce, who at first shared the idealistic vision of his master and brought a valid contribution to the understanding of modernism. Gentile's temperament, however, was influenced by his more dynamic nature. Soon he considered Croce too static, and began speaking of idealism in terms of concrete activity, as if it should guide and inspire day-to-day life. Because of these ideas, or sentiments, as they might more correctly be called, Gentile was closer to pragmatism. When he spoke of 'actual idealism' he meant something very near to Bergson's idea of a 'vital impulse', Blondel's 'action', and Nietzsche's '*Wille zur Macht*'. While Croce felt that liberty should guarantee free inquiry and the full assertion of the spirit, Gentile was more concerned with action and with the necessity of getting things done. Idealistic or logical motives concerned him less. It is therefore no wonder that he became the champion of literary and political tendencies that Croce strongly opposed. Eventually he became the official philosopher of Fascism.

After ten years of co-operation, the two men parted. Henceforth they were to follow different roads. Political events helped to widen the gap. Of the two, Croce had the greater influence on subsequent Italian life. During the Fascist regime his periodical was miraculously to continue publication, although it criticised prevailing methods and opinions. Croce himself wrote the greater part of it. Though it chiefly dealt with cultural problems, and was limited therefore to a few intellectuals, it soon became the only free voice to be heard in Italy. Its editor's personality remained unfailingly vigorous and was a constant inspiration to free-minded people.

Chapter 5

The Crisis of Liberalism (1915–22)

IT HAD long been felt that if war came to Europe the first spark would ignite in the Balkans, the powder-keg of that continent, where the presence of several nationalities provided fuel for a possible fire. Two Balkan wars had already shown how easily a crisis could arise in a zone where so many conflicting imperialisms met. The main danger was the existence of the Austrian Empire, which, like all pluri-national States held together by force or skilful diplomacy, could easily disintegrate in times of aggravated passions. And passions in southern Europe were extremely violent. A great number of Slavs living under Austrian sovereignty looked to Serbia for guidance and fulfilment of their aspirations to independence. In this they were much like the Italians living within those same borders who regarded Italy as their fatherland.

There had been internal unrest in Italy after the Libyan War. Yet, on the whole, the country was morally and economically in good shape. The Triple Alliance between Italy, Austria, and Germany, which had created stronger commitments for the nation, had also helped to consolidate her international position. The main weakness of this treaty was the presence of the large Italian minority within the Austrian Empire. Nationalists, in fact, were constantly demanding the cities of Trento and Trieste, thus focusing public attention on the problems of those two areas.

Following the murder of the Austrian Archduke Franz Ferdinand and his wife at Serajevo on June 28, 1914, Austria sent an ultimatum to Serbia imposing conditions that were incompatible with that country's independence and dignity. By so doing, Austria had violated the spirit and the letter of the Triple Alliance, which had been conceived and worded solely as a defensive treaty. Premier Salandra told the Austrian Ambassador on July 25, 1914, that he believed Vienna deliberately wanted to provoke a conflagration. This seemed to be proved by the Austrian rejection of the note by which Serbia accepted nearly all the conditions put forward in the ultimatum. War broke out between the two countries, and if it had been confined to the Balkans it would have resulted in a swift Austrian victory. Unfortunately, the ties, the alliances, the disagreements and feuds of European diplomacy turned the conflict into a continental war, the most tragic the world had ever experienced. In a few weeks Austria and Germany were clashing against Serbia, Russia, France, Belgium, and Great Britain.

The two central empires had treated Italy as a second-rate Power, dealing with her in a most undiplomatic manner. This naturally embittered her and strengthened nationalistic tendencies. Apart from psychological factors, there had been a violation of the Triple Alliance, according to which Austria or Italy could alter the *status quo* in the Balkans only by agreement between the two Powers. This agreement was to be based on the principle of mutual compensation for all new territorial or other advantages that either Power might acquire and also on the principle that any such change would have to satisfy the interests and legitimate claims of both parties. Italy was therefore right when she proclaimed her neutrality in a conflict in which one of her allies had acted with such contempt of commitments. Her neutrality enabled France to release her divisions located along the Alps. This strengthened Franco-British resistance against German invasion in the North. History is not an account of events that might have happened if something had been different. Nevertheless, one can easily visualise how different the course of humanity would have been if during the summer of 1914 France had been forced to defend her south-eastern frontier. The Battle of the Marne, which turned the tide of events, might have had a different outcome.

The months between the outbreak of war and Italy's intervention were troubled ones. Giolitti, practical as usual, felt that the nation was militarily unprepared and should remain out of the conflict. Neutral tendencies were also backed by Socialists and by Catholics. One wonders what would have happened if Giolitti had been in power during those crucial months, and if the country would have sided with the Entente, as it eventually did.

Di San Giuliano, the Foreign Minister in the Salandra Cabinet, died in October, 1914, and was succeeded by Sidney Sonnino, a Florentine, and the son of an English mother who had many British connections. Propaganda favouring intervention in the war on the side of the Entente became stronger, fanned by the nationalist party and by a daily paper printed in Milan, *Il Popolo d'Italia* (The People of Italy), edited by Benito Mussolini, who only a few years before, as the editor of the Socialist daily paper, had violently denounced the Government for having fought the Libyan war. After expulsion from his party, he had founded this paper, which proclaimed itself Socialist in programme, but soon began to favour intervention. It was rumoured that French money encouraged this change of trend. The result of his propaganda was effective, because it came from a man belonging to the working-class and was backed with inflamed speeches that profoundly impressed audiences.

Meanwhile Sonnino, although favouring the Entente, tried to keep Italy out of the war. He requested the Austrian Government to hand to Italy Trentino and other territories inhabited by Italians. Vienna flatly rejected these requests with the exception of the one concerning Trentino, which was to be transferred to Italy only after the war. Sonnino therefore turned to the Allies, who were quite ready to comply with Italian requests concerning territories which at the moment did not belong to them, but in the event of success would be part of the victor's spoils.

On April 26, 1915, the Pact of London between Italy, England, France, and Russia was signed. According to its provisions Italy was to receive Trentino and the Alto Adige region up to the Brenner Pass, Trieste, the Istrian peninsula, part of the Dalmatian coast, part of Asia Minor, if this was to be partitioned after the Turkish collapse, and some part of the German colonies. Several clauses of this most controversial treaty were destined not to be observed, and eventually caused bitterness and resentment among the Italians.

Much can be said as to the constitutional value of this treaty, which was practically imposed on Italy by her Government. It committed the country to intervention in a war without the approval of Parliament. The constitution provided that the Government was responsible for making peace treaties, alliances, trade agreements, and for giving notice of them to Parliament only if the interests and security of the State would allow it, but it also added that treaties involving financial expenditure or territorial changes would be null and void without parliamentary approval. The Pact of London, however, fixed a date by which Italy would have to start military operations against Austria, and gave no consideration to the fact that Parliament would not be asked to ratify it.

The signing of the treaty was accompanied by violent nationalist propaganda in favour of intervention. Mussolini and his paper inflamed the most irresponsible section of the public, which, though extremely noisy, was not the most numerous. This noisiness impressed the parliamentary majority. Groups of rioters began using organised violence and threats against anyone opposing intervention on the Allied side. After the war this same technique was to be used by Fascists only too successfully. Although many people shared Giolitti's opinion that neutrality was the most advantageous course, they were overruled by a wave of emotional enthusiasm favouring the war, which, according to the prevailing belief, would be short and would ultimately free all Italians living under Austrian rule. How far emotions could be stirred was proved by the excitement caused by a letter that Giolitti was said to have written. Allegedly the former Premier had said in it that Italy could obtain 'a good deal' without actually going to war. This frank opinion caused an outbreak of protest, and Giolitti was accused of being the servant of foreign interests. After the declaration of war he retired to his mountain birthplace in Piedmont and kept out of public affairs for some years.

Although from a moral and constitutional point of view the Government could be criticised for the way the nation had been led into the conflict, the people nevertheless displayed patriotism and a sense of duty. This should be emphasised, because it has become a widely circulated legend that Italy's conduct was below the standard of other countries. The temporary retreat of the Italian army at Caporetto in 1917, for instance, was certainly less serious than those of other armies in the field. Yet that unfortunate battle was given immense publicity in order to belittle Italy's contribution to the common victory. The lack of understanding shown by the Allies must be regarded with regret, for many tragedies might have been spared the world had Italy's war effort been given due recognition.

When entering the war Italy was unprepared for the terrible ordeal. Because of the frontier fixed in 1866, her strategic position, in comparison with that of Austria, was very unfavourable. The enemy was firmly entrenched on the Alpine passes leading to the Po Valley. Any Italian offensive therefore demanded a much greater sacrifice of men and war materials. Despite these obstacles, General Luigi Cadorna (1850–1928), who had been appointed Chief of General Staff eleven months prior to the declaration of war, succeeded in building the army up efficiently.

Operations followed the pattern of other fronts. The first Italian advance across the Isonzo River was heavily opposed by the enemy entrenched in the Carso region. From then on there were few changes, until the spring of 1916, when the Central Powers, believing victory was within their reach, launched a great offensive. Germany tried to break through the French lines at Verdun, while Austria started a heavy surprise attack in the Trentino. General Cadorna rushed troops from the Isonzo River to the assistance of units already resisting in the mountains. Despite the enemy's careful planning and the use of heavy artillery, the Battle of Asiago, as it is generally known, was a victory for the Italians. Cadorna then moved the greater part of his forces back to the Eastern front and attacked along the Isonzo River, capturing the allegedly impregnable position of Mount Sabotino and the city of Gorizia. These operations were carried out with the same gallantry as displayed during the previous year, but with greater technical skill. More than a year of active war had taught the Italians many lessons in strategy and tactics. By now slit trenches were more ably made, dug-outs were safer, and suspended cable lines brought materials up to the highest positions. On the home front a rapid development in the industrial field assured front-line troops of a constant stream of heavy artillery, weapons, ammunition, and food supplies.

In March, 1916, Salandra's Cabinet received an encouraging vote of confidence in the Chamber of Deputies (394 to 61). A few months later, however, the parliamentary situation became less stable, and the Premier resigned. The next Government was headed by Paolo Boselli (1838–1932), an old and respected statesman, who formed a Cabinet of national unity in which nearly all groups were represented. Sonnino retained the Foreign Ministry, while Cabinet posts were accepted by Reformist Socialists Bonomi and Bissolati, by Catholic Meda, and Republican Comandini. The key post of Minister of the Interior was given to Vittorio Emanuele Orlando (1860–1953), a Sicilian, who, although belonging to Giolitti's majority, had in 1915 favoured Italy's entry into the war. This Government declared war on Germany, for until then Italy had been at war only against Austria.

The darkest year for the Allies was 1917. The people and the soldiers of several countries were feeling the strain of the ordeal and began thinking that their efforts and sacrifices were in vain. The resources of the Central Powers seemed inexhaustible. Some nations had already collapsed. Serbia had been completely overcome and her King and army had been brought to safety on the Greek island of Corfu by the Italian navy. The heavy defeat of the Russian army had led to the political and military collapse of the Czarist regime. Rumania was on the verge of defeat and Allied operations against Turkey on the Dardanelles were turning out to be one of the most unsuccessful ventures of the war. Even on the French front there was no advance, despite the combined efforts of the French, British, and Belgian armies. The French were suffering from moral depression—the *caffard*, as it was called—which spread not only among civilians, but also reached the fighting man in the field.

Considering the general situation, Italy's reaction to the moral strain was better than average, although General Cadorna, who had proved his ability as a strategist, showed little understanding in treating the men under his command. A firm believer in discipline, he was ready to enforce it at any price. Previous wars had shown that while Italians do not lack personal courage, they always need powerful moral leadership. Though aware of this trait, Cadorna kept his men under constant strain. Amusements and entertainments were reduced to a minimum, for he believed these things might weaken their morale. On the contrary, the lack of such diversions and long periods of service in the line had a detrimental effect on the men, who felt that, while they were risking their lives, their country had forgotten them. Socialist propaganda did not help. In July, 1917, Claudio Treves, a Socialist deputy, said in Parliament: 'Next winter not a man will be in the trenches', a phrase that was widely publicised, although its meaning was not very clear.

A different attitude was that of the Church. Horrified at the inevitable bloodshed, she had opposed the war from the beginning. Pope Pius X had done his utmost to prevent it, and when his efforts proved to be vain died of a broken heart. Benedict XV, his successor, also declared his opposition to what he called 'a useless carnage', and refused to side with any of the contestants. Despite this official attitude of the Holy See, the Italian lower clergy was making a valid contribution to the war effort. Many parish priests co-operated with civil and military authorities and displayed faith in victory. The animosity towards the State which had deprived the Vatican of its temporal sovereignty had gradually died out. Several army chaplains were killed in action, and others were awarded medals for gallantry.

The Battle of Caporetto took place in this atmosphere of mixed sentiments. In August, 1917, Italy's Second Army began a successful attack against the Bainsizza mountain bastion, while the Third Army advanced towards Trieste. The units were still under the strain caused by this offensive move when, on October 24, the Austrian High Command launched its great offensive, preceded by heavy bombardment. Operations had been carefully planned. Divisions released by the Russian collapse had been brought into the line and six German divisions bolstered the attacking army. From the very first moment things went badly for the Italians. The lines broke near Tolmino and, in the South, near Caporetto. The Second Army gave way, and this compelled the Third and Fourth Armies to retreat. The enemy advanced, re-conquering former Austrian territories which, at the cost of terrible sacrifices, had been held for over two years. In addition, the provinces of Udine and Belluno, and part of those of Venice, Treviso, and Vicenza were overrun; 300,000 soldiers were taken prisoners, and great quantities of materials and 2,500 guns were captured. It seemed that the front had collapsed and that the enemy would advance down the peninsula. In reality the situation was less precarious. Although some units had given way, the army was soon able to regain its spirit. General Cadorna did not lose control of the situation and ordered his men to withdraw to the River Piave, where the line was shorter, so that an effective defence could be set up. In the new strategic disposition, Mount Grappa was the bastion round which the whole defence pivoted. These events caused grave concern in Italy and among her allies. Yet both the country and her armed forces displayed a great spirit of resistance. It was thus possible to strengthen the line on the Piave and to stop the Austro-German offensive. An attempt made by the enemy to cross the river was immediately checked, and it was soon apparent that the most critical period had passed.

Mistakes had undoubtedly been made during this phase of operations. Some commands, taken by surprise, had not faced the situation with sufficient decision and skill. This may have been caused by the fact that many officers had been killed, and replacements from civilian life, commissioned after short periods of instruction, lacked experience. There had been disorder in the retreat. Communications had been hindered at the crossing of the River Tagliamento. Despite these mistakes, the worst had passed and the country was again in a position to fight strenuously. The best comment on the Battle of Caporetto is to be found in the following excerpt from the *Encyclopædia Britannica*:

> 'When retreat became inevitable, the prospects might well have seemed desperate for those who had to organise it. For the army, long used to the war of positions that had been the rule for 28 months, was in no condition to move. The retreat, with all its confusion, its mistakes, and its tragedies, remains an astonishing achievement. The resistance which followed it, when the retiring armies turned and stood at bay on the mountains and on the Piave, was the greatest of Italian victories.'

Behind the battle-front other events influenced the situation. General Cadorna was relieved of the post of Chief of General Staff and replaced by General Armando Diaz (1861–1928), who immediately set to work to strengthen resistance and fill the gaps. The whole country backed his efforts. Industry went to work on an unprecedented scale. (The Fiat automobile factory at Turin succeeded in producing 1,700 lorries a month.) By December the French and British had also sent reinforcements.

The Boselli Cabinet resigned after Caporetto and was succeeded by one headed by Vittorio Emanuele Orlando, the former Minister of the Interior. Orlando worked vigorously to provide the armed forces with everything they required and to boost the national morale. His exuberant temperament, while successful in restoring confidence, was a drawback after the war, when he had to represent Italy at the Peace Conference. His juridical background hampered him in diplomatic contacts, for he seemed unable to discuss or negotiate without indulging in subtleties.

The year 1918 began under better auspices. The enemy's attack had been bravely checked and the situation seemed to be under control. The United States had entered the war, and their contribution in men and materials was looked upon as a decisive factor for an Allied victory. During the spring the Central Powers, feeling they might yet achieve success before the full weight of the American war-machine was launched against them, prepared a massive attack on the French front. This was successful in the beginning and created a dangerous crisis. On that occasion an Italian army corps was sent to France, where it took part in the Battle of Bligny. Casualties suffered by Italy's soldiers on the French front were more than those suffered by her allies on the Italian front. The part taken in a common cause can certainly not be judged simply on the basis of the numbers of dead and wounded, but the comparison of figures should be kept in mind, for all too often Italy's contribution to the Allied victory has been greatly under-estimated.

The building up of the army to replace losses suffered during the last months of 1917 was speeded up to such an extent that by the beginning of 1918 General Diaz headed a very efficient war machine. Some English and French divisions were soon withdrawn and sent to the French front, where the situation, following the German offensive, had become especially grave. In July, 1918, Austrians and Germans launched a last desperate offensive on the Italian front in the hope of breaking through the line and of achieving the strategic success they had missed the year before. But after a few days the offensive was completely repulsed. The moral consequences of this victory were of the greatest importance. The Austrian people were profoundly demoralised when they learnt that the Italian army, previously compelled to retreat, was brilliantly resisting all attacks.

After these events there was much discussion among Italian statesmen on the question of resuming offensive operations. Some thought it sufficient to the general outcome of the war that the Austrian army should be pinned to the ground. Foreign Minister Sonnino felt instead that the nation should end the war holding strong territorial positions that would enable her to bargain with more authority at the Peace Conference, where old antagonisms and enmities were bound to reappear, even among former allies. This idea prevailed and the General Staff was soon preparing for an attack. This was launched on October 24, 1918, on the first anniversary of the Battle of Caporetto.

The River Piave was crossed and the enemy's line broken at the village of Vittorio Veneto. On October 30 Austria requested an armistice. The vanquished army was obliged to withdraw behind the line fixed in 1915 by the London Pact. Sea-borne troops landed at Trieste, and fast units reached Trento and Bolzano up to the Brenner Pass. The dream of the Risorgimento had been fulfilled with the union of all Italians under one flag. The 'unredeemed' were at last united to their fatherland and the Austrian Empire was beaten. These events left Germany's southern border entirely unguarded. Pressed by the Allied offensive on the French front, Germany also asked for an armistice. This was signed on November 11, exactly one week after the Austrian one.

The sacrifices made by Italy in three and a half years of war were astounding. There had been over 600,000 killed, and over 1,000,000 wounded. The gravity of the financial situation can be shown by the following comparison: in the last peace budget (1913–14) public assets had practically balanced liabilities at about 3 billion lire. In the budget of the fiscal year 1917–18 expenditure had swollen to 33 billions, while the public debt had grown from 15 to 94 billions. In addition, a further debt amounting to 22 billion gold lire had been incurred with the United States and England. Yet Italy's contribution to the common cause was unfortunately not given due recognition by her allies. International public opinion did not accord her the goodwill she deserved, while the foreign Press, for psychological reasons difficult to understand, showed a constant tendency to side with her adversaries. The world papers began putting forward the opinion that Italy's Government and people intended to assume in south-eastern Europe the aggressive role of the former Austrian Empire. This idea was prevalent in Paris, where the Government was busy establishing on the Continent a network of alliances and connections of which France was to be the central element. It was, therefore, in an atmosphere very adverse to her interests that Italy took part in the Peace Conference which met in Paris on January 18, 1919.

Premier Orlando headed the Italian delegation. This statesman, who had spent his professional life as a lawyer in the courts and his political life in the Chamber of Deputies, proved unfit to deal with the diplomatic difficulties of such a task. From the beginning, England's Lloyd George and France's Clemenceau outplayed their Italian partner. Woodrow Wilson, the American President, dominated the conference and advocated policies which were not only disapproved of by the majority of his own countrymen but appeared highly impractical and required the sacrifice of more immediate and concrete aims. Lloyd George and Clemenceau soon realised that by accepting Wilson's idealistic projects they could achieve backing for their aims. Thus, by complying with his view that there should be no annexation of enemy colonial territories, which should either be made independent or administered by the League of Nations, Britain and France gained nearly all Germany's colonies and a part of the Turkish Empire. They were appointed trustees of these territories, and their administration of the German colonies continues to this day.

Prior to the Peace Conference there had been some disagreement within the Cabinet concerning the new frontiers. Foreign Minister Sonnino insisted on the enforcement of the London Pact. Even the problem of Fiume called for a solution. Although this city was not included in the provisions of the London Pact, yet, as its predominantly Italian population had asked to be annexed, Sonnino felt that it should be added to the regions specified in the treaty. Other ministers, especially Nitti and Bissolati, favoured more limited requests. An agreement was eventually reached within the Cabinet, but at the Peace Conference Italian demands were received unsympathetically by Wilson. At one point the American President decided to ignore Italy's official representatives and to address himself directly to the Italian people. He had, however, under-rated the Italian character by thinking that the citizens of a country could be dealt with like students of a university. It will be recalled that as president of Princeton University, Wilson had at times ignored the opinion of the board of trustees and had turned to the students directly. In this case he was disappointed, for the Italians rejected the message addressed to them and Parliament voted in favour of Orlando, who, together with Sonnino, had left the Paris conference and returned to Rome.

From a diplomatic point of view, Italy's aims at the Peace Conference should not have been difficult to achieve, for President Wilson was so committed to his project of a League of Nations, and Lloyd George and Clemenceau were so anxious to get the treaty signed by all the Allies, that they might well have granted Italy's desires had Orlando pressed his case more forcefully and effectively stressed his country's contribution to victory.

Unfortunately Orlando was not a great negotiator and was

easily defeated by Wilson, Clemenceau, and Lloyd George, who often formed a common front against him. When he and Sonnino returned to Paris, they found that in their absence the three Allied leaders had already agreed on the conditions to be imposed on Germany in the peace treaty signed at Versailles on May 7, 1919. This diplomatic defeat compelled Orlando to resign. He was succeeded by a Cabinet headed by Francesco Saverio Nitti. Under his premiership the Treaty of Saint Germain was signed with Austria (September 10, 1919), by which Italy obtained Trentino, Alto Adige, and Venezia Giulia, but not the port of Fiume. In an attempt to solve the problem of Fiume by force, a group of volunteers led by the poet Gabriele D'Annunzio marched on the city and occupied it. Nitti's Government dealt with the situation indecisively and in a most vacillating way, creating widespread discontent.

The parliamentary scene changed completely after the general election of 1919. Under pressure from Socialists and Catholics, the old electoral law was replaced by a proportional system by which the country was divided into a few large constituencies, each of which was to elect a certain number of deputies. This method favoured organised parties which could control the electorate and counteract Government patronage. The result of the voting was a surprise to all. Socialists increased the number of their deputies to 156, and Catholics, who had formed their own party, elected 100 members. This was the beginning of a new phase in Italy's political life. Up to that time deputies, although professing to be liberal or democratic or radical, had seldom been actual members of the party to which they owed allegiance and to which they were not indebted for election. This enabled them to change their policies so long as they did not displease their electorate. Now, on the contrary, the backing of a party became necessary, for without it a candidate was unlikely to be elected.

The result of the 1919 election made Nitti's situation increasingly difficult. Socialists, dominated by the extremist faction, kept the country in a state of turmoil by constantly demanding wage increases that employers could not grant. These demands were backed by a series of strikes, the purpose of which was obviously that of preparing the ground for a revolution which, following Russia's example, would hand over power to the workers.

Public sentiment was more outraged by the Socialists' antipatriotic approach than by their economic programme. The war effort was in fact constantly spurned, as if its aim had been not to serve the nation, but to strengthen capitalism.

Nitti's Cabinet was so unable to deal with a situation that was drifting more and more towards anarchy that under Socialist pressure it granted deserters an amnesty. Nitti was also unsuccessful in solving the most urgent economic and financial problems. Few people realised that the existing state of affairs was chiefly a result of the enormous expenditure on the war and that only a real effort by the people could put the country on its feet. The workers continued, however, to demand higher wages and better working conditions.

In an attempt to maintain some sort of order, Nitti created a new police organisation called 'La guardia regia' (the royal guard). This military body soon proved ineffective in fighting extremism because it lacked the necessary leadership and often clashed with the regular police. The Government's weak approach to problems of public order was most dangerous, not only because it allowed things to go from bad to worse, but especially because it relinquished the responsibility of fighting Socialism to other political groups, mainly to ex-service men and members of a reactionary organisation founded in March, 1919, under the name of Fasci di Combattimento. The leader of this new group was Benito Mussolini, the former Socialist, who had strongly supported Italy's joining the Allies. A bitter conflict began between Socialists and the new organisation, and this frequently led to battles in the streets and city squares. Nothing could be less favourable to the survival of a democratic State than the clashes between two factions under the eyes of an impotent police force.

Nitti resigned in March, 1920, but was asked to form a new Cabinet. In May he resigned again, but the task of forming a Cabinet was given to him once more. A decree that increased the price of bread brought about his final resignation a few weeks later.

His successor was Giolitti. This elderly statesman seemed to be indispensable to his country. He had first come to office as Premier nearly thirty years before, and had been active in political life ever since. He now seemed to be the only man capable of handling the difficult situation. Many factors were in his favour. He had achieved outstanding results before the war and had shown his ability in dealing with Socialism by bringing it within the frame of the parliamentary State. He might be able to perform this miracle again. It was also hoped he would receive support from the Catholic Party, of which, in a sense, he had been the ally in the 1913 election. The new Cabinet was formed, and Count Sforza, later to emerge as an anti-Fascist, was appointed Foreign Minister.

Socialism had never been so violent and, as a consequence, reaction to it was equally strong. Giolitti soon found himself in the middle of the clash. His background, past experience, and education had been consistently inspired by liberal principles. He believed in moderation and thought all problems could be solved by compromise. Yet, his middle-of-the-road policy aroused so much controversy, that in the end he was criticised by everybody. Socialists accused him of having armed the Fascists, who, in turn, believed him to be responsible for Socialist strength. This phase of Giolitti's life exemplifies the tragic fate of moderate people in a world of violence.

He intended his Cabinet to be one of national union, in which all parties would be represented. Yet the official Socialists—those known as 'maximalists', and who could count on a strong parliamentary group—did not take part in it. The support of reformists, headed by Bonomi, who had seceded from the official party before the war, was, of course, less important, because of the few deputies it could count on. Socialists were tied to obsolete political formulas, according to which no co-operation could be given to *bourgeois* governments. They believed the Russian example was to be followed and that power could be achieved by force. They also thought they could control the mob. But the war had given other people, besides them, the taste for violence.

Having refused to co-operate with the Government, the Socialists began a policy of what they called 'direct action'. This implied the occupation of industrial plants by the workers. The reason given was the refusal of the employers to grant wage increases, but the real aim was to start an armed revolution. Socialists believed that after the occupation of factories, political control of the country would follow automatically. Giolitti felt that the Socialists would ultimately abandon this policy and that the occupation of factories would come to an end when labour found that it could not run them efficiently. He therefore acted as he had done fifteen years before, at the time of the first agrarian strikes in the Po Valley, and refused to re-establish order by force. Since Socialist leaders were not the type to lead the revolution they had so constantly preached, they agreed to meet with representatives of the Government and the employers. Upon obtaining some concessions that enabled them to save their face, they withdrew the workers from the factories. Giolitti had again been right, but at an enormous cost to the national economy. The whole industrial set-up had been at a standstill, many factories being idle for weeks. The worst harm was psychological, for the principle of private property on which the State was based had been directly challenged. Citizens had been allowed to seize buildings and machinery not belonging to them, and to escape prosecution. That the policy of direct action had other objectives besides those of improved wages and conditions was proved by the fact that many cleverly concealed weapons were discovered all over the country when the occupation came to an end.

Fascists, less numerous than Socialists, but better organised and more efficient, took advantage of the moment, and of the mood the country was passing through. Financed by capitalists, and chiefly composed of young people and ex-service men, their movement spread quickly, especially in industrial districts. The introduction of weapons into political disputes was, of course, a consequence of the war and of the Russian Revolution, which had taught many a lesson. Armed fights became regular occurrences, with many on both sides being killed and wounded. It was an alarming state of affairs, and showed that the country was in grave danger. The Fascists formed special *squadre d'azione* (action squads), with which they stormed the strongholds of their adversaries in towns and villages. As their uniform consisted of a black shirt, it was under this name that they began to be known. In their ventures they were generally successful, even if they were outnumbered. After grave incidents and agitations that led to the murder of Giulio Giordani, an ex-officer who had been awarded a high military medal for gallantry in action, Fascist squads concentrated their action on the Socialist centres of the Po Valley and the Emilia region, and especially on the city of Bologna.

At a time when national sentiment seemed to have been put aside by people who were quick in declaring their moral dependency on Soviet Russia, Fascist propaganda was most effective on all classes by speaking of 'patriotism', 'national pride', and 'rights deriving from the 1918 victory'. Fascist methods were, of course, detestable, but not very different from those the Socialists had been adopting since the end of the war. Violence cannot easily be stopped, and it was not long before all political parties, including Catholics and Liberals, became the object of Fascist violence.

At Leghorn in January, 1921, the Socialist congress revealed the deep rift in the party. Members who adhered most completely to the Moscow line bitterly opposed the more moderate leaders, such as Filippo Turati (1885–1932) and Claudio Treves (1869–1933). When the contending resolutions were voted upon, and it appeared that the moderate one was getting the majority of votes, the extremists broke away to form the Communist Party, which was recognised by Moscow as the Italian section of the Communist International.

While these events were taking place, Italy reached at Rapallo an agreement with Yugoslavia concerning her eastern frontier. (The moment was favourable for a settlement, because President Wilson, the chief Yugoslav protector, had been defeated in the United States.) Foreign Minister Sforza conducted the negotiations, and the Rapallo treaty was signed on November 12, 1920. Italy renounced her rights on the Dalmatian coast granted her by the London Pact, except for the city of Zara. Yugoslavia gave up her claims on Trieste, Istria, Gorizia, and the islands of Cherso and Lussin. Fiume, still held by D'Annunzio's forces, became an independent State. This sensible solution of the frontier problem between the two countries was reached with reciprocal goodwill. Unfortunately Fascists seized upon it as a propaganda issue, stating—quite falsely—that the nation's rights had not been properly safeguarded.

Giolitti would not intervene in the civil war now taking place in the streets between the opposing factions. Instead, since he was a master of parliamentary combinations and a successful 'maker of elections' in the Government's interest, he believed the time had come for calling the electors to the polls. Accustomed to a Chamber of Deputies elected by limited suffrage in small constituencies, where the weight of Government support could be of great value to candidates, he knew little of proportional representation dominated by party machines. In an attempt to overcome this difficulty, he managed to unite the scattered liberal forces he had controlled before the war into a coalition. This was merely the temporary alliance of local politicians with a certain following. The old Premier's efforts met with some success, for in the general election held on May 15, 1921, out of 535 deputies elected, 275 belonged to this combination. Had the other groups not been organised by a very strong party discipline, this could have been a sufficient majority. Returns were as follows: 122 Socialists (as compared with the previous 156), 16 Communists, and 107 Catholics (instead of the previous 100). The greatest surprise was the election of 35 Fascists. The party which had never had any parliamentary representation immediately arose to an outstanding position. In addition, some liberal deputies favoured Fascist policies and strengthened its influence.

The opening of Parliament in June, 1921, found the Chamber of Deputies deeply divided. The conduct of Foreign Minister Sforza was bitterly criticised, and on this issue Giolitti resigned, although he obtained a narrow majority when a vote was taken. The new Cabinet was headed by Ivanoe Bonomi, the reformist Socialist, who relied for a majority on Catholic and Liberal votes.

But the situation was precarious. Italy faced a major crisis when the large and powerful Banca di Sconto went bankrupt with grave consequences to the nation's economy. Socialists and Fascists continued to fight each other with ever greater violence. Strikes, apparently inspired more by political aims than by economic necessity, paralysed production. Fascism was by now gaining great influence among the masses, while labour leaders, who had previously been at the peak of their power and popularity, were gradually losing ground. They had missed the opportunity of becoming the country's leading force. Under threats of Fascist violence, many Socialist municipal councils resigned and were replaced by temporary Government Commissioners or by new conservative administrations. For the same reason, many trade unions and workers' co-operatives, which for years had been dominated by Socialists or Catholics, were abandoning their former allegiances and passing over to Fascism.

The day Fascism would come to power seemed imminent. Its leaders did not intend to be kept on the back benches of the political scene, nor to be considered the defenders of the liberal State. But there was also a constitutional problem to solve. Mussolini was fundamentally opposed to the monarchy, yet he was the last person who would renounce power for the sake of defending a formula. He had switched from extreme Socialism to uncompromising nationalism when he saw that the first, being divided by internal feuds and disputes, would probably never be successful. As he now realised that the majority of his followers believed in the monarchy, he made it clear that the King had nothing to fear from him, and declared at the Fascist congress of Rome in 1921 that he was a republican only in tendency. Cynical and unscrupulous, he was ready to enlist the support of widely different sections of public opinion.

Agrarian interests in the North began to enlist the aid of and to finance Fascist squads against peasant unions, which had become powerful and were in a strong bargaining position. The accusation that Fascism was nothing but the armed servant of large landowners, while not true in the beginning, became so eventually, despite the fact that the party had promised to satisfy the aspirations of poor peasants. Deliberately lacking a definite programme, Fascism was so elastic that it could stretch to include the defence of any interest so long as it served its aims, particularly those of its ambitious leader.

The numerous but weak Cabinets that governed Italy after the war helped to pave the road to its success. Giolitti, the only leader who might have resisted the movement, had strengthened it at first by indulging in his usual policy of letting opposite extremes fight it out and, later, by withdrawing his support from the Bonomi Cabinet, thus causing it to fall in February, 1922. When the King asked Bonomi to form a Cabinet again, Giolitti's party voted him down. This attitude increased public dissatisfaction with parliamentary methods. The next Cabinet was headed by Luigi Facta, who had previously served as Minister, and who was one of Giolitti's faithful followers.

During Facta's term of office the economic congress of Genoa took place (April 10–May 19, 1922). This was an important event, because Soviet representatives took part in it. The official reason given by the Russians for their first visit to the capitalist world was to offer trade agreements, but what they really wanted was legal recognition of the Soviet Union. This was in contrast with previous Soviet policy, according to which no compromise could be reached with capitalist Powers. Italian Socialists and Communists, who had looked to the Soviet representatives, and particularly to Chicherin, the Commissar for Foreign Affairs, for example and inspiration, were deeply disappointed and bewildered to see the Marxist principle of non-co-operation with capitalism (on which they had founded their parliamentary policy) denied by their Russian comrades.

The situation in Italy was swiftly deteriorating. In the summer of 1922 Socialists and Communists launched what they termed a 'legal strike' (*sciopero legalitario*) in order to demonstrate to the Government that they were still powerful and could control public opinion. It turned out to be a complete fiasco. In three years extremism had lost ground, and, as a result, many workers did not obey the call-out. Fascists stepped into the breach, and took over the most vital services in some cities, such as Milan. The way was paved for action. Fascist popularity had now reached its peak.

Mussolini, with his finger on the public pulse, decided that the moment was ripe for a national insurrection. The election held the previous year had given his party good results, but it was doubtful if an absolute majority would ever be obtained. Only through military action could he obtain power.

For a long time Fascists had been talking of a 'march on Rome'. It had been considered rather as a joke, or as an expression of that provincial mentality still prevailing in some Italian regions where it is believed that everything done in Rome is wrong and that direct action would be necessary to clean the house and put things straight. But in this case a march on Rome meant an armed revolt that would enable Fascism to reach power. Despite the general weakness of the State, a venture of the kind would never have been successful had it not been for a series of favourable circumstances.

If one considers these events in the light of what we know about them to-day, one must conclude that the march was a miracle of unpreparedness and disorganisation, and that very little would have been needed to defeat it.

On October 22, 1922, a congress of blackshirts was held in Naples, and all was decided for the uprising. Mussolini temporarily handed the command over to four of his lieutenants—namely, Bianchi, secretary of the party (who died in 1930), Balbo (future Governor of Libya, who was killed at the beginning of World War II), De Bono (a retired general who was for a time commander of Italian forces in the Ethiopian campaign, and in 1944 was condemned to death by Mussolini), and De Vecchi (who served in office several times during the Fascist regime). Mussolini did not lead the insurrection, but remained in Milan, perhaps to be able to flee to safety in Switzerland if the revolt failed.

The headquarters of the insurrection was set up in Perugia in

Central Italy, while general mobilisation of the blackshirts was ordered. While this was taking place in several provinces Fascists were seizing by force State buildings and taking control of public services. Little resistance was met, for nearly everywhere officials and army commanders, lacking orders from the Government, did not know what to do or whether resistance should be offered. Besides, it was extremely difficult to fight against people who declared their only aim was to rebuild the country and bring back the army to the position it had reached with the victory of 1918.

Later propaganda has divulged the legend that Fascism, when starting the march on Rome, had taken an uncompromising attitude towards all other parties and the liberal State as a whole, and that it would be satisfied with nothing less than complete power. There is now evidence that in the beginning Mussolini would not have refused the solution of a Cabinet formed by Fascists, but placed under the premiership of such a man as Orlando or Salandra, both of whom were regarded as not entangled in party feuds. Fascist spokesmen were already in Rome at the moment the march started, with orders to prepare the ground for a solution of this kind. Only after events had taken a most favourable turn did Mussolini's conditions become more unyielding.

On October 28, 1922, when news of the insurrection had already reached Rome, Premier Facta asked the King to sign the decree proclaiming martial law. This meant that civil powers would pass into the hands of the army and that military resistance would be set up. Facta firmly believed that the sovereign would sign the decree, and had issued instructions to the provincial authorities and informed the Press. But the King refused to sign and ordered the Premier to cancel all measures already taken. This meant that no resistance would be offered to the columns advancing on Rome on foot and by rail, and that there would be no defence of the capital. Fascism had won the battle because a royal signature had been refused. The army, although favourable to the movement, would certainly have obeyed orders if any had been issued, but when the King's decision became known it took it as an approval of Mussolini's action, and fraternised with the Fascist squads.

Although numerous (it was said they were 100,000 strong, but the figure was probably exaggerated), Fascists would have been in no position to resist armed opposition.

After his success became known, Mussolini was summoned to Rome to take over the premiership. Legend has it that when addressing the King and presenting him with the new list of Ministers he said: 'I bring you the real Italy of Vittorio Veneto, restored by the new victory'. In truth, he was carrying the death sentence of the liberal State and of the parliamentary system. Both were to be supplanted by a dictatorship based on the exaltation of power and force, according to the teachings of Nietzsche of which he had been a follower all his life.

Chapter 6

Fascism (1922–40)

THE TERM Fascism derives from the Latin word *fasces*, meaning a group of rods containing an axe, carried before the Roman magistrates, as a sign of authority. In Italian, the word *fascio* (plural *fasci*) means a group or a bundle. Before Mussolini used it to characterise his movement, this word had already occasionally appeared in political terminology. At the end of the nineteenth century the uprising in Sicily was known by the name of Fasci Siciliani. During World War I those members of the Chamber of Deputies who had favoured intervention and wanted war to be carried on energetically formed the *Fascio parlamentare di difesa nazionale* (parliamentary group for national defence). After Caporetto several *fasci* were created for the purpose of boosting resistance and of counteracting defeatism.

The *fascio* as a symbol was also used by the French Revolutionists. Covered by a phrygian cap, it forms a decorative motif in pictures and sculptures of the neo-classic period. During the nineteenth century it came to symbolise liberty united to authority with a republican colouring. It is, for instance, to be found as an ornament on the equestrian monument of Garibaldi erected on the Janiculum hill in Rome. In previous centuries it was also occasionally used as an emblem and is found in the coat-of-arms of Cardinal Mazarin.

Since 1919, when Mussolini formed his movement, the word Fascism, having entered the vocabulary of all countries, has come to indicate any centralised government favouring strong policies and exerting strict control on the people's activities. The word has now become a synonym of dictatorship.

We have already spoken of the movement's development, and of events that brought Mussolini to head Italy's Government. His first Cabinet, the list of which he handed to the King, was founded on a coalition. Two non-political personalities served in it. They were General Armando Diaz and Admiral Thaon de Revel, who were Chiefs of General Staff of the army and the navy respectively at the end of the war. All other members belonged to political parties. Some were nationalists (therefore near to Fascism but still separated from it), others Liberals or Catholics. Although it was later denied, when greater emphasis was placed on the revolutionary significance of the march on Rome, Mussolini was anxious to ensure a parliamentary majority. This he reached through the combined vote of the parties he had called to co-operate with his. It may not seem quite clear why other political movements agreed on this co-operation. An explanation for the Liberals is easily found, for they were not really a party but a group of politicians with a certain following, temporarily united for electoral purposes. The 275 deputies belonging to this group who had been returned in the 1921 election were without a leader, nor did they follow a party doctrine or discipline. Theoretically 'liberals' or 'democrats', they were ready to serve any strong man who could provide them with Government support, so that they might be returned to Parliament in their constituencies. They had gladly served Giolitti after the turn of the century, when he had been Italy's strong man, and were ready to do the same now that the baton of command had passed into the hands of an even stronger leader. Mussolini soon understood that the small number of Fascist deputies could be increased only by getting from the Liberals the support they seemed anxious to give.

Support from Catholics was of a different nature. Their party had been formed in 1919 with a programme of social reforms inspired by the Church. As they believed these reforms could be achieved only through democratic methods, Catholics opposed those movements of the right that did not conceal their anti-parliamentary approach. But parties, like States, are not in a position to choose their allies. They must take them as they come. The most logical solution was, at that time, an agreement between Catholics and Socialists, provided the latter abandoned their revolutionary programme. Unfortunately, the Socialists were unwilling to give this co-operation and preferred the seclusion of the citadel of insurrectional activity. Although they were returned in both post-war elections in considerable numbers, the *popolari* (as the Catholics were called) did not control a majority. This could be reached only through agreements with other parties. After the fall of Bonomi it was suggested that they might form the Government with Filippo Meda as a possible Premier, but this project did not materialise.

When Mussolini's Cabinet was formed, a few *popolari* were authorised to serve in it, not as representatives of the party, but on a personal basis. This was done in an attempt to control the Fascist Government from within and to compel it to follow more democratic policies. It was an unsuccessful experiment, as Premier De Gasperi was later to acknowledge. Mussolini was not a man to be checked in his striving for complete power, and Catholic ministers soon resigned.

Mussolini had hardly taken over his new post when he asked Parliament for 'full powers', claiming that he needed them to restore finances and public order. The 1848 constitution contained no provision that the Government could be granted such powers. It is not astonishing that the Premier should have made such a request, but it certainly is that Parliament should have granted it by a majority of 275 votes to 90. Liberals voted in favour of the measure. Yet Mussolini had made no attempt to conceal his intentions, or his contempt for the elected assembly. In a speech delivered on November 16, 1922, he used the following insulting words: 'Having 300,000 armed men under my orders, I might have punished all who had defamed and attempted to destroy Fascism. I might have turned this dead and grey hall into a bivouac of armed squads. I might have locked and closed Parliament and formed a government solely of Fascists. I might have done so, but at all costs in this first period, I refused to do so.' In admitting that he had no constitutional scruples and that respect for the law would not stop him, Mussolini could hardly have been more explicit. Nothing but his own will had kept him from performing excesses, and he flatly implied that his will might change. Having received full powers, he could now issue orders-in-council. From that moment on, the course of Fascism was set towards a dictatorship, although outwardly democratic forms and terms were still observed.

In a democratic State there is, apart from the written law, the unwritten principle of decency and self-respect. Liberal governments are not simply made up of elected bodies. The citizens' approach favours a method inspired by liberty, to be followed in every sphere of life. The public attitude towards the person heading the Government is simply that he is a citizen who, for a limited period of time, is governing the nation. It is naturally implied that his appointment is temporary, and that he may soon hand over his powers to someone else. No one, not even his most ardent follower, would dream of exalting a democratic

Premier to the point of comparing him to Caesar, or stating that his mission is inspired by God. The case of a dictator in the making is different. Propaganda organised by Press bureaux or State agencies enters the picture and focuses everyone's attention on the would-be dictator and his movements. When such propaganda goes into action, dictatorship is a certainty. These periods of history must be lived through to be described, for they can seldom be understood by outsiders. This explains why books and films on Fascism or Nazism, written or made by people who have not actually been acquainted with them, rarely hit the mark. The impact of moral fear must be taken into consideration. It has been said that life is dominated more by terror than by love. No phrase could better explain the rise of a dictator. As a man he may even declare himself the follower of strict ethical principles. Through his speeches he may even appear open-minded and ready to understand other points of view, but when daily events show that he condones violence and inspires fear his words become worthless.

After 1922, violence, instead of coming to an end, grew in intensity. The Opposition had been greatly weakened. The police and the army, controlled by the Government, were in no position to check the excesses and crimes of Fascist squads, which continued to assault whomever they considered their opponent, whether Socialist, Communist, Liberal, or Catholic. Many were beaten and thrown out of office, their homes were ransacked, their social positions ruined. There was no law against a man criticising the Government, but if a man did so in public he would pay severe penalties for his act. It soon became a general practice to refrain from political remarks even in private. In every province, in addition to the prefect who represented the Government, directed the police, and looked after all matters affecting public security, there was a Fascist provincial chief whose position became more and more powerful, for he controlled the Fascist squads and his activity was unchecked. If his men stormed the homes of those who opposed the Government, the police never intervened. Only a few of these acts of violence were sufficient to create the atmosphere of terror that would paralyse opposition. Soon after the march on Rome, Mussolini had these action squads incorporated into the armed forces. They became the *Milizia Volontaria per la Sicurezza Nazionale* (Voluntary Militia for National Security). Their oath of allegiance was given to Mussolini, from whom they took orders.

As time passed, more emphasis was placed on military organisation. Up to 1922 Fascism had been a political movement with armed bodies at its disposal, but it soon became an army with a political doctrine. Mussolini was addressed as Duce, a word of Latin origin, meaning leader and chief. The title gradually replaced that of Premier and ultimately was used in official documents and in the heading of decrees. A military aspect soon crept into the new Government's methods, replacing ways linked to the parliamentary period. Uniforms were gradually replacing formal dress on ceremonial occasions. While Mussolini, after the march on Rome, had officially appeared in civilian dress, he wore a military uniform and rode a horse when the first anniversary of the march was celebrated.

But the switch to dictatorship required more than uniforms. New laws had to be enforced, and for this purpose a new parliament was needed in which Fascism could count on an absolute majority. Yet no majority could be hoped for in an election in which the proportional system was followed. Voting in 1921 had given meagre results to Fascist candidates, nor was there any evidence that popular support would increase. The electoral system had to be reformed. A new Bill was therefore introduced providing that the party achieving a relative majority of votes in the country would also obtain an absolute majority of seats. This system, while not necessarily anti-democratic, immediately became so when it was evident that electoral results would certainly be juggled in order to suit the Government's plans. The Bill had to pass through the existing Chamber of Deputies, where Fascism still disposed of few votes, yet even this measure was approved. Mussolini ran things with the greatest skill. He let it be known unofficially that if Liberal members supported the law he would make it a point of accepting them, if not into his ranks, at least as candidates in his electoral lists. This would mean their re-election, and was therefore quite a tempting proposition. Few could resist the offer, and the Bill was approved. The 1924 elections were run as anticipated. Armed squads intimidated the electors, the secrecy of the vote was violated, opposition speakers were disturbed and their meetings broken up. On several occasions ballot-boxes were open and the counting of votes interfered with. Giolitti had often been accused of 'making elections' through patronage and active local supporters, but his methods were scrupulously fair when compared to the Fascist ones.

Fascism enjoyed an absolute majority in the new Chamber. Some Liberals were elected in its lists, but most of the deputies who had voted in favour of the Government and had helped to set up a totalitarian regime were not returned to office. Their policy of appeasement had borne no fruit. Opposition was so reduced that it could no longer carry on any useful work.

During 1924 Fascism passed through a grave crisis. Giacomo Matteotti, a Socialist and one of the more courageous and outspoken members of the opposition, disappeared on the eve of a day he was to deliver a speech in Parliament. It was rumoured that he was going to bring to the country's attention proofs of Fascist crimes against liberty and human rights. A few days later his body was found in a wood near Rome. Some blackshirts had forced him to enter a car, had taken him to the wood and murdered him. After their arrest it was said that they had acted under orders of top-ranking Fascist chiefs, including De Bono, one of the four leaders of the march on Rome.

This created great public excitement. The country, which as a whole had not reacted too strongly to the violation of personal liberty, now took a different attitude. The circumstances in which the crime had been committed were widely publicised by the opposition, and many people resigned from the Fascist party, surrendering their membership cards. A wave of indignation swept the nation.

In an attempt to pin the responsibility of the murder on the Fascist chiefs, the opposition made its greatest mistake. It withdrew from Parliament as a protest against the Government's tardiness in conducting inquiries into the crime and in clearly establishing the moral and political responsibilities of the Fascist chiefs. This withdrawal is generally known as the Aventino. The opposition's absence from the Chamber of Deputies turned out to be a great drawback when Matteotti's body was found and Fascist guilt became more evident. The men who were materially responsible for the crime declared they had no intention of killing Matteotti, who had died of a heart attack caused by the beating he had suffered. Had the Fascist Government really given instructions, as alleged, for his liquidation, it would certainly have been a grave error. Probably no such order had been issued and the men who had kidnapped Matteotti had acted on their own initiative to ingratiate themselves with their superiors.

During the autumn of 1924 anti-Fascists seized the opportunity provided by the Matteotti affair to launch heavy attacks against the Government. Yet they could not be echoed by Parliament, where opposition was absent. Public opinion had been moved by these events to such an extent that it seemed Fascism had lost all support. The enthusiasm of two years before had become contempt and hatred, so much had the people been impressed by the Matteotti crime and its implications. If the Chamber of Deputies elected in 1921 had been in existence, a vote of no confidence would probably have been passed. But in the new Assembly, where the Fascist majority was overwhelming, a similar vote was now impossible. The only hope was that the monarchy, interpreting the popular trend, would dismiss the Government, for the King was not obliged by the constitution to retain Mussolini as Premier if he did not enjoy his confidence. Yet, when he was requested to take action, he lacked sufficient courage and replied that a vote of no confidence by the Assembly was required. Since this was out of the question, the answer was tantamount to a refusal. For the second time the monarchy was allied to Fascism, and for the second time Mussolini owed his office to the King.

While the opposition discussed the various moves it might make, it lost valuable time and opportunities, and Mussolini again took the initiative. On January 3, 1925, he delivered a speech in the Chamber of Deputies announcing that he was taking on himself full responsibility for what had happened during the previous years and that new and decisive steps would restore order in the country. This was the beginning of a new, more anti-democratic line. Freedom of the Press was reduced and the police were given the right to confiscate newspapers opposing the Government. Anti-Fascist editors and publishers were compelled to resign and were replaced by Government supporters. More authority was given to prefects, who were instructed to repress opposition energetically. The most illiberal measure enforced was the so-called *confino di polizia* (police confinement). This was an administrative decree ordering a citizen, although not guilty of any crime, to live for a certain time in a given town or city, from where he could not move without permission. Special *commissioni di confino* (confinement commissions) were set up. Their decisions were swayed by sectarianism or private revenge.

Political emigration had begun by this time. Several opponents chose voluntary exile (mainly in France) to escape local violence. Having reached a free land, they did not hesitate to express in speeches and articles their opposition to conditions existing in Italy. As a measure of retaliation a law was passed depriving them in certain instances of their citizenship and ordering confiscation of their properties. Secret agents were sent among them with orders to report their activities.

Local elections were abolished. Elected mayors of cities and towns were replaced by Government nominees (called *podestà*), whose term of office lasted five years and who naturally enforced the policies of a government to which they were indebted for their appointment.

Mussolini's official position was also strengthened. All through the parliamentary period the Premier had been a minister very much like the others, with the task of co-ordinating policies and choosing his colleagues. He was spoken of as *primus inter pares* (the first among equals). Mussolini was now given the title of *Capo del Governo* (Chief of the Government) to stress his supremacy over other members of the Cabinet. Special penalties aimed at protecting his life were incorporated into the criminal law. There had been four attempted murders of Mussolini (once by an Irishwoman), all of which had been unsuccessful, but they had nevertheless stirred his wish for protection.

The Law for the defence of the State was approved in December, 1926, and became the basic juridical instrument of the new regime. It sanctioned dictatorship by giving the widest definition of the so-called 'plot against the State', which included the propagating of political doctrines such as Socialism and Anarchism. Crimes of this nature were to be judged not by ordinary courts but by the *Tribunale speciale per la difesa dello Stato* (Special tribunal for the defence of the State), against whose sentences there was no appeal. High-ranking officers of the Fascist Militia enforced the new laws. This tribunal, set up as a temporary body, was never abolished and became the country's most dreaded institution. There is evidence that in various instances Mussolini himself fixed penalties or ordered clemency to be granted.

Although the election of 1924 had given Fascism complete control of the Chamber of Deputies and placed it in a position to obtain unquestioned approval of all legislation that might be put before it, parliamentary procedures were nevertheless regarded as too slow. A law was therefore approved in 1926 enabling the Government to issue orders-in-council. This soon became the normal form of legislation, with Parliament remaining a body deprived of any power of control.

The Matteotti crisis gave Mussolini the opportunity to dissolve the opposition. The Aventino attempt to organise a moral resistance by absenting themselves from Parliament was destined to fail from the beginning. After Mussolini had again taken the situation in hand, an attempt was made by some members to re-enter the Chamber of Deputies, from which they had been absent so long. This they were unable to do, for their reappearance produced the strongest reaction in the Fascists, who expelled them by force. In December, 1926, members of the Aventino group were deprived of their immunity and formally prevented from entering Parliament. This action was patently unconstitutional, but failed to cause the popular reaction it might have done at other times, probably because it was not yet clear that the last vestiges of democracy had thus been suppressed.

The Matteotti case was soon closed. The henchmen who had committed the crime, defended in court by the secretary-general of the Fascist Party, were condemned to light sentences. The chiefs believed to be also responsible were acquitted. Public indignation soon abated because the Press was rigidly controlled.

The disappearance of any opposition marked the end of all parties other than the Fascist, which thus retained the monopoly of political life. Liberals and radicals, being little more than electoral committees backing certain candidates, were dissolved, since elections were run solely by the Government in its own interest. The Catholic Party also came to an end. Its members had been quite active at the time of the Matteotti crime. Their daily paper, *Il Popolo* (The People), had been especially active in denouncing moral and juridical responsibilities, but after the dismissal of nearly all its deputies and the enforcement of new police laws, it was shorn of any power or influence. Persecutions started against its leaders, and Luigi Sturzo its founder was compelled to go into exile. He was succeeded by a triumvirate which included Giovanni Gronchi, later one of Italy's Presidents of the Republic. The last secretary was De Gasperi, assisted by Giuseppe Spataro, later a minister in various post-war Cabinets. They boldly kept the organisation together, until the end of 1925 when they were obliged to retire from public life. De Gasperi was soon arrested and condemned to four years' detention.

The two Socialist parties (Reformists and Maximalists) were also prevented from carrying on activities. Most of the leaders went into exile, especially to France, where the two movements were set up again and were eventually united in 1930. In Italy very little remained of the organisation that had been so active during previous years in stirring up discontent and creating the circumstances which had greatly strengthened Fascism. The Communists were the most efficient among Marxist parties, because they were tied to a severe discipline and could draw moral and financial support from Russian sources. Although going into exile, their party retained several links with groups operating in Italy. Many Communists were condemned by the Special Tribunal. Antonio Gramsci, who died while in detention, is today considered the martyr of Italian Communism.

A special law was enforced against secret societies, particularly against Freemasonry. Many Masonic lodges were invaded by Fascist squads, and violence became, as usual, the first step leading to dissolution.

The Government took a severe attitude towards public servants who had been members of subversive parties. Their dismissal was authorised in cases where it could be shown that they had been members of Marxist organisations or had been guilty of conspiracy against the State. If judged according to democratic standards, this seems a logical measure taken to strengthen a modern State. In the hands of a dictator it became a weapon to compel civil servants to carry out his instructions. The Fascist regime was now firmly entrenched in the country. Opposition had become little more than a secret society, meeting in restricted circles or friendly homes. Italians went underground. Everybody became fearful of expressing their opinions in public or of taking any initiative that might appear as a form of resistance. This was detrimental to the national mind, for it could hardly be through hidden activities or by concealing one's opinions and hopes that the national character could be welded together. The spiritual unity among Italians, which had long been one of the Risorgimento's aims, was now broken. A tyrannical unity, imposed through police measures, had taken its place. Italians were obliged to undergo again the moral and material ordeal they had been confronted with during previous centuries, when they had fought against domestic and foreign despotism.

Up to 1925 the history of Fascism is that of a party fighting against other political forces trying to oppose it. Until then a separation still existed between the political movement and the nation. But from then on the distinction can no longer be made, not because the nation backed the Government's policies, but because it had no way of voicing its opposition.

Although Fascist methods of maintaining power must be condemned, certain solutions it gave to public problems were of advantage to the nation. Much of the legislation enacted during this period is still in force. The law codes (civil, criminal, and of procedure) were reformed and, with few changes, are still applied.

The same may be said of the conciliation with the Church and the resolution of the so-called Roman Question. This problem had kept the Italians divided for over fifty years, and an immediate solution was needed that would take into consideration the interests and rights of both parties. This was accomplished by the Vatican Pacts of 1929.

Italy's international situation after World War I had not been one of strength. Although the peace treaty had enabled her to attain her natural borders on the Alps, this had not taken place without an intense struggle. A frontier question with Yugoslavia had been left unsolved, that only the Treaty of Rapallo (1920) had succeeded in closing, at least temporarily.

Furthermore, when she had passed through a period of economic crisis and social unrest, she had not found from her former allies the co-operation she might have expected. Her contribution to the war effort did not seem to entitle her to any consideration. In several instances her economic weakness had offered the occasion to impose on her political conditions. It is no wonder that she viewed with resentment and suspicion all the talk there was about the League of Nations. Much was then being said about the so-called 'spirit of the League', an expression implying that tolerance and unity would now oblige nations to come closer to one another. Unfortunately events were not influenced by this spirit. When Italy's Government had been weak and internally unstable, it had been very difficult to resist outside pressure. After Fascism had achieved power, a firmer and more efficient policy was followed. A first stand was made in August, 1923, when an Italian mission in Greece, entrusted with the task of finding a solution to certain border questions, was attacked by Greek bandits and its members murdered. Mussolini ordered the occupation of the Greek island of Corfu, which was not evacuated until full satisfaction was given to the demand for reparations advanced by Rome.

At that time, however, Mussolini intended to remain at peace with the rest of the world. In his first speech on foreign policy, delivered after the march on Rome, he proclaimed that treaties had to be respected even if their clauses were objectionable. In 1925, when the Locarno Treaty was signed (which its makers hoped would settle military antagonism between France and Germany), Italy was called on, together with Great Britain, to be one of the guarantors of its provisions. Mussolini personally went to Locarno during the last period of the negotiations. A policy of amity and appeasement was followed with other Powers, first of all with Yugoslavia, with whom a treaty of friendship was signed in 1924. The question of Fiume was settled on this occasion, and the city was given to Italy. Treaties were also signed with Rumania, Greece, Bulgaria, and Turkey. With this last Power an agreement was concluded at Lausanne on July 24, 1923, which acknowledged Italian sovereignty over the islands of Rhodes and the Dodecanese, occupied during the Libyan campaign. A treaty with Albania recognised Italy's extensive rights on that country.

As to Africa, the border between Libya and Egypt was rectified so as to include the oasis of Giarabub on the Italian side, and an agreement was reached with England granting Italy a strip of land south-east of Somaliland, known as Jubaland. The nation's policy was one of friendship towards her former enemies. Especially towards Germany she showed understanding by refusing to join France in the occupation of the Ruhr in 1924. All in all the Fascist regime, in its first years of power, showed a serious and dignified approach to foreign problems. Internal stability, even if forced upon the people through violence and unconstitutional measures, was nevertheless effective in international affairs.

The country's position also improved in the economic field. When Fascism came to power the situation was one of bankruptcy. The problem was taken in hand by a Fascist economist Alberto De Stefani, who made it a point to restore finances as quickly as possible. Taxation was reorganised and many economies enforced in State expenditures. Great emphasis was placed on exports. The trade deficit was reduced, while the budget deficit disappeared altogether. Yet the lira, due mainly to speculative manœuvres, had been shifting in value. A new

Minister of Finance was appointed in the person of Giuseppe Volpi, a businessman and diplomat, who restored its value. A policy of revaluation of the lira was therefore followed, the appropriateness of which was the object of much controversy. Mussolini's financial policies were in fact criticised by businessmen and industrialists, who saw them withholding prosperity. Yet a few years later, when the great world crisis broke out, the consequences of recession were felt less seriously than they might have been if the nation had been passing through a period of expansion.

To-day the doctrinaire mind of Mussolini can be traced in his policy concerning the increase of population. His so-called *politica demografica* (demographic policy) started on Ascension Day, 1926, with a speech in which the people's attention was called to the decreasing birthrate, and in which they were reminded of their duty of having more children. Even this line was inspired by desire for prestige. More informed advisers pointed out that something should first be done to reduce infantile mortality, which was scandalously high, especially in the South. Yet Mussolini paid no attention to this advice and persisted in his policy.

Gradually Italy became what is known as a totalitarian State. New Government organs were set up to turn the regime from the dictatorship of a man into an organised system. In 1928 a law was issued fixing the tasks and responsibilities of the Fascist Grand Council. This body, formed of the major chiefs of the party, had existed from the beginning, but its powers were now increased to enable it to deal with all major problems of the State, such as royal succession, preparation of a list of suitable people from which the King could choose the next Premier, annexation of territories, etc. A new electoral law gave it the task of choosing the candidates for the Chamber of Deputies. Candidates had to be proposed by trade unions, but the final list of names was determined by the Grand Council. The list as a whole was put before the electors, who voted for or against it.

It was not an election, it was a plebiscite. Fascist organisation, lack of secrecy, violence, and intimidation saw to it that the outcome was what the Governments desired. The numerical results of the 1929 and 1934 elections carried out in accordance with this law bear therefore little significance.

Soon after the march on Rome, anti-Fascist trade unionism came to an end because of the persecution of Socialist and Catholic leaders. In 1926 all unions were organised on a nation-wide basis and practically placed under Government control. They were recognised as the juridical representatives of the workers with the right to bargain with management. Strikes were declared illegal.

Where no agreement could be reached on working conditions, the controversy had to be taken to court, the decision of which was final. Fascist unions did little to defend the working man, but merely echoed his necessities. Although Fascism always denied it, its origin had chiefly been one of reaction against the mounting demands of the working class; and this could hardly fail to affect its policies. The outlawing of strikes was probably the most effective measure taken to favour management.

In 1928 a national programme of land reclamation was launched aimed at the resettlement of poor peasants. Although the regime was pressing people to have larger families, land was scarce and bound to become even more so as time passed and population increased. Unfortunately Italy was, and remains, a country with too many mountains and little arable land. Every scrap of it had therefore to be reclaimed and cultivated. The most impressive success was the draining of the Pontine marshes, a large expanse of land south of Rome, which for many centuries had been abandoned and where malaria was endemic.

Agriculture was given considerable attention, the chief emphasis being placed on wheat production. Italy is a great consumer of cereals, these being the principal ingredient of the people's diet. National production was not sufficient to meet the needs of consumption, and great quantities of wheat had to be imported yearly, as a result of which Italy had a large trade deficit. The Government launched the *Battaglia del Grano* (wheat battle), which encouraged farmers to produce more by awarding prizes for the best yields.

Great importance was placed on public works. The Government, claiming to have inherited its doctrine from Rome, was naturally interested in archaeological research. Roads were opened around ancient ruins and gardens laid out, so that the surroundings enhanced their historic glory. Highways were built or improved to deal with modern traffic. Railways were electrified to save on the import of coal. Electric power was produced from water resources in the mountains, many of which were harnessed to new dams. Public buildings were erected in several cities to serve the increasing needs of the population.

The country's stability put it in a position of superiority towards France and Germany, both of whom were afflicted by internal unrest. Rome became a centre of international dealings. After a period of friendship, however, relations with Yugoslavia became tense again. Belgrave objected to Italy's increased influence in Albania, and strengthened her ties with France. This was the beginning of Italy's friendship with Austria and Hungary, who found in her a defender of their policies for a revision of the peace treaties.

A success widely publicised by the Fascist Press was the Treaty of Rome, signed on June 7, 1933. Nazism had reached power in Germany that year, and the moment seemed to have come for an agreement among the major European States for the preservation of peace. This was signed by Italy, Germany, Great Britain, and France, but was never ratified. If it had been, it might have provided a substitute for the League of Nations, increasingly unable to deal with the great issues of the times.

Italy and Germany were bound to clash over the problem of Austria. Mussolini and Hitler met in Venice in June, 1934, and seemed to have reached an agreement concerning that country's independence. Yet two months later the Nazi revolt broke out in Vienna, and Chancellor Dollfuss was murdered. The plot had been organised in Germany, and was the prelude to annexation. Mussolini was quick in mobilising four divisions (approximately 50,000 men), and in sending them to the Austrian frontier. This meant intervention if annexation took place, and as a result Germany, still disarmed under the provisions of the 1919 Peace Treaty, refrained from attempting anything of the kind. Italy's influence in Austria and Hungary became very strong from that moment. This made relations with Germany difficult, and such they remained up to the time of the Ethiopian conflict.

The year 1935 started under good auspices. A new treaty was signed with France, settling certain colonial problems. In March Premier MacDonald of Great Britain and Premier Flandin of France met Mussolini in Stresa and agreed to collaborate for peace. But a new crisis was in the air. Italy and Ethiopia were on the eve of liquidating a critical situation that had lasted for half a century. Much has been said about the Italo-Ethiopian conflict, generally to the detriment of Italy and her armed forces. She is generally accused of having violated the Covenant and of having attacked a member of the League of Nations. If, juridically speaking, she may be to blame, morally there is much to say in her defence.

For centuries colonial expansion was never considered a crime. Often it was regulated by international agreement. Colonisation contributed to the formation of all independent States in North and South America, to the setting up of nations in which natives are enjoying the material and moral benefits of civilisation and in many cases are now ready for self-government. But colonialism also brought wealth to European States. Every major Power is indebted to it for its prosperity and strength. Why should Italy have been deprived of it just because she had achieved national unity late and had been unlucky in her first attempts? Besides, not many people realised that what they called the independent State of Ethiopia, to which membership of the League of Nations had been granted, was nothing but the domination of a few Abyssinian chieftains over a large territory, many parts of which had been only recently conquered. For instance, the vast Harrar region in the eastern part of the country had been annexed as late as 1887. Italy could not understand why this State should be entitled to so much protection by the League of Nations. She was right in thinking that this enmity was caused by the wish to keep her out of Africa and to deny her the economic outlet and territorial expansion to which she believed she was entitled. Fascist propaganda was also active in pointing to the vast benefits that England, the British Dominions, and France had achieved after the Peace Treaty of 1919, when they had received several territories belonging to Germany and Turkey. This was bound to stir the imagination of the people.

The crisis started in 1934, when the outpost of Wal Wal, on the border with Somaliland, was attacked by Ethiopian troops. Although the episode did not interest world opinion, it was in reality the origin of the conflict. At the beginning of 1935 Italy mobilised two divisions of her regular army and sent them to Eritrea and Somaliland. General De Bono was placed in command. Ethiopia made an appeal to the League of Nations, where a commission was set up to study the question. Yet nothing came of it, for the points of view of the interested parties were too divergent. Italy was determined to take this opportunity to extend her colonies in East Africa, while the world appeared to be equally determined to make it impossible for her to achieve this goal. Her Press and Government did not conceal their purposes nor that the crisis was to be considered the starting point of a colonial enterprise. In June, 1935, Anthony Eden, the British Minister for League of Nations Affairs, came to Rome and suggested that the crisis should be solved by exchanging certain territories. Italy would receive Ogaden, a desert land on the borders of Somaliland, while Ethiopia would be given the port of Zeila in British Somaliland. It was a highly unsatisfactory proposal, unacceptable to Italy. In August a conference between representatives of Italy, France, and England took place in Paris, but it soon adjourned without having reached any conclusions.

Because of these events, and in the face of Italy's determination to carry out her projects, Great Britain thought the moment had come to show her strength. The Home Fleet was ordered to the Mediterranean as a display of naval might. But Mussolini sent several divisions to Libya, warning that in the event of a naval war against him he would certainly attack Egypt. The British move was a tactless one, for Italy has always resented her naval inferiority. By displaying her strength, Britain was touching Italian susceptibility and pointing to her weakest spot. The natural result was that preparations were carried on more swiftly until war against Ethiopia started on October 3, 1935.

Operations were based on plans for a short campaign. This was required not only by the international situation, but also by Ethiopia's internal conditions. The feudal structure of this State was a fragile one, and it was felt it would soon disintegrate. The Italian army, 250,000 strong, was well supplied and protected by a strong air force. In a pincer movement troops marched south from Eritrea and north from Somaliland. Adowa and Makallè, both of which had witnessed Italian sacrifice in previous wars, were soon occupied. From the South troops pivoted towards Harrar.

Meanwhile the League of Nations declared Italy an aggressor and ordered economic sanctions against her in accordance with Article 16 of the Covenant. This meant that war materials would not be sold to her and that her products would be unacceptable to countries supporting the sanctions. The measure was ineffective for several reasons. Not all States, to begin with, belonged to the League. The United States of America, for instance, although quick in proclaiming their neutrality, could supply important materials. Austria and Hungary were members of the League, but refused to adopt any sanctions, thereby reaffirming their friendship. Other countries, though adopting sanctions in principle, were slow to enforce them. Italy, on her part, retaliated by ordering the so-called counter-sanctions, a measure by which nothing would be bought from countries that had accepted the policy of the League. Industrial firms were invited to develop their plants and produce locally what would normally be bought abroad.

In the meantime military operations were proceeding according to schedule. After the initial phase, De Bono was replaced as commander-in-chief by Marshal Pietro Badoglio (b. 1871), Chief of General Staff. Ethiopia's army had been divided between the northern and southern sectors. The advance units were beaten in successive battles, until only the best forces remained under direct orders of the monarch (generally called the Negus): these were dealt with in the Battle of Lake Ashianghi and routed.

Confronted with complete defeat, the Negus fled from his country. Addis Ababa, the capital, was over-run by the mob, formed in greater part by prisoners who had been released from jail. Marshal Badoglio was requested by the diplomatic corps to occupy the city and restore order, which he did on May 5, 1936. Some resistance from troops still faithful to the Negus was encountered in other parts of Ethiopia. Operations were continued for several months, but organised opposition was nonexistent. Annexation was proclaimed four days after the occupation of Addis Ababa on May 9, 1936. Mussolini made the announcement in his usual theatrical way by calling on the people to congregate in the city squares, where his radio speech was broadcast. Ethiopia was proclaimed an empire and the title of emperor bestowed upon the King of Italy.

The new colony was divided into several administrative units, according to ethnic and geographic principles. Much was done from the very beginning to improve economic, social, and sanitary conditions and to free the various races and religions from domination by the Abyssinian minority. Slavery was abolished. An outstanding achievement was the construction of a network of highways connecting all parts of the country.

Italy had achieved all her aims in a short time and at a relatively low cost in human lives, but the diplomatic aspects of the annexation had to be dealt with. Sanctions ordered by the League, although still in force, were being applied with less enthusiasm. Now that the war had reached an end little could be done, except to take notice of the new situation and recognise it. Sanctions had been a failure. More effective measures would have been an embargo on oil and the closure of the Suez Canal, but Italy had made it clear that she would consider these as a declaration of war and would react accordingly. No country was willing to face a conflict to save Ethiopia. Besides, the League had lost much of its prestige, and this also had to be taken into account.

Meanwhile new events were taking place in the international field. The estrangement between Germany and Italy caused by the Austrian issue had been quickly healed. During the Ethiopian crisis, Germany, although not a member of the League, was invited to take part in the sanctions. It was an absurd request, for Hitler was anxious to take advantage of the situation to serve his own interests. He had in mind rearmament and expansion, intended annulling the provisions of the Versailles and Locarno treaties, and knew that all this could not be done without Italian assistance. He also sensed that by agreeing with Mussolini he would get what he wanted, for the Fascist dictator was really the only obstacle in his path.

Thus the two regimes came closer together. During the Austrian crisis of 1934 newspapers and propaganda had stressed the differences between the two doctrines, but this policy was now reversed. It was emphasised that both States had fought Communism and had much in common. It is hard to believe that in so short a time such changes could take place. Yet modern propaganda can do anything, provided it is rightly organised. What is incomprehensible is why Mussolini was in such a hurry to conclude a written agreement. But his approach to international affairs was always influenced by his irrational nature. In the first decade of office his attitude had been more prudent, but after the Ethiopian campaign his moderation ended. Military and political success produced in him the feeling that he could deal with any situation. The wisest policy would have been that of strengthening what he held without getting involved in more difficulties, but dictators never know when to stop and are always over-confident. Rarely surrounded by friends, but only by servants ready on all occasions to approve his decisions, no matter how absurd these may be, a dictator's policy is not inspired by geographic, ethnical, or economic interests so much as by dreams of prestige and power. Calculations of strength, balance of forces, and traditional diplomacy do not interest him, for he would rather take a chance than yield to sensible advice.

In his policy towards Germany, Mussolini was not aware that he was being played off. He did not understand that, being the weaker partner, he would lose the role of leader he had held in recent years. There was a profound contrast between Germany on the one side, and England and France on the other. If he had been as Machiavellian as he proclaimed earlier (he had written an essay with the title 'Return to Machiavelli'), he would have made no commitment with either of the two sides, and acted as a mediator between them. But Hitler's attitude touched his pride by making him think he was leading, not following, events. Alliances between States of different strength generally turn out to serve the interests of the strongest partner. Italy was still stronger, but it was open to doubt if she would retain this role for long. Her superiority was linked to the fact that Hitler was still unarmed. While the Ethiopian campaign was caused by a legitimate need for expansion, the policy towards Germany was bad statesmanship and could in no way serve the nation's interests. Yet, on October 23, 1936, the protocols of Berlin were signed between Hitler and Ciano, Mussolini's son-in-law, who had become Foreign Minister. This was not yet an alliance, but a commitment between the two nations to follow the same international policies and to consult each other on the main problems. Mussolini, who enjoyed finding impressive words to indicate plain realities, soon declared that this agreement was no obstacle to an understanding with other countries, but an axis around which European affairs would gravitate. Hence the word 'Axis', a recurring term during the following years.

Barely a year had elapsed since the successful conclusion of the Ethiopian affair, and Mussolini was already searching for new adventures. The first occasion was offered him by the outbreak of civil war in Spain in July, 1936. It could not, of course, be foreseen that this conflict would last nearly three years, that so much blood would be shed, or that its international implications would be so grave. Be that as it may, Mussolini seemed eager to support and assist Franco's movement from the very beginning; why he should have done this will probably never be known.

The Ethiopian campaign had turned Italy into a major African Power, and English realism was anxious to reach some accord, at least of a temporary nature. This also seemed to suit Mussolini. On January 2, 1937, a gentlemen's agreement was in fact signed between the two countries which committed them to defend the *status quo* in the Mediterranean. Agreements of this kind have little chance of lasting or of having any real influence. However, this one helped to break the international deadlock in which the two nations found themselves. That same year an agreement with Yugoslavia was signed in Belgrade by Premier Stoyadinovic and Minister Ciano which seemed to bring to an end the rivalry between the two Adriatic Powers. Friendship with Austria and Hungary continued, although these two nations looked with some alarm on the improvement of relations between Italy and Germany.

The Spanish conflict was lasting longer than anticipated, and Italy was deeply involved in it. She was now sending whole divisions of so-called volunteers. What had started as a civil war had become a conflict for European and Mediterranean supremacy, contrary to the spirit, if not to the letter, of the gentlemen's agreement signed with England. Italy was also losing the position of mediator between other Powers, while Germany was making capital gains, and was gradually attracting her within her ideological orbit. Frequent meetings took place between high officials of the two States. More emphasis was placed on the identity of the two regimes than on friendship between governments, since the latter was expected to follow as a consequence of the first. This new intimacy influenced Fascism profoundly. Changes were so radical that by 1937 it was hard to recognise in Fascism the same movement that had come to power in 1922. It seemed as if, having always lacked a programme and having achieved success just on the wave of reaction against Communism, Fascism was at last filling the gap and, absurdly enough for a nationalist party, was getting its doctrine from a foreign country.

In September, 1937, Mussolini visited Germany. Dictators seldom travel abroad unless as victors, and rarely pay a friendly visit to the head of another State. His journey, therefore, was evidence of the intimate relations between the two regimes and underlined that in a short time a partnership had been formed in which Italy played an important role. But his journey also proved that Germany had something to teach the Italian dictator. In 1937, after four years of Nazi government, everything had been done to turn the democratic Weimar republic into a totalitarian State. During his stay Mussolini saw a country that in an amazingly short time had set up armed forces and was quickly making up for the period when rearmament had been forbidden. He perceived that the German brand of Fascism was ahead of his in methods adopted and its determination to challenge democracy. Any other statesman witnessing German power would probably have followed a more prudent policy and would perhaps have tried to strengthen existing ties with France and England. But Mussolini got more and more entangled with German politics. Nothing seemed to restrain him. On November 6, 1937, Italy signed, together with Germany and Japan, the anti-Communist pact. This also was not an alliance, but an establishment of common policies directed against the Communist International and, of course, Russia. Never had Italy taken such an attitude. She had recognised the Russian regime as far back as 1924. The fight against Communism within her borders, the elimination of the party, and the imprisonment of its leaders were a strictly domestic affair. Enmity towards Moscow was part of the German and Japanese plans, for these two Powers knew that sooner or later their expansion would clash with the Russian colossus. But Italy had no territorial claims against that country, nor could she receive any advantage from an aggressive war in that direction. The signing of the pact was for her just another piece of bad diplomacy.

Meanwhile Mussolini continued to give substantial support in arms and materials to Franco's cause, so that nationalist victories were considered by the Press as victories of the Italian army. That of course made the world speak of an Italian defeat when, in March, 1937, in face of enemy pressure, nationalists temporarily withdrew from the sector of Guadalajara. This event was of little military significance, but it was built up by the world Press into a grave defeat. The Fascist Government was also backing Nationalist Spain in the London committee set up to prevent foreign intervention, and its representative in that committee lost no opportunity of challenging the interests of France and England.

Italy's entanglement left Germany free to pursue her policy

of aggression. In March, 1938, the annexation of Austria took place. This marked the failure of Mussolini's policy towards Austria, since he had strenuously defended that country's independence. Two months later, in May, 1938, Hitler visited Rome. He was triumphantly received, chiefly because he had just declared that he considered the Brenner Pass an inviolable boundary between the two nations.

In this picture of mistaken diplomacy, lacking all preparation or continuity and often caused by the plain impulses of an emotive kind, the only intelligent move was the policy of closer ties with England. After the 'gentlemen's agreement' of 1937, it was felt that some wider understanding could be reached between the two Powers. It was not easy for them to get together, as there were so many differences between them. Contacts had already been made in Rome during 1937, but negotiations became smoother in February, 1938, when Foreign Secretary Anthony Eden, who had opposed any appeasement, resigned from the Cabinet. Two months later an agreement was signed in Rome. It provided for the maintenance of the *status quo* in the Mediterranean and the exchange of naval information. It also dealt with mutual policies in East Africa and the area of the Red Sea and Arabia.

Relations with France were also strained, due to the Spanish war. The French, with a few exceptions among the Right and the Catholics, generally favoured the Government of Madrid against Franco, and had sent it supplies and armaments, while allowing volunteers to be recruited on their territory. However, after the League authorised member States to recognise Italian sovereignty over Ethiopia, France sent André François-Poncet as the new ambassador to Rome with the task of establishing cordial relations between the two countries. He was accredited to the 'King of Italy and Emperor of Ethiopia', which implied a recognition of the constitutional changes that had taken place. Alas, his efforts were not destined to succeed.

The German intention to expand into Czechoslovakia was causing a new crisis. The pretext was the presence within that State of a German minority. It was to become part of the greater Reich, although it had lived for centuries under the Bohemian crown. The annexation of Austria had only been the beginning of Germany's expansion. In September, 1938, the crisis broke out as German troops were about to attack Czechoslovakia. This meant war. Chamberlain asked Mussolini to act as a mediator and to obtain a twenty-four-hour delay. The Munich Conference, attended by Hitler, Mussolini, Chamberlain, and Daladier, sealed Czechoslovakia's tragic destiny. All the territory of the Sudeten mountains was annexed by the Reich. Czechoslovakia was deprived of her military defences and reduced to the rank of a satellite.

Europeans began thinking that after recent events, and in the face of democratic weakness, German aggression could not be checked. This must have also been Mussolini's opinion. At the Munich Conference he had acted as a mediator, and had apparently been successful. The fact that the whole world, even the democratic one, had praised him as the saviour of peace should have finally opened his eyes and shown him where Italy's most favourable policy lay. This, unfortunately, was not his reaction. While he was fighting the war in Spain, with no concrete result, Germany was annexing important countries densely inhabited and with rich industrial resources. This may have been the reason why, hardly two months after Munich, a new crisis appeared on the horizon. On November 30, 1938, Ciano delivered in the Chamber of Deputies a speech on foreign affairs in which for the first time he mentioned the 'natural aspirations' of the Italian people. At this point the deputies rose and launched the slogan: 'Tunisia, Suez, Jibuti, Corsica, and Nice'. The whole affair had been arranged in advance, and it was no coincidence that these territories had been named. Fascist expansion, it was now being madc clear, was bent on French territories thickly populated by Italians, or where Italian interests were strong. The hope of reaching an agreement with France, similar to the one signed with England, collapsed among the dreams of hopeful diplomacy. France reacted violently. Prime Minister Daladier delivered anti-Italian speeches, declaring that his country would never yield to intimidation.

In January, 1939, Neville Chamberlain and Lord Halifax visited Rome, meeting Mussolini and Ciano. Although nothing concrete came of this encounter, it was a success for Fascist diplomacy which became even more apparent when, two months later, the Spanish war ended with Franco's victory.

Events moved swiftly. In March, 1939, Germany broke the Munich agreement, and incorporated a large part of Czechoslovakia in the Reich. This took place with the most complete disregard of Italy's position. Some resentment was felt among Fascist ranks, and it was hoped that the country might turn to more sensible and realistic policies. Unfortunately Mussolini's attitude was more and more one of political blindness. He believed that by inventing magnificent myths about German–Italian relations, and by making his people believe them, he was serving his country's interests. Ten days after the annexation of Czechoslovakia he declared that the event had been necessary and that friendship with Germany remained unaffected. Yet, frustrated by Hitler's success and in need of action to bolster his own position, he ordered, on April 7, 1939, the invasion of Albania. Of all the moves of Fascist diplomacy, this was probably the most childish. Albania had always been within Italy's orbit. Its invasion added nothing to her position in the Adriatic and violated the agreement with England. Mussolini was industriously applying his talents to create the world's resentment.

Two months later a formal alliance was signed with Germany. Until that moment, although several agreements had been reached and many declarations had been made stressing their common ideals and programmes, there had been no definite obligation for mutual assistance in the event of war. Mussolini was evidently not satisfied with this fortunate position, which still enabled him to avoid direct military intervention, and urged the Germans to sign an alliance. He was so anxious to reach it quickly that he insisted that the announcement of its conclusion be publicly given while it was still being negotiated. Drafted in Berlin, it was of the most absurdly aggressive nature. Evidently, Mussolini had lost all touch with reality. Feeling that Hitler's diplomacy had been more successful than his, he hoped to conceal his mistakes by insisting more and more on them. A queer treaty it was indeed. Although binding to an incredible extent, it was never ratified, so that it really never came into existence.

It had scarcely been signed when World War II broke out. Mussolini was asked by Hitler not to fight, under the pretext that his aid was not yet needed. In reality, he could not intervene, for his armed forces were unprepared. It seemed as if something in Italy's destiny was keeping her out of major entanglements, although she did everything to get into them. For ten months, in fact, she remained in the unusual position of being Germany's ally without actually fighting, and of maintaining diplomatic relations with all the belligerents.

For eighteen years prior to the outbreak of the war, Italy's history was dominated by the actions of one man. Yet, after

World War II, little distinction was made between the Italians and the Fascist Government which held them in a firm grip. The people were made to pay heavily for the mistakes of their leader although they had no part in the decisions taken. Many upper and middle-class Italians, who had originally supported Fascism, found it exhausting to live at concert pitch in a tense atmosphere of crisis. Alarmed by the dangerous turn of events, they would have preferred Mussolini to follow a more cautious policy. Working people had never been warm supporters of Fascism, which had failed to improve their standard of living. Fascism had influenced the masses emotionally when the national 'ego' had been stirred by successes in Ethiopia and Spain, but this enthusiasm had quickly evaporated, while the policy of friendship with Germany had never been popular. Soon reason replaced emotion among many who, although lacking proper information, did not succumb to propaganda and were still capable of a rational analysis of their country's position. If free elections had been held, Fascists would have been defeated. This was so profoundly felt by the Government that, far from being made free, elections were abolished. The Chamber of Deputies elected in 1934 was the last elected assembly. In 1939 legislative power was given to a new body formed by party leaders and by representatives of economic, financial, and industrial interests, and known as the Chamber of Fasces and Corporations. If a man occupied a certain position in the party, he automatically became a member of the new body. On the other hand, if he was dismissed from his post, he lost the seat. The Chamber had no real power and only approved decrees issued by the Government. Budgets were passed practically without discussion.

These radical reforms were certainly inspired by the Nazi regime, which had formally placed all power in the hands of the Führer, nullifying the importance of legislative bodies. German influence was also obvious in the solution given to the racial problem. Up to the time of the Ethiopian campaign there had never been any doubt as to the right of the Jews to take part in Italy's life. There had never been any discrimination or persecution. In an interview with Emil Ludwig, the writer, Mussolini had denied the existence of a Jewish problem in Italy. A few Jews had even risen to high positions. No emphasis had ever been placed upon the ethnical purity of the nation, and the word 'race' was never used with the meaning given it by Hitler.

Fascist propaganda now began to spread the myth of Aryanism, as a pretext to persecute the Jews. A Government-sponsored journal, *The Defence of the Race*, was published with the aim of building up the scientific and political foundations of Aryanism. Yet this anti-Jewish policy was not accompanied by acts of cruelty. Jews were never compelled to wear the infamous yellow star, nor sent to concentration camps. Economic restrictions were placed upon them, and they were expelled from certain professions and prohibited from owning certain types of property. Mixed marriages were forbidden. Considering that Italian Jews had always made great contributions to Italy's advancement and progress, and that their numbers were few, having never exceeded 100,000, their persecution was an extremely stupid act. In fact many intelligent and loyal citizens were compelled to emigrate.

The tendency to modify the structures of the State became more radical during the final months preceding the war. Security measures were strengthened. The police were allotted more financial support and the whole nation was placed on a military footing. No effort was spared to make the country self-supporting. This was not only intended as an economic measure for the protection of industry, but as a military one in order to keep factories in operation if, in the event of war, supplies became short. New industries were set up which in ordinary circumstances would quickly have become bankrupt. Costs seemed to be unimportant, and any product which cut down imports was viewed with favour. As a result, a protectionist mentality developed among factory-owners which lasted throughout World War II. This economic policy was called 'Autarchia' (autarchy).

Dominated by a political dictatorship which controlled every aspect of life and had transformed the country into a prison where people were afraid to speak or act, the nation was morally depressed and uncertain of its future. This was the unhappy position in which Italy found herself at the beginning of World War II.

Chapter 7

Italy in the Great Tragedy (1940–45)

IN AUGUST, 1939, when World War II started, Italy was unprepared for a major conflict, for the equipment used in the Ethiopian and Spanish campaigns had never been replaced, despite the large funds set aside for rearmament. News of the real situation reached the public's ear, causing substantial damage to Fascist prestige. Yet people were relieved when an official *communiqué* was issued announcing that, at least for the moment, the Government intended to keep out of the war. Neutrality was never proclaimed, Italy's position being that of a non-belligerent State. This meant that, although non-combatant, she favoured her German ally morally and politically. During the summer and winter months of 1939 it seemed more and more likely that Mussolini intended to keep out of the war, and that Italy would pass from a non-belligerent state to a neutral one. Neutrality was championed within the Duce's intimate circle by Foreign Minister Ciano. Even King Victor Emmanuel III opposed intervention and, although his influence had considerably decreased, his opinion was still not to be ignored. Great Britain and France naturally preferred a neutral Italy, especially as Germany was at this period far superior to them in military strength.

Had it not been for Mussolini's temperament, this situation might have lasted indefinitely, but he was an impulsive character and prone to make sudden decisions. So impressed was he by German victories in Norway and Denmark, and later in Holland, Belgium, and France, that he never doubted that these victories were decisive. Current events led him to believe that the war was nearly over and that Britain, after the fall of France, would give up fighting. This explains why on June 10, 1940, when the French and British armies were retreating under heavy enemy pressure and the Maginot Line had collapsed, he declared war against France and Great Britain. It was said that when asked why he had intervened, his answer was that he needed a few thousand dead to enable him to participate on the winning side at the peace conference. So much was the declaration of war simply a political move that in the beginning he paid scant attention to military preparedness. In 1939 he had said it would take at least three years before he could intervene in the war. In 1940 conditions had not changed and no attempt had even been made to stir up public opinion.

So determined was Mussolini to 'get in before it was too late' that he ignored all offers of mediation and appeasement. Both Roosevelt and Churchill sent messages advising him to reconsider his decision, and the French Premier, Daladier, hinted that if he kept out of the war, claims made by Italy on certain French territories might, in due course, receive favourable consideration. At this point, however, nothing could stop him, so strong were his convictions that the war was almost over and so avid his desire to take part in the dividing of the spoils. Rarely has a nation's leader made such a gross mistake.

Although France capitulated a few days later, Mussolini's belief in a short war was soon shattered when, after the Battle of Britain, Hitler gave up his attempt to invade that island. From then on problems of military preparation became more and more predominant. Great Britain's naval strength, which up to then had been of little consequence against the Germans, was soon to be in force against Italy, a much more vulnerable target owing to her long coastline and distant colonial territories. The Italian navy and air force had been caught off guard. Had the declaration of war been a military rather than a political move, a massive attack would probably have been launched against the British on the western and eastern sides of the Mediterranean. Had such an attack been made during the first days of the conflict—when the R.A.F. was fighting in the Battle of Britain and no planes could be spared—it would have provided Italy with initial superiority. Nothing of the kind, however, was done, and the British navy, from its strongholds in Alexandria and Gibraltar, was in a position to close the Mediterranean and to menace Italian sea communications.

Italy had never before been at war against such a strong naval Power, and the extreme weakness of her position became more and more evident. Mussolini had placed great importance on the construction of a strong navy, and in this respect had gone beyond the financial resources of his country; yet, in spite of this, it was open to doubt whether he had any chance of success.

Efficient co-operation between navy and air force was another strong point in favour of the British. With aircraft carriers and a large number of planes under their command, the British navy placed Italy's navy in a critical condition. Chiefly for economic reasons, Italy had not built aircraft carriers, and to avoid difficult explanations the public had been told that 'Italy in herself was an aircraft carrier' and had no need for such ships. Should air support be required during a battle it would suffice for a message to be sent to all air bases of the peninsula. What, however, was not taken into consideration was timing and co-ordination. In the course of a battle immediate air support may be the deciding factor. If to get it a navy commander has to contact a base—perhaps an hour's flying distance away—the battle, more likely than not, will be over before any aircraft has a chance to appear on the scene.

This is exactly what happened during the battles of Punta Stilo (known also as the Battle of Calabria) on July 8 and 9, 1940, of Cape Spada on July 19, 1940, and of Cape Teulada (known also as the Battle of Sardinia) on November 27, 1940. On these occasions lack of co-ordination was responsible for Italian lack of success. The same may be said of the Battle of Cape Matapan, March 27 and 28, 1941. Radar was also an invaluable asset to the British, for Italian ships, unequipped with this important device, floundered helplessly in the face of an enemy who could see their movements beforehand and act accordingly.

These battles gave the British ample opportunity to seriously hinder troop and supply ships on their way either to Africa or to the Balkans. With increasing demands from the army for reinforcement and supplies, the situation became more difficult. Although the Italian navy had formed a group of 'Commandos' which raided enemy ports (Souda, Alexandria, and Gibraltar were successfully attacked and several ships were destroyed), neither these tactics nor the use of submarines changed the course of the war on the seas.

The combat area between the British and the Italians was an extensive one. The two countries faced each other over a wide territory which covered Egypt, the Sudan, Uganda, Kenya, Ethiopia, and Somaliland. Sooner or later the situation in Ethiopia was bound to become critical. Conquered four years before, it was hardly ready for another major conflict. Italian hopes lay in a quick victory in Europe, but should the war last it was inevitable that Ethiopia would pass into the enemy's hands.

During the first phase of the Ethiopian campaign the Italians swept through British Somaliland, crossed the Sudan frontier, and occupied Kassala. These victories had a moral effect on the public, and even in England they were viewed with concern. Yet, the situation changed after the British succeeded in sending supplies and armaments. Admittedly these reinforcements were meagre, but they were sufficient to tilt the scales in their favour. Italian man-power was double the British, but it was not enough to win a war. By the end of 1942 the whole of Ethiopia, Eritrea, and Somaliland had been occupied by the British.

Cyrenaica, however, was a far more vital sector. Had Italy's entry into the war been more carefully planned, her first logical move would have been to attack Egypt from the Libyan border, where her forces outnumbered the British. Occupying Suez and Alexandria would have been relatively easy during the summer of 1940, when British war efforts were concentrated on the Battle of Britain. Marshal Graziani, Commander-in-Chief in Libya, lost precious time, and three months passed before he occupied the stronghold of Sidi-el-Barrani, a village hardly a stone's throw from the border. Instead of carrying on with the attack, he again paused, giving the enemy a valuable breathing-space and time to reinforce both man-power and supplies. The British attack launched in December, 1940, succeeded beyond expectation. Modern tanks—Italian tanks had little protection and were armed only with machine-guns in fixed turrets, while those of the British were mobile—and efficient co-ordination between navy, army, and air force were the cause of this. The towns of Tobruk and Benghazi fell within a few days. By now the situation had become so serious that German reinforcements were urgently needed. Therefore some special German units, equipped for the war in the desert, under the command of General Rommel, were sent to North Africa. With strengthened artillery and air support, the Axis forces attacked the British on April 1, 1941, and drove them back to the Egyptian frontier. Tobruk remained in British hands. Towards the end of 1941 the British counter-attacked and, despite strong Axis resistance, succeeded in re-occupying Cyrenaica. Sollum and Bardia resisted for two months before being occupied.

While operations in Africa were in progress with this series of advances and retreats, Italy went to war against Greece, attacking her from the Albanian border on October 28, 1940. The occupation of the Greek peninsula would probably have improved the Axis position, making Alexandria and the Middle East more vulnerable. But it is doubtful if Mussolini ever considered the problem in this light. Prestige was, as usual, the main reason for launching this campaign. Germany had by now spread over most of Europe, while Italy had made no progress at all. This, to a man who entered the war only for reasons of prestige, was, to say the least, galling. Military organisation was at its worst. Erroneous intelligence reports had led Mussolini to believe that the Greeks would not resist an attack and operations would take only a few days. Troops were ill-equipped and badly trained for mountain warfare. The Greeks put up a strong resistance, for they were better equipped and their morale was higher. This enabled them to launch a counter-attack which sent the Italians a few miles in retreat towards the Albanian frontier.

In a war of such magnitude a small campaign of this kind is of little importance. Yet, psychologically speaking, the Greek resistance provided Great Britain with excellent propaganda ammunition. If prestige was Mussolini's aim, he certainly did not find it in the Balkans. The soldiers he used as cannon-fodder were undoubtedly stalwart fighting men, but the odds were against them. In March, 1941, Mussolini personally took part in the spring offensive, but again things went wrong and the attack was repelled. As in Libya, it soon became evident that German intervention was needed, for British forces and supplies were arriving regularly. The R.A.F. was also in a better position to attack the Italian mainland and the oilfields of Rumania. This state of affairs could not continue if German plans against Russia were to be carried through.

In January, 1941, Germany occupied Rumania. In March her troops marched into Bulgaria and political pressure was brought on Yugoslavia to side with the Axis. As this project did not meet with success, armed force was used against Yugoslavia, who was compelled to ask for an armistice. At the same time German troops advanced into Greece and broke through the Metaxas line. The Greek forces gave way, while the British were compelled to re-embark for Africa. A few weeks later the island of Crete fell to the German paratroopers and all opposition to the Axis came to an end. Italy participated in the last attack on Greece and in operations against Yugoslavia. Among the Yugoslav regions, Slovenia was split between Germany and Italy, while Croatia became an independent State under the dictatorship of Ante Pavelich. Certain areas of the Dalmatian coast, inhabited chiefly by Italians, were annexed. It is common knowledge that had it not been for the campaign in the Balkans, Germany would have attacked Russia in May instead of June, 1941. This would have enabled her to occupy Moscow and Leningrad before the winter months. Had these plans run to schedule the outcome of the Russian campaign might have been different. War in the Balkans turned out to be a costly affair.

In November, 1940, the naval base of Taranto was attacked from the air by the British, who were in control of Grecian airfields. Anti-aircraft artillery and fighter planes proved inadequate and several warships suffered serious damage.

By this time Italy's morale was low. Her people had shown little—if any—enthusiasm when war was declared, and the course of events had certainly not brought about a change of attitude. Mussolini's poor leadership had caused even his staunchest supporters to become critical. In the past his speeches had been forceful and worthy of attention. Now they sounded meaningless and blustering. Defeats suffered by the Italian forces showed only too well why he had been nick-named 'the sawdust Caesar'. The concern of the public was growing daily as German influence increased. Hitler had never seriously considered Mussolini as a partner, but had always looked upon him as an underling. Often he did not even bother to consult the Duce before making an important decision. Meetings between the two dictators became more frequent, but seldom, if ever, did they reach any definite conclusion. The Führer completely dominated the situation. Meetings between Ribbentrop and Ciano were of the same kind, for the Germans always took the upper hand and issued the orders. It was not long before they also took over military control. Although security measures were tightened and new ones enforced, the public was beginning to speak more openly against the Government, defeatism was spreading, and anti-Fascism mounting. Underground parties, after years of persecution, were reappearing, and were certainly of no help either to the war effort or in strengthening the home front. Italians had never been told that the outcome of a war of such dimensions could mean the life or death of their country.

Whereas common danger had rallied other nations around their governments and had linked them intimately, Italians were not feeling a sentiment of that kind. In fact many welcomed the idea of defeat simply because it would free them from the fetters of Fascism. Dictatorship is, after all, basically weak. Originating in violence and fear, it rarely stands up to the hard test of difficult times.

Did the Italians understand what defeat would mean? That it would bring in its wake both moral and material misery? The minority probably did, but the mass was more influenced by Allied radio propaganda. Used for the first time in history on such a large scale, this weapon of war contributed greatly to the weakening of the people's morale. Distinction between the people and the regime was constantly emphasised and it was implied that the Allies only wanted to destroy Fascism, while after the downfall of the regime the Italians would regain their rightful place among nations. Many people believed this and genuinely looked upon the Allies solely as liberators. History should have taught them that few military campaigns have been undertaken merely for the purpose of liberating a nation, the outstanding exception being the liberation of Vienna from the Turks in 1683, spontaneously undertaken by John Sobieski, King of Poland.

External affairs were dominated by military events. As the Germans were virtually in control, their opinion predominated everywhere and Italian diplomacy could do nothing but agree to decisions already made. Hitler, for example, attached little importance to the Duce's African strategy, and it was only after the first British advance that he decided to intervene in Libya. The same can be said of Malta. This Mediterranean stronghold was a decisive factor in Allied strategy, but the Führer, believing that the final phases of the war would take place in northern and western Europe, refused to make any special effort to occupy it. He was also convinced that Spain should declare war on the Allies, for this would enable him to occupy Gibraltar without difficulty. Diplomatic relations between Germany and Italy on one side and Spain on the other were rather pathetic. The Spanish regime owed everything to the Axis, especially to Italy. Yet it never yielded to the pressure brought to bear on it. The only positive action taken by Franco was the sending of a division of volunteers (the so-called Blue Division) to fight in Russia.

On September 27, 1940, a formal alliance was signed in Berlin between Germany, Italy, and Japan. As it contained a clause indicating that Russia was in no way implicated, it was clearly directed against the United States. Hitler's and Mussolini's knowledge of America was extremely limited and, amazing as it may seem to the ordinary man, they acted as if they knew nothing of that country's vast resources and of the fact that America helped to tip the scales in the First World War. The Axis made a tremendous effort to bring other countries into the alliance. In this it failed, as only the States already within its orbit were willing to join. Spain consistently refused to have anything to do with it.

When the attack on Pearl Harbour came, the Axis lost no time in declaring war on the United States. Mussolini proclaimed that this new enemy had already been helping Great Britain for a long time and that open warfare would in no way alter the situation. His statement was grossly untrue. Admittedly the United States were providing material aid to Great Britain, but they were at least still at peace with Germany and Italy. It would have served the Axis purpose for things to continue this way, while open war meant that American planes, warships, and soldiers would now reach Europe in vast quantities.

The Russian campaign was not running to schedule. The Germans had calculated that within a few months all territories west of the Urals would be occupied, but strenuous resistance and unexpectedly cold weather slowed down their plans. On this front Italy contributed at first with an army corps, then with an army. Her soldiers showed courage and endurance, although they had to fight against a stubborn enemy and under conditions to which they were not accustomed. At first they took part in the general advance, occupying a sector of the Ukrainian front. The advance was checked when the Russians started their great offensive. During the retreat they were engaged in rearguard battles. Over 100,000 Italian prisoners were captured and subjected to long, deadly marches and to the horrors of concentration camps. Few of them ever returned to their country, for the majority perished of disease or exhaustion.

The year 1942 was one of great events in North Africa. After having withdrawn west of Benghazi, the Axis troops started a new offensive during the month of January, compelling the

British to abandon nearly all Cyrenaica, which they had occupied only a few weeks earlier. In June they were on the offensive again, and after having captured Tobruk, they pushed on into Egyptian territory, reaching El Alamein, approximately sixty miles west of Alexandria. At this moment, however, their success came to an end. Even with the African base almost within sight, their victory was doomed through inadequate supplies and, above all, shortage of fuel. On October 24, 1942, the great Allied push started under the command of General Montgomery. Heavily reinforced with modern weapons, the Allies counter-attacked, and Axis forces, although resisting for eleven days, had to withdraw. Supply lines had stretched, and it was very difficult to provide soldiers with equipment needed in the field. The Allies broke through and advanced rapidly, meeting little resistance. They recaptured the territory lost to the Axis during the previous months and reached Tripoli in January, 1943.

During November, 1942, the Allies invaded North Africa and in a few days occupied several important bases. The Axis retaliated by occupying the French regions which the armistice of 1940 had left unoccupied—southern France, Corsica, and Tunisia. Italian and German troops, retreating from Libya, made a new stand in Tunisia, but could not resist the growing might of their enemies, who had by then succeeded in uniting the two theatres of war.

After the North African invasion the Allied air force began a constant and methodical bombing of Italy's most important bases. Theoretically these attacks were aimed at military and industrial targets, but in fact they caused an enormous amount of damage to non-military objectives. The power of resistance of the population, harried unmercifully, was rapidly nearing breaking point.

To eliminate defeatism the Government tried enforcing discipline through police measures and party pressure. This policy had little success. The people were by now so depressed that indifference was the only emotion they were capable of feeling; belated Fascist threats had little effect on them. The police force, sensing that things were going badly with the regime, was less inclined to arrest anti-Fascists than it had ever been in the past. Following the well-known principle, 'whilst governments fall the police always carry on', it was not in its interest to arrest persons who, sooner or later, might be the nation's new leaders.

Some measures aimed at strengthening the war effort were never put into force, or were applied in a half-hearted manner. The Fascist party was rapidly weakening, and was no longer the bulwark of which Mussolini had always boasted. Many leaders already sensed that the war was lost and that nothing could be done to avoid the final and inevitable crash. The population had always blamed Italy's entry into the war on the Fascists. Party leaders went one step further, and put the entire blame on Mussolini. For years official propaganda had proclaimed, '*Mussolini ha sempre ragione*' (Mussolini is always right). Little wonder that after all the past catastrophes he was held responsible for the whole affair.

In the early part of 1943 the Duce, sensing unrest in the party, decided to remove from key positions certain possible trouble-makers. Ciano, as Foreign Minister, was the first to go. Although he had served throughout the war in that capacity, it was general knowledge that he disapproved of Italy's participation in the conflict. After the fall of Tunisia, Mussolini hinted for the first time at a possible invasion of the Italian mainland. He failed, however, to convince the people that the Axis could possibly win the war. On July 6, 1943, the text of one of the Duce's speeches, in which he emphasised the necessity of strong resistance in the face of an invasion, was not only received with a distinct lack of enthusiasm, but openly ridiculed. Two days later the Allies landed in Sicily, backed by a military force of such might that history has seldom witnessed its equal. Troops on the island, including the IXth Italian army and 70,000 Germans, were unable to resist. It is possible that at this period Mussolini would have liked to ask for a separate armistice. Several of his advisers, including the King himself, favoured that move. He also believed that a separate armistice with Russia was still possible, in which case the whole war effort could be concentrated on Great Britain and the United States. In his dream of splitting the Allies he had entirely overlooked the fact that Churchill and Roosevelt were working in close co-operation with Stalin and that their attitude towards the Russian dictator was at that period a friendly one.

On July 19, 1943, Hitler and Mussolini met at Feltre, in North Italy. The Duce intended to discuss the present state of affairs and insist that something be done to relieve it. But, as usual, the meeting developed into a monologue, with Hitler doing all the talking. Of late, relations between the two men had become strained. Military setbacks had not lessened Hitler's determination to carry on the war. In a sense they had strengthened it, for they seemed to bring forth all the stubborn and irrational qualities of Hitler's character. Mussolini reacted differently; his feelings were those of a man defeated both morally and physically. The meeting at Feltre ended abruptly when news reached the two dictators that Rome had been subjected to its first heavy air attack and had suffered much damage.

This attack hastened the crisis. The discontent in the Fascist party, already brewing for many months, had reached boiling point. A group headed by Grandi decided that the Fascist Grand Council should be convened and a vote of confidence called for. The Grand Council was one of the constitutional organs of the State with the right to designate the names of those from whom—in case of need—the Premier was to be chosen. If confidence was withdrawn, this fact alone would mean the downfall of Mussolini. Yet this legal device was little more than a sophism, the truth being that Fascism was dead. Created by a dictator, it certainly could not unravel its internal problems by assuming new and apparently democratic forms.

Although the Grand Council had not met for years, Mussolini did not sense any danger in its convocation. The Assembly was convened in Rome on July 24, 1943, and the outcome of its last session has a permanent place in Italian history. When a vote was taken, nineteen members voted against the dictator, seven in favour, and one abstained. The next day the Duce tendered his resignation and was put under arrest. Marshal Pietro Badoglio was called in to take his place and form a new government. The conqueror of Ethiopia was a staunch defender of the monarchy, and in the early part of the Greek campaign had resigned his post as Chief of the General Staff and retired from active service.

Events were now taking place so rapidly that the nation—unprepared for such an emergency—had completely lost its sense of equilibrium. With the fall of Fascism people thought the war was over and expressed their relief openly in the streets. Unfortunately so much joy was not justified. Technically speaking, what had happened was simply a change in the Government. Italy was still at war with the Allies and perhaps in a more vulnerable position than ever. The Germans held a key position, and any false step could cause serious consequences. All the new Government could do was to carry on where the others had left off and hope for the best. Its first step was to abolish several Fascist institutions. The Grand Council, the Chamber of Fasces and Corporations and the Fascist Militia were suppressed. This caused little concern, for even the party's leaders were indifferent to the whole affair. The most incredible aspect of the fall of Fascism was that, although the party and its leader had been all-powerful for over twenty years and had formed an aristocracy of their own, when the final crash came this class not only failed to defend itself, but surrendered without any show of resistance. Internal corruption was probably the reason for this. The restriction of freedom had not only reacted detrimentally on the public, but had also had unfavourable repercussions on those responsible for it. Servility and lack of initiative had seeped into the party and spread, reaching even the senior ranks.

Mussolini had no friends. He considered people either servants or enemies. When he was placed under arrest, not one member of his bodyguard made the slightest effort to help him. The Militia was not in a position to react, and Fascists were far too concerned with their own troubles. It is said that after his arrest he wrote a letter to the King avowing his fidelity to the Crown. If this is true, it only goes to prove what a complete farce Fascism really was.

After the new Government took over, many internal problems called for immediate attention, but the most important were those connected with the war. The Allies, in fact, were not interested in the fact that a few Fascists had been imprisoned or certain institutions dissolved. What they wanted was, plainly and simply, the end of hostilities and the nation's surrender. Yet, as time passed, more and more difficulties arose. At the time of the fall of Fascism the Führer had only seven divisions on Italian soil, but within a month their number had increased to seventeen. German units poured into the country from Austria, France, and the Balkans.

In August Badoglio was contacted by the newly formed Committee of National Liberation. This political body had been organised by the representatives of the six most important parties —Communists, Socialists, Actionists, Labourites, Christian Democrats, and Liberals—under the chairmanship of a former Premier of pre-Fascist Italy, Ivanoe Bonomi. The formation of political parties had been prohibited by the new Government, but public sentiment was by this time so determined that it was impossible to suppress them. Thus the Committee of National Liberation became the most important political body in the country. It urged the Government to end hostilities with the Allies and to avoid, if possible, a complete takeover by the Germans.

The first contact between the Italian and Allied authorities was made in Lisbon. In the meanwhile war operations were carried on as usual. On August 6, 1943, the new Foreign Minister, Raffaele Guariglia, and the Chief of General Staff, Ambrosio, met Ribbentrop and Von Keitel at the Brenner Pass. The two officials stressed that Italy would carry on the war on the German side, but emphasised that the people's morale was at a dangerously low level. With the fall of Messina on August 17 the Battle of Sicily ended and left the way open for an Allied landing on the peninsula.

Events which led up to the signing of what is generally known as 'the short armistice' are common knowledge. The Italian High Command had tried, through its special delegation, to arrive at some sort of agreement, but owing to the adamant Allied attitude not to accept anything but unconditional surrender, this move failed. The armistice was signed at Casibile, in Sicily, on September 3, 1943, with the Allies reserving the right to announce the truce at their own convenience. This they did unexpectedly five days later, when the landing of their troops at Salerno took place. It had been hoped, and more than half expected, that Rome would be the Allied first target, and that by means of airborne divisions the Eternal City would quickly be rid of German occupation. This, however, was not to be, and Rome, left to the entire mercy of a vindictive army, suffered many reprisals. The Germans were now recovering and were in a far stronger position than they had been a month and a half before. Their units, greatly increased in number, lost no time in occupying the country and in taking over its military establishments and strategic points. This move had evidently been carefully planned in advance.

The Badoglio Government lacked the necessary qualities of leadership. The King, who virtually controlled its moves, had not foreseen such a German reaction and was incapable of handling the situation. Commanding officers of the army were without orders, and when the armistice was announced many of them did not know whether they were supposed to resist the Germans, who succeeded in disarming several Italian units during the general confusion. Other units were simply disbanded. In spite of the chaos, heroic stands were made in different places, especially at Rome and on the Greek island of Corfu. A more critical situation could hardly be found. No government or recognised authority existed nor was there even the possibility of knowing what was happening.

The King and Marshal Badoglio fled by car and reached the Adriatic coast. Here they embarked for Apulia, a region already occupied by Allied forces, where they set up the Government again. This act has been both criticised and praised. Some Italians consider it was high treason for two commanders to abandon their army in the field, whilst others believe that, in the circumstances, the act was fully justified. It was, however, the main cause of the monarchy's downfall three years later. Many people had lost faith in a sovereign who, together with his Government, had failed to cope with the situation while the country could have defended itself until the arrival of the Allies. First-class units would have been able to resist had proper orders been issued.

The strategy of the Allies is not beyond reproach. Why did they not land near Rome instead of choosing a spot near Salerno, so far south and so unsuited to operations? The Germans, in fact, with only a few men, were able to hold off their advance long enough to set up strong resistance in the North. This was the origin of Italy's severe ordeal during the following eighteen months. Had there been swifter action, more knowledge of geographical difficulties, and better understanding of the people, much suffering would probably have been avoided to the Allies and the Italians alike.

On September 29, 1943, the so-called 'long armistice' was signed at Malta between Marshal Badoglio and Generals Eisenhower and Alexander. Its forty-four articles were specially onerous for Italy and gave the Allies complete control over the nation. A few days later Italy declared war on Germany.

These events had given Hitler the opportunity to occupy northern and central Italy, whilst the Allies only held the South. After their landings in Calabria, at the toe of the peninsula, and at Salerno, they met stiff resistance all along the front from the Garigliano to the Sangro.

Nazi reaction to Italian events was one of violence and cruelty. Certain atrocities during this period can only be compared with those practised by the Russians in occupied territories. The tragic fate of the Italian 'Acqui' Division in the Greek island of Corfu parallels that of the Polish officers brutally murdered at Katyn. In both cases thousands of men were unmercifully slaughtered. Many more were disarmed, sent to Germany, and put in concentration camps. These reprisals deepened the already bitter enmity existing between the two countries. Being incapable of practising the art of persuasion, the Nazis ignored the technique of getting co-operation from occupied countries. In this, as in other psychological aspects of the war, the Allies were far superior.

After his arrest Mussolini was sent to Sardinia and later transferred to Campo Imperatore, a winter resort not far from Rome. From here he was spectacularly rescued by S.S. officers and taken to Germany, where immediate plans were made for the setting up of a new Fascist Government. His first move was to organise an army that would work in co-operation with the Germans. Volunteers were called for, but as there was scant response and little enthusiasm, compulsory drafting had to be put into force. Results were highly disappointing, because Italians preferred joining the partisans and taking part in guerrilla warfare.

The period from September, 1943 to April, 1945, was one of the most disastrous in Italian history. Facing each other along a line which split the peninsula were two armies strongly equipped with modern weapons of warfare and determined to fight to the end. Incessant bombing of cities by both former and present allies brought utter destruction in its wake. More damage was caused after the armistice than during the three previous years of hostilities. Supplies became scarce and the rationing system collapsed.

Some uncharitable remarks have been made as to the Italian reaction to this period. It has been said that black-marketing and prostitution were the people's main sources of income. These criticisms are unfair. Despite the country's pitiful condition caused by war and foreign occupation, the people's morale was sufficiently high. Weaknesses and shortcomings naturally existed, but considering the ordeal Italians were going through they showed an extraordinary will to resist. Families, though starving, did not abandon their moral principles. The same may be said of their political and social ideals. Under Fascism people were allowed no part in the country's affairs and so, politically and socially starved for so many years, their one desire was to assert their rights and to see the totalitarian State replaced by an efficient democracy.

Hatred of Nazi oppression inspired many deeds of heroism. Five days before the fall of Naples the Neapolitans courageously rebelled against the Germans. Unfortunately the Allies did not always understand that the people genuinely regarded them as liberators, and not as conquerors. Ever since their landing on the peninsula, Italians were in fact most anxious not only to co-operate, but also to fight on their side, although they were under no obligation to do so. A group of volunteers, consisting chiefly of army cadets, saw action for the first time at Montelungo, on the Garigliano front, and suffered heavy losses. These forces were eventually strengthened and became a fully fledged division known as the Italian Liberation Corps, which fought brilliantly throughout the campaign. Had the Allies permitted it, more fighting units of the kind could have been formed. Italian man-power, however, was used on auxiliary tasks, also of great importance to the war effort.

Consistently with the Army's requirements, which had first priority, the Allies tried nevertheless to expedite the revival of Italy's democracy. The Allied Military Government, set up in liberated territories, had in fact the task of administering the people under its control with the aid and co-operation of those who had opposed the Fascist regime. The first steps in the direction of democracy after the fall of the regime were, therefore, assisted by Anglo-American personnel, the good intentions of whom must be recognised, even if results were at times unsatisfactory.

With the Anzio landing in January, 1944, hopes of a speeding up of the Allied advance were high. But they were quickly dispelled by stubborn German resistance. So the war dragged on and the country daily suffered more destruction.

Italians living in the South soon developed a keen interest in politics. They were, at times, inclined to forget that the war was by no means over. 'Should Italy remain a monarchy or become a republic?' was the topic of the day. Parties represented in the Committee of National Liberation were deeply divided on this issue. This emerged clearly at a Congress held at Bari in January, 1944, which was attended by representatives of several anti-Fascist movements. Differences of opinion were in fact so great that co-operation between parties became practically impossible and Marshal Badoglio was forced to form a 'Caretaker Government'.

A change came about when Palmiro Togliatti—for years one of the leaders of the Communist International and the recognised chief of the Italian Communist Party—arrived from Russia. His approach was a practical one. He claimed that controversies should be shelved and more emphasis placed on supporting the war effort. This ended the deadlock. A month after Togliatti's return King Victor Emmanuel III, although not yet abdicating, designated his son Humbert to become Lieutenant-General of the Realm. This move was an attempt to place constitutional powers in the hands of a man who during Fascism had never held other than minor posts. In April, 1944, a new Cabinet was formed, again under the premiership of Marshal Badoglio, in which all the major parties were represented.

That the champion of such a compromise should be Togliatti was, to say the least, surprising. The Communist Party had been noted for not wanting to co-operate with other parties. The reason for the change of tactics soon became evident and similar methods were later adopted by Communists all over Europe. Their idea was that taking part in a democratic government would assure them a position of vital importance in the event of an armed revolution. The idea was brilliant and well planned, but in Italy it did not have the success it achieved elsewhere.

The atmosphere in Rome had been a strained one during the nine months of occupation. Acts of violence perpetrated by the Nazis—the grimmest being the execution of 355 hostages in the Ardeatine Caves south of Rome—had kept the population in a constant state of fear. Yet the Committee of National Liberation, working secretly, had planned and prepared the policies of the future Government. Underground propaganda had been circulating rapidly and military measures had been taken to organise officers and men who refused to co-operate with the Germans.

After the Allies occupied Rome and military operations were moved north to the so-called Gothic line, the Badoglio Cabinet resigned. From this moment the Committee of National Liberation, in the absence of an elected parliament, became the body from which Government members were selected. The Chairman of the Committee, Bonomi, was chosen to be Italy's first democratic Premier. His ministers and under-secretaries were all men who had worked side by side with him in the underground movement.

The first Bonomi Government ended in December, 1944, when the leftist parties accused the Premier of leaning too much to the right. Finding a new formula was no easy matter, and once again the Communists solved the deadlock by agreeing to the formation of a government under Bonomi's premiership but without the participation of either Socialists or Actionists.

Military operations, not running according to schedule, had allowed the situation in the North to become more stabilised. The powers of the Fascist Government set up by the Germans were limited, but as time passed, and the Allied advance slowed down, they were strengthened and founded on a new constitutional structure. The Italian Social Republic was in fact proclaimed and great emphasis placed on its social programme. Mussolini tried hard to revive his past republican and socialist ideas. He seemed to believe it possible that twenty years of dictatorship could be easily forgotten. His new State called for the support not only of Fascists but also of all left-wing parties. Some of his actions proved his vindictive nature. He was certainly responsible for the trial at Verona of the men who had caused his downfall at the last meeting of the Grand Council. So a few months after the famous meeting which had provoked many important events, several among the men who had taken part in it had been eliminated.

Armed resistance to German occupation was a great burden to the Nazis and played an important part in helping the Allied war effort. This partisan movement proved that Italians are brilliant soldiers when they are convinced of the justice of their cause. Mussolini, either through short-sightedness or lack of understanding of the character of his countrymen, had overlooked this important factor. The Italians had no desire nor could they see any just reason to enter the conflict in 1940, but when the change came and they joined the Allies they gave birth to a strong partisan movement. This was formed of volunteers, disbanded soldiers, deserters from the Fascist army, and members of anti-Fascist parties. Young and old alike were inspired by a genuine wish to serve democracy. Credit must be given to these men for their bravery and resourcefulness. In a few months units and commands were set up and military discipline adopted. Most of them had a different political background. They were chiefly Communists, Socialists, and Christian Democrats, but a few had no political affiliation. The central command was headed by a Communist, Luigi Longo, an Actionist, Ferruccio Parri, who had suffered many years' imprisonment under Fascism, and a general of the regular army, Raffaele Cadorna. Political differences between the leaders and lack of legal status did not hinder the actual fighting.

The Germans regarded these units as formed by rebels who, if captured, were not entitled to any international protection. Tragic incidents occurred when partisans, seized together with Allied soldiers, were executed without trial, whilst their Allied comrades were made prisoners of war. In spite of these tragedies, they carried on courageously, their spirit unbroken. Even the amnesties offered them from time to time if they would surrender did not deter them.

Although at one time after 1943 there were over one million Italians in Germany—either workers or prisoners captured after the armistice—the Germans found it difficult to recruit sufficient men to form military units. Most of these Italians were living in pitiful conditions in concentration camps and were fed on the lowest possible rations. Their moral resistance was also low. Yet when recruiting started among their ranks and better living conditions were offered to volunteers, only a small percentage accepted.

The important part played by partisans in the war was recognised both by the Germans and the Allies. Their warfare consisted of guerrilla actions, sabotage, open attacks on outposts, communications, and supply depots. At times open and direct war was waged against entire enemy units. The German High Command entrusted the Italian Social Republic with the task of dealing with the situation, but when its forces proved inadequate, German soldiers were brought in. Partisan activity became even more effective when lighter units, known as GAP and SAP (Partisan Action Groups and Partisan Action Squads), were formed for the purpose of destroying the enemy's military equipment and cutting communications right along the front line.

The Allies decided to assist the partisans by supplying them with weapons and money. They also dropped officers behind the lines for liaison purposes. This last move was not always welcomed by partisan leaders, who feared it might interfere with their plans and restrict their freedom. On the other hand, their growing strength and independence of action soon began to cause considerable anxiety in Allied circles, with the result that in February, 1945, further assistance was cut off.

In April, when the Allies broke through the Gothic Line, the signal for a general uprising in the North was given. Partisan brigades attacked, and entire German units were either destroyed or taken prisoner. Nazi and Fascist resistance broke down. This uprising had disastrous effects on the enemy, hastened its surrender, and cleared the way for the Allies, who found the Germans retreating everywhere. Civil power passed to the hands of the Committee of National Liberation for northern Italy with headquarters in Milan, which now acted as a regular government. One of its primary tasks was to defend the factories to prevent the Germans from destroying or dismantling their equipment.

The insurrection in the North was the cause of several acts of violence. Some ruffians seized the opportunity to loot, murder, and carry out personal reprisals. These acts are to be deplored, even if they can be blamed on the existing state of affairs. So much blood had, in fact, been shed and so much cruelty suffered that uncontrolled violence was bound to break out in the end. Conflicts between Fascists and anti-Fascists had taken on all the aspects of a civil war.

About this time Mussolini came to Milan, but realising that the situation was hopeless and his cause absolutely lost, he tried to escape in the direction of the Swiss frontier. The past months of worry had reduced him to a shadow of his former self. He suddenly became a tired old man who spent his days writing an account of the latest events. He was finally caught by Communist partisans hiding in a truck of a retreating column and, together with other Fascist leaders also fleeing the country, was put to death after a mock trial. Their bodies were taken to Milan and strung up by the feet in a public square. Among those who died was Clara Petacci, his mistress. Although this young woman could have escaped, she preferred to stay by her aged lover's side to the bitter end. Several writers have already tried to build up the death of the two lovers into one of history's greatest romances. Mussolini was lucky to be spared the ordeal of a trial which would have inevitably ended in a capital sentence.

The conflict ended and Italy was finally reunited. A civil war had been fought on her territory leaving deep scars. Would it be possible for her to regain her status among other nations, or was she destined for many years to come to bear the burden of Fascist blunders? What treatment would she receive from the Allies? Her contributions to their war effort had often received their recognition, but did this mean that she could count on their co-operation and thus receive credit for it at the Peace Conference? These and many other grave problems faced the nation after the last cannon had been silenced.

Chapter 8

The Aftermath (1945–53)

ITALIANS were now confronted with the difficult task of rebuilding their country. Firstly, what exactly was their position? Were they to be considered as vanquished enemies or as co-belligerents? Was Italy to receive any benefit from the fighting of the partisans and the regular army, both of whom had been on the side of the Allies throughout the Italian campaign?

On March 24, 1944, Winston Churchill, in a speech in the House of Commons, declared: 'I can say here that we are doing our best to equip the Italian forces, who are anxious to fight with us and not under the German yoke. They have earned their place in the line on more than one occasion. Their fleet is carrying on a useful and important service, not only in the Mediterranean but also in the Atlantic, and the loyal Italian air force has also fought so well that I am making special efforts to refurnish it with new and modernised machines of British make.'

In spite of these reassurances, the first approaches were not encouraging and did not come up to the country's expectation. On the eastern and western frontiers, Yugoslavia and France were trying to annex parts of Italian territory, and only through Allied intervention were Tito's troops removed from Trieste, after forty-five days of occupation during which several serious incidents took place. France also attempted to gain control over the province of Cuneo, and only Churchill's strong-handed opposition succeeded in averting this move. Many problems called for immediate solution, the most urgent being that Italy was, juridically speaking, still at war with most of the world.

For years Fascism, war, and foreign occupation had forced all political movements underground. By 1945, however, they had become the foundation of the country's new life.

Among them Socialism enjoyed great prestige. After the 1924 election it had declined rapidly. Local and national leaders, victims of Fascist violence, were forced to flee the country. Many of them took refuge in France, where the two parties (Maximalists and Reformists) were formed once again, at least on paper. The going was difficult for them, and the main weakness lay in the fact that their leaders outnumbered their followers. In 1930 the Socialist Party was reunited, and in 1934 it signed an agreement of joint action with the Communists which is still in force. In 1942 Socialism reappeared in Italy in the organised form of secret groups and circles, set up especially in industrial areas.

During the Fascist period Communists continued their underground work. They set up an organisation which enabled them to carry on a minimum of propaganda. Some of their leaders were arrested and given heavy sentences by the Fascist Special Tribunal. Among them was Antonio Gramsci, chief of the party, who died in prison. His successor, Palmiro Togliatti, escaped to Russia, where he lived for many years. During the partisan war, Communist-led brigades were considered the best organised and the most active, although their record was often marred by violence. In April, 1944, Togliatti returned to Italy and offered to co-operate with the Government. Thenceforward for more than three years the Communists were members of all Cabinets.

The 'Partito d'Azione' (Action Party) is also to be numbered among leftist movements. Its programme lay between Socialism and Liberalism. It agreed with the first on the improvement of the worker's condition and with the second on the necessity of safeguarding free enterprise. Although morally and intellectually the party's influence was strong, it could count on few followers, and after a brief period of success its popularity faded.

At the centre of the political line-up, equally distant from right and left, were the Catholic-inspired Christian Democrats. After the breaking-up of the Partito Popolare in 1925 many of their leaders had remained united, preparing for the fall of Fascism. Together with a younger generation of people coming from Catholic organisations, they formed the central nucleus of Christian Democracy, which officially saw the light of day in 1942. The policy of this party lies in its name. Democracy was interpreted and applied in the political and social sense as aiming at the improvement of the working-man's conditions. The party advocated the splitting up of large estates and the formation of a class of small landowners. Strongest support, of course, came from the Church, which generally advised Catholics to back the party and vote for it. Christian Democrats were prominent in all Cabinets from 1944 onwards.

The Liberal Party was historically linked to the Risorgimento, when the entire ruling class had proclaimed itself Liberal, although no party, in the modern sense of the word, actually existed. Despite the Government's persecution, Italy's liberal intelligentsia continued to meet during the Fascist period. Its spiritual leader was Benedetto Croce, guide of Italian culture since the beginning of the century and the most outspoken opponent of Fascism. In 1943 the party was formed again, and although it polled few votes it was represented in many Cabinets.

Among the other parties of the time were: the Democrazia del Lavoro (Labour Party), which advocated social reforms on a moderate scale; the Republicans, whose chief ambition was to abolish the monarchy; and the Monarchists, who, on the contrary, were committed to its defence. A movement which advocated a government composed entirely of technicians was the Fronte dell' Uomo Qualunque (the Common Man's Front). Its programme was taken both from Socialism and Liberalism.

Bonomi's Cabinet resigned in April, 1945, after having accomplished the task of co-operating with the Allies. Things by now had changed considerably. The North, with its recent experiences of armed conflict, was strongly influencing domestic policies. New ideas coming from recently liberated areas were generally known as the 'Northern wind'. This wind blew from the left. The northern Committee of Liberation, led by the Marxist parties and organised on a provincial and communal basis, had in fact gained control of the country. The leftists intended using it for the purpose of upsetting the central power and of taking over, as the Soviets had done in Russia during the 1917 revolution. With the arms left over from the war and vast numbers of people experienced in their use, Italy had never been so dangerously near to revolution. Taking this into consideration, it was fortunate that the first Cabinet after the liberation of the North was led by Ferruccio Parri (b. 1890), a northerner who had led the partisans during the resistance. As a member of the Action Party, he was backed by Socialists and Communists, who held some of the key posts in his Cabinet. Even the other three parties (Christian Democrats, Liberals, and

Labourites) were represented. This Cabinet succeeded indirectly in avoiding the danger of a revolution. Extremists saw no reason to risk a revolt when they held very strong positions and believed future elections would be favourable to them. With the passing of time, however, events did not work out this way. The prestige which surrounded extremism in the early post-war days was on the decline. The population had suffered too many years of sorrow and strife, and now the excitement of combat had died down. People were tired and did not welcome the return of past miseries in the form of an economic and political revolution.

Leftist parties were backed by the Italian General Confederation of Labour. With the death of Fascism, free trade unionism had again come into being and all unions had merged into one large organisation, controlled by special committees. These included Communists, Socialists, and Christian Democrats, but were practically dominated by the first two. Communists took advantage of this situation by playing a double game. Although they were part of the Government, they would also attack it from outside. Whenever the Cabinet did not comply with their requests, the Confederation of Labour would call a strike, and street demonstrations would take place. Communists would often occupy public buildings, and the police (at that time badly organised and in no position to maintain order) had a hard time resisting the party's attacks.

The Parri Government remained in power until the end of 1945. In December the right wing of the Cabinet (Christian Democrats, Liberals, and Labourites) sensed that Parri, a weak man, was being completely dominated by the left. The basic principle of the Committee of National Liberation was that Cabinet decisions required the unanimous vote of the six parties which formed it. If one party voted against the Government, this was enough to cause a crisis. Such was the case when the Liberals, seconded by the Christian Democrats, opposed Parri's policies and forced him to resign. Alcide De Gasperi (1881–1954), leader of Christian Democracy and a member of past Cabinets, was asked to form a new one. A native of Alto Adige, he belonged to the Italian minority formerly under Austrian rule. Supported by the Catholics, he had been elected to the Vienna Parliament before World War I. After the annexation of Trento and Bolzano he had become an Italian citizen and had taken an active part in politics, serving in the Popular

Party. Elected to Parliament in 1921 and 1924, he fought strenuously against Fascism and was arrested and imprisoned. With help from the Holy See, he regained his freedom and for many dreary years worked as a librarian in the Vatican. His first Cabinet was again formed by the Committee of National Liberation, as this could hardly be done away with before general elections had been held.

Much depended on the result of these elections. Whether Italy was to be a monarchy or a republic was still the leading question of the day. Republicans wanted an elected assembly to decide the matter, but Monarchists insisted that the people should be given the right to choose. The latter opinion prevailed. On May 9, 1946, King Victor Emmanuel III abdicated in favour of his son Humbert II. This move was intended to strengthen the royalists' cause, but it had very little effect. Though Communists, Socialists, and Actionists were on the republican side, their influence was insufficient. Christian Democrats were the deciding factor, as they had a large following, especially among people who took no part in everyday demonstrations, but quietly turned out on election day. The party did not adopt an official line on the question until it met in Rome a few days before the elections. The majority of its members, influenced by the North, pledged themselves to back the republic. This move was probably the death-knell of the monarchy. Elections took place on June 2, 1946, and the Monarchists polled two million votes less than the republicans.

This margin showed the trend of public opinion. However, the Monarchists would not admit defeat, and King Umberto, although leaving the country, refused to recognise the results as authentic. This attitude created the impression that the figures had been faked and that something had gone wrong, although up to the present time nothing in the way of evidence has been produced to bear this out.

The people had also elected a Constituent Assembly, and results had proved that Communists and Socialists had more bluster than power. The two parties together won 219 seats. Socialists polled more votes than their Communist fellow-travellers because many middle-class people voted for what they believed to be a diluted form of Marxism and for a party which they thought was genuinely interested in bettering the working man's conditions and in the country's rehabilitation. They were disappointed when they found that the movement was torn by internal feuds and practically under the control of the Communists, who, with their disciplinary measures and power of organisation, were far superior in strength. Actionists were almost completely wiped out. Liberals and Labourites together gained 41 seats. The majority was held by the Christian Democrats, who won 207 seats.

The 1946 elections were an outstanding event. Had it not been for Premier De Gasperi's experience and knowledge of men, their consequences might have been different. The King's refusal to recognise the electoral results could have created an awkward situation with grave consequences, even possibly civil war. De Gasperi sized up events magnificently and ably led the country until the Constituent Assembly elected the provisional chief of the State. This was Enrico de Nicola (b. 1877), a man of considerable experience who had often held office before the advent of Fascism and had later retired to private life.

The new Cabinet, still headed by Alcide De Gasperi, was formed by Christian Democrats, Socialists, Communists, and Republicans—four parties which had supported the republican cause. This coalition, however, was undermined by many conflicting elements. Communists showed no desire to co-operate and insisted on their system of 'running with the hare and chasing with the hounds' by being in the Government and by attacking it from the outside. This absurd situation was the cause of De Gasperi's resignation in January, 1947. He was again asked to form a government, and, as before, the three major parties took part in it. It was felt, however, that this formula, generally known as the 'three-parties system' (*tripartito*), had outlived its usefulness. The belief that the final rupture was caused by De Gasperi's visit to the United States in 1947 was circulated by Communists, but this was untrue. The time was ripe for a major change and for the formation of a government without the two leftist parties.

The world in general was in a chaotic state. War-time alliances had broken down and the cold war had set in. Aid given by the United States to Europe was frowned upon by the Soviet Union, which regarded it as a form of expansion and not as a bona-fide attempt to solve the Continent's economic crisis. The danger of a further Soviet expansion in Europe was also feared. Not only had Communist dictatorship been established in eastern Europe, but it seemed as if the next move would be against countries like Italy, where the already existing partisans of

Communism might guarantee success. The fear of war against Russia, accompanied by the certainty that resistance to aggression would be of no avail, was in everybody's mind. This situation was bound to be reflected in Italy's domestic affairs.

On May 31, 1947, De Gasperi resigned, but was again entrusted with the formation of a Cabinet. This time Communists and Socialists were ejected and, apart from a few Liberals and outside experts, the Government was for the first time truly Christian Democratic. Chosen from among the Liberals, Luigi Einaudi (b. 1874) was appointed deputy Premier. Isolation of the Leftist parties began and was destined to increase during the following years. The Government gained more strength towards the end of 1947, due to the split in the Socialists. One group, headed by Pietro Nenni (b. 1891), favoured the existing alliance with Communism, whilst the other, led by Giuseppe Saragat (b. 1898), formed a new party and decided to cooperate with the Government. (This was the birth of Social Democracy.)

The main task of the Constituent Assembly was the drafting of a constitution. This took longer than originally planned, for the life of that body, scheduled to last eight months, was prolonged to twelve, and later to nineteen. An agreement concerning the future structure of the State was reached between parties. Committees were set up and each was given a special problem to solve and report on.

All constitutions express the doctrines prevailing at the time they were drafted. The Italian one reflects the widespread anti-Fascist feelings of the people and their reaction to twenty years of dictatorship. Of special interest are Articles 1 to 54, containing the principles on which the republic is founded, together with the rights and duties of citizens. Article 1 reads as follows: 'Italy is a democratic republic based on work. The people are invested with sovereign powers and exercise them in the manner and within the limits of the constitution.' The Social nature of the Charter constantly reappears as the document's leading theme. Any form of discrimination is condemned by Article 3, according to which:

> 'All citizens are invested with equal social dignity and are equal before the law, without distinction of sex, race, language, religion, political opinions, and personal and social conditions. It is the task of the Republic to remove

all obstacles of an economic and social nature limiting the freedom and equality of citizens, preventing the full development of human personality, and the participation of all workers in the political, economic, and social organisation of the country.'

Legislative power is based on a bicameral system. The two assemblies are the Chamber of Deputies and the Senate of the Republic, both elected by the people, and the members of which, meeting in a common session, elect the President of the Republic. The Premier and the Cabinet Ministers form together the Council of Ministers. They have executive powers, and only on given occasions and within strict limits may they issue orders-in-council (generally called decree laws).

The Council of Ministers, according to the English pattern, is responsible to Parliament. Complete autonomy is given to the judicial power. Autonomy is also guaranteed to communes, provinces, and regions. This was an important innovation inspired by the Christian Democrats, who have always believed in local self-government, against the opposite opinion shared by Risorgimento statesmen and by Fascism, according to which Italy can be governed only by a highly centralised system. Although embodied in the constitution, regional governments have not yet been set up, with the exception of those in Sicily, Sardinia, the Valle d'Aosta, and Trentino–Alto Adige. In these territories local conditions made the granting of wider autonomy more urgent than in others. Despite some inevitable defects, the 1948 constitution remains a document of well-considered legislation, in which several doctrines and political tendencies are blended so as to provide the country with sound government and administration.

The Constituent Assembly was also confronted with the ratification of the Peace Treaty. This question is examined more completely in the chapter dealing with post-war foreign policy. A few observations may, however, be made now. The drafting of this document was jointly carried out by the United States of America, Great Britain, France, and the Soviet Union. Italy took no part in the dealings, although her point of view was heard.

The treaty dealt with the problem of the eastern frontiers and of Venezia Giulia, where Italians and Slavs live side by side. It had been proclaimed during the war that the ethnical principle would be followed and that any new settlement would be based on the respect of minority rights. Unfortunately this commitment was not carried out. Yugoslavia's claims were of a most imperialistic nature and she demanded the annexation of several territories. Her demands were strongly backed by Russia. As a result of this powerful influence famous Italian cities like Fiume, Pola, and Zara were awarded to Yugoslavia.

The treaty also sanctioned Italy's surrender of other territories, such as the districts of Briga and Tenda on the French frontier, the islands of Rhodes and the Dodecanese to Greece, and her colonies, which were handed over to the Allies, who were later to arrange for their disposal.

Italian diplomacy could do little to change decisions already made by the Big Four, yet a real success was won by Premier De Gasperi on the Alto Adige question. The Italian hold on this region was in great danger because the Government of Vienna had been allowed to appear before the Paris Conference, which in general favoured its annexation to Austria. De Gasperi, however, seized the opportunity offered by the presence in Paris of the Austrian Foreign Minister to discuss the matter with him. A satisfactory understanding was reached confirming the existing frontier.

One of the most deeply felt losses was that of Pola. Ever since Dante's time this city had been considered an outpost of Italian civilisation on the nation's historic and geographic frontier. The Italian delegation at the Paris Conference pleaded that the city should remain under Italian rule or, failing this, that it should be included in the so-called Free Territory of Trieste. But all this was of no avail and the city was given to Yugoslavia. At the beginning of 1947, when Pola's fate was made known, the exodus of the population began. It was the most striking example of attachment to a motherland ever shown on the part of a population which had lived in the area for centuries.

The ratification of the treaty came up at the meeting of the Constituent Assembly in the summer of 1947 and was the object of much controversy. During the first months of the year Italy's home policies had changed. The 'three-party' system had split, so that Communists and Socialists, now forming the opposition, were always on the alert and ready to grasp any opportunity to attack the Government. De Gasperi and his party fortunately understood the treaty's deep implications on the country's future. A policy of non-co-operation would certainly not have changed the fixed provisions, while it would be interpreted as an attempt to boycott peace. Grave problems called for immediate action. Military occupation had to come to an end, for the nation's moral and material reconstruction was not possible unless she was given complete freedom of action. Christian Democrats and Social Democrats took on themselves the responsibility of pushing the treaty through the Assembly for approval. Right and left were both opposed to ratification, although their reasons differed; the former believed the treaty went too much against Italy's interest to be acceptable, while the latter opposed it because it was backed by a government in which they were not represented. The debate before the Constituent Assembly lasted several days. Fortunately the point of view of the centre prevailed, and the treaty was ratified.

Immediately after the war domestic disorder had reached the highest level, and if the situation had been allowed to develop further it would have caused the complete destruction of State authority. Communists were largely responsible for this state of affairs. During the partisan war their actions had been justified by alleged patriotism, but now the war was over it was essential that order be restored. This the Communists, who were successfully keeping the country in a state of turmoil, did not intend to allow, as a constant feeling of unrest among the people furthered their chances of gaining control. Whenever they wanted to force an issue, either national or international, they would organise a revolt. They also had at their disposal large quantities of weapons and ammunition left over from the partisan war. Public order was also difficult to enforce because the Government could not always rely on its police. In fact after the insurrection in the North, many persons had been taken into the Government's service solely on account of their political creed and war record. Communist leaders were frequently put in charge of large provinces or appointed as chiefs of police. They were therefore entrusted with the enforcement of the law they were anxious to infringe. An especially difficult area was Emilia, where extremism, traditionally strong, could count on many followers. In the beginning the Allied Military Government kept them in check, but when control was handed over to the Italian authorities, the situation became serious and it seemed as if Communism were gaining the upper hand. Acts of cruelty and violence took place. One district became known as 'the triangle of death', owing to the number of murders carried out by Communists.

Although cases of political delinquency were more frequent in the North, the South also had grave problems to solve, the most serious being the revival of banditism in Sicily. Here, during the years following the armistice, a movement had developed favouring political separation of the island from the rest of the nation and the setting up of an independent Sicilian State. Nothing could be more unreasonable, for in an epoch of fading nationalism, regionalism is absurd and obsolete. Yet this movement provided a political justification to people who thought they could challenge the State. Police authorities had great difficulty in dealing with the problem, owing to lack of co-operation from local inhabitants.

This and other matters were keeping Italy in a constant state of restlessness and made reconstruction difficult. Mario Scelba had the responsibility of re-organising the police forces and restoring order. Appointed as Minister of the Interior in January, 1947, he retained that post until 1953. Under his leadership the Ministry of the Interior regained its lost power and prestige. New funds were allotted to it for the organisation of mobile armed units. Reinforcement of the police was most opportune, as the Communists, having been ousted from the Government, were now in the position to carry out with greater efficiency their revolutionary programmes. Had they not met with powerful resistance, they might have seriously impaired the country's reconstruction. A major crisis broke out in November, 1947, when the prefect of Milan—a partisan who had obtained his position because of his war record—was removed from office. This act was considered by Communists as a challenge to their party, and a general strike was proclaimed. The move was made in the belief that such a measure would force the Government to reconsider its decision and withdraw it. This fortunately was not the case. The authorities remained adamant, and the newly formed police force coped brilliantly with the situation, restoring order almost immediately.

De Gasperi's Cabinet, formed in May, 1947, was voted in by only a narrow majority. In December its position was strengthened by the inclusion of Social Democrats and Republicans. This enabled it to tackle the domestic situation with greater assurance and determination. Important measures were taken to improve the country's economic position and to check inflation.

The Constituent Assembly having been dissolved on January 31, 1948, the problem of setting up the bodies created for the administration of the new Republic became most urgent. Parliament had to be elected so that legislation could be carried out in a normal fashion. Up to that time the Government had covered both executive and legislative functions. A general election was held on April 18, 1948, based, like the previous one of 1946, on proportional representation. The Christian Democrats' victory was overwhelming. They polled more than 12 million votes and gained an absolute majority in the Chamber of Deputies and a relative one in the Senate. These results confirmed the Catholic Party's position as leader of Italy's political life. There were several reasons for the party's success. Many voters were tired of violence and could not believe any good could possibly come from the Communists' programme. The constant threat of an impending revolution alarmed them. The Communists' policy had in fact been a strange mixture of Latin temperament and oriental shrewdness. They tried to give the impression that they were supporting democracy when they were actually preparing to launch an attack on the State. In the 1948 elections Communists had pushed their Machiavellianism to an extreme by presenting common lists of candidates with the Socialists. This electoral alliance was disguised under the inconspicuous name of 'Popular Democratic Front'. Giuseppe Garibaldi's image was chosen as a symbol to replace the traditional hammer-and-sickle emblem. This act of deceit did not pass unnoticed by the public, and was probably one of the reasons why Christian Democracy gained an overwhelming majority. The Communists' method of campaigning was also open to suspicion. The money spent and the quantity of propaganda material used were enormous; the source from which they came was never made clear. It was a mixture of bullying, cajoling, and vindictiveness. The impression it endeavoured to give the people was that Italy was already in the hands of Communism and that it was only a question of weeks before they would actually take over control from the Government. It is a known psychological fact that the ignorant are easily influenced by such blatant propaganda and are inclined to follow the party which they think is a sure winner, getting, as the Americans say, 'on the band wagon'. In this case, however, that theory did not work out as expected, for the Popular Front polled only 30·7 per cent of the total vote, whereas the Christian Democrats alone polled over 48·7 per cent.

For the first time since the end of the conflict, Fascism reappeared, under the name of Movimento Sociale Italiano (Italian Social Movement). Although its programme had been carefully worded so as to avoid giving the impression that it favoured a rebirth of a totalitarian State, its members and supporters were either former Fascist leaders or people who had fought on the German side after the armistice of September, 1943. Their propaganda had been loud and active, and it was feared they might poll a large number of votes. This, fortunately, did not happen, as they received only 2 per cent of the total vote.

The Christian Democrats' victory was supported by two international events: the Marshall Plan, by which the United States committed themselves to provide material aid to Europe, and the Three-Power Declaration of April, 1948, when the United States, Great Britain, and France promised they would help to restore Italian sovereignty in the Free Territory of Trieste. The cold war was already in progress and was affecting Italy's affairs, and in the electoral campaign much stress was placed on Italy's international position and future. Communists and their allies were proclaiming that by accepting American help Italy had become a satellite of Washington and that material aid coming from abroad was only making the country's reconstruction more difficult. The other parties, on the other hand, reminded their voters how foreign aid had helped Italy to recover and that, although the Peace Treaty had been a harsh one, it was unfair to say, as the Communists did, that only the Western Powers were responsible for it. On the controversial issue of Trieste, only the West had taken attitudes favourable to Italy, while Russia had constantly backed Yugoslavia. They also pointed out that Palmiro Togliatti and other extremists might say what they liked about United States aid, yet they were eating bread made from American wheat and using American petrol to run their cars. After the election, Communists tried invalidating its disappointing results by claiming that many electors had voted under the clergy's moral pressure. An absurd accusation, if one considers what methods of propaganda they had been using and that the clergy had simply used their right to enlighten the people.

The Parliament's first task was to elect the President of the Republic. The choice fell on Luigi Einaudi, at that time Deputy Premier. A statesman of great experience and a professor of economics, Einaudi gave the high post he held the prestige and dignity it deserved. At a moment when the country was not yet on its feet, it was appropriate and desirable that such a man should be the head of the State. He was an example of moderation and his devotion to duty was an inspiration to all.

The Government's stability was, of course, strengthened by the success of Christian Democracy, but De Gasperi was not a man who allowed success to blind him. He showed great qualities of leadership by inviting the three small democratic parties (Social Democrats, Liberals, and Republicans) to join the Cabinet. In Italy, where formulas and questions of principle are more important than elsewhere, the new Cabinet was called a centre–left formation. This indicated that while formed of moderate persons, its programmes were also those of the working-man and it favoured reforms.

Communist animosity became greater than ever. In 1947, when the party was excluded from the Government, it had always believed this to be a temporary eclipse and that after the general election it would return to power. As this now appeared improbable, it decided to oppose the Government on every possible occasion. Opportunities to do so were certainly not lacking. Even measures taken in favour of the working class met with Communist resistance. When the Minister of Labour, Amintore Fanfani, suggested a plan that was bound to ease the grave housing shortage, instead of getting Communist support he met with violent opposition. The Communist Press called his plan 'a tragic joke at the workers' expense'. On July 13, 1948, Togliatti was wounded by a nationalist student who believed his action would express the anti-Communist sentiments of the nation's majority. Communists proclaimed that De Gasperi's Cabinet was responsible for what had happened and mobilised their military organisation. The General Confederation of Labour called a general strike, but the Government reacted in a powerful and forceful manner. Riots were immediately quelled and order restored. It soon became apparent that Communism had lost much of its former strength. The situation had indeed changed since the days of the uprising in 1945. After 1948 Communist agitation and intimidation became much rarer. This was not due to any change of tactics, but rather to the energetic manner in which the Government was enforcing law and order.

Following the outbreaks of violence caused by the attempt on Togliatti's life, a certain reaction arose among the workers. Since the fall of Fascism trade unions had been united within the General Confederation of Labour, led by Communists, Socialists, and Christian Democrats, but for some time public opinion had been pressing Catholic unions to abandon the Confederation and to set up a new and more impartial organisation. After the 1948 events, when the Confederation proved its partiality by siding with the Communists, collaboration between the three groups became impossible, and eventually ended in October, 1948. A new organisation was then set up by Catholic and other free unions.

With the country in a more stable condition, De Gasperi's Government was able to devote its attention to the solution of some of the nation's outstanding problems. The most urgent was fiscal reform. For centuries tax evasion had been a common practice. Quite probably the origin of these fiscal ethics can be traced back to the times when citizens, deprived of all liberties by foreign governments, considered the State their greatest enemy and refused to co-operate with it. This mental attitude had unfortunately remained even after unity. It was no secret that taxpayers declared only a small portion of their income. The tax collector always doubled the declared sum and after much bargaining an agreement was concluded. Not all tax evaders could be traced, however, and the Government lost a part of its revenue. The reform carried out bears the name of the Minister of Finance, Ezio Vanoni. Parliament obliged by law every taxpayer to make a yearly declaration of his income. This was a practice not unfamiliar in other countries but entirely new to Italy. In the spring of 1951 the first income-tax declaration was performed.

The Government took a very firm attitude towards limiting expenditure and balancing the budget. The credit for reducing the deficit belonged to the Minister of the Treasury, Giuseppe Pella, who succeeded in strengthening the currency. The country's economy gained in stability, for capital previously invested abroad returned to the home country.

After the tragic years, when the fight for survival had overshadowed everything and excluded any idea of economic planning, the outlook was brightening and Italians were beginning to place more trust in their future. Trust is the first sign of recovery, especially in a country where a policy is needed to reduce expenditure without affecting investments capable of producing employment. Italy had also to limit her trade deficit, a difficult matter in a land of few natural resources troubled with over-population and unemployment. War damages were faced bravely. Works of all kinds were accomplished in an extraordinarily short space of time through public aid and private enterprise. One of the most striking features of this programme was the reconstruction of the railway system. Not only was pre-war efficiency restored, but the State Railways improved their service to meet the increasing demand of passenger and freight traffic.

It was also felt that if basic problems were to be solved, if the country was to be brought up-to-date, the Government must take the initiative and prepare better conditions under which private enterprise would develop trade and industry. This programme was of special importance to the South, where a provincial mentality and an economy based exclusively on agriculture were prevailing. A special agency was therefore formed called the Cassa del Mezzogiorno (Fund for the South), the purpose of which was to put into effect a policy of heavy public investments. Since 1950 the South has slowly developed. Inhabitants are changing, both in their way of thinking and living, and this is a major victory and an example of national solidarity. The sums of money thus invested come, in fact, from the North, by far the country's greatest industrial region, which bears the heaviest burden of taxation.

Among obstacles to be eliminated for a better understanding between Italians was the antagonism between Republicans and Monarchists. The monarchy's defeat in 1946 had left much resentment and suspicion on the losing side. The King's supporters had been made to understand by propaganda that the elections had not been fair and that voting had been 'arranged'. Even here the Government's action was well timed and inspired by devotion to duty. The first two presidents of the newly created republic, De Nicola (elected in 1946) and Einaudi (elected in 1948), had both been Monarchists. Their election had partially bridged the gap between the King's supporters and his opponents and had eliminated bitter feelings.

Much consideration was given to youth education. This task

had been a difficult one, as Fascists had paid great attention to 'young Italy'. If the new generation was to be taught to love Democracy and its ways, Fascist indoctrination had to be eradicated. Even in this the Government was successful. Through appropriate schooling the love of freedom is gradually penetrating the minds of the young.

An important scheme was the distribution of land to landless peasants. In a country where so many events have taken place over the centuries and where foreign occupation has been accompanied by political and economic disorder, it is understandable that several large holdings should have fallen into the hands of a small group of people. On the other hand, where rural workers are numerous and poverty-stricken, extremism may easily spread, while if they can become small proprietors, more conservative ideas are bound to develop. Hence the necessity of breaking up and distributing large estates, so as to give peasants a chance to earn a decent living. Up to the present day land-reform has been carried out only in a few regions where its necessity was more urgently felt. The distribution of land has been accompanied by its improvement. This scheme has contributed greatly to the social and moral uplift of the Italians. Confiscation of surplus land not only implies that farms are transferred to workers who may be more capable of making them produce; it also awakens landowners to added competition, compelling them to modernise their property. This means more employment for the working-class and a larger circulation of capital. Success of the reform is proved by the animosity Communists have shown towards it. After years of preaching that their aim was to turn poor peasants into proprietors at the expense of large landowners, they should have been pleased with a reform that was, at least partially, putting their doctrine into effect. On the contrary, they fought against it energetically, thus proving that their aim is not to reform society, but to create discontent. A large class of small landowners would, in fact, undermine their strength, for contented farmers are their greatest enemies. Their approach to the problem was outlined with exceptional clarity by Ruggero Grieco, the party's spokesman on agricultural problems. He said: 'The Communist Party is against the reform because it creates a class of strong farmers who own the land which they cultivate. Communism advocates instead that land ownership should belong entirely to the State.'

Italy's international position improved between 1948 and 1953. At the beginning of the legislature the occupying armies had just withdrawn their troops but the leading class was still under the influence of American and British tutorship. After five years what is known as the 'armistice complex' had completely disappeared and the Government was following a line of firm and dignified defence of national interests.

Confronted with the conflict between East and West, the nation shouldered all her responsibilities and sided with Democracy. When the Marshall Plan and NATO came up for approval, Communists fought them both. Opposition was especially violent in Parliament, where they tried to delay ratification through useless filibustering tactics which only widened the gap between them and the Government. Results of De Gasperi's policy became evident when the revision of the Peace Treaty began and some of the clauses limiting Italy's rearmament were modified.

During the first republican legislature political parties underwent certain changes. Communists violently opposed Christian Democrats and fought hard against all Government schemes, especially those of a social nature. Socialists, led by Pietro Nenni, followed the policy of previous years by remaining attached to their fellow travellers. The results of the 1948 elections came to them as a shock, for the number of their members of Parliament was heavily reduced. This caused the loss of more of the autonomy they had already forfeited. A queer condition was that of Social Democrats, who never found their stability. They were split up internally between those who wanted to co-operate with the Government and those who opposed it. This perennial discussion weakened the party considerably. De Gasperi still carried on his policy of calling on them to co-operate, but his offers were not always accepted. Thus a party which could certainly have contributed greatly to Italy's recovery slowly faded and is to-day reduced to only a few members of parliament. The small Republican Party led by Randolfo Pacciardi co-operated with the Christian Democrats for five years. Pacciardi, as Minister of Defence, started the rebirth of the armed forces. Liberals, split by inter-party feuds, insisted on maintaining for a time a position of constitutional opposition. An interesting development was that of the rightists. After the 1948 election, in fact, when the Communist danger was no longer considered imminent, the rightist movements—Monarchists and Neo-Fascists—started a violent campaign against the Government.

Local elections were fought in 1951 with incredible intensity, and gave the impression that the whole country's future depended on their outcome. Their results were taken as an indication of public opinion and, in general, did not show any major gain for the Communists. Voting took place according to a new revised law which granted an absolute majority of seats in city councils to the party or group of parties which obtained the largest number of votes. During the parliamentary debates of 1950, when this law was discussed and approved, Communists and Socialists did not object too strongly, hoping it might turn out to their advantage. But when they found out that the majority of the public had once more voted against them, their approach changed. They decided in fact to fight against that electoral system, when the Government suggested that it should be adopted also for national elections. The new project, introduced in Parliament in 1952, allowed political movements to ally themselves. If a group of parties obtained at least 50 per cent of the total vote, it would get 65 per cent of the seats in the Chamber of Deputies, thus disposing of a clear majority. Communists and Socialists and the two rightist parties (Monarchists and Neo-fascists) were so sure that the four democratic parties of the centre would obtain the minimum of votes necessary that they launched a heavy attack on the law. Hence those filibustering tactics which at times reached the extreme in violence. Only a government with strong determination was able to face such a storm and combat a carefully planned battle which had become a matter of principle and prestige. The Cabinet asked that the approval of the new law should be linked to a motion of confidence. Confronted with the danger of a crisis, Parliament rallied round the Government and the law was approved. The two Houses were dissolved and a general election called for June 7, 1953.

This parliamentary debate was the cause of much discussion and the country found itself divided between supporters and opponents of the law. The electoral campaign had indeed started long before it was officially opened. Public opinion was distracted from more essential issues and its attention chiefly directed to electoral technicalities.

When the campaign started amidst much noisy publicity, the main topic, which the opposition pushed as a moral question of great importance, was the electoral law. Christian Democrats were the victims of this propaganda, in which both left and right were united, thus causing them to lose many votes. Their record was an excellent one. During the previous five years they had proved how effective and far-reaching their work had been. Through perseverance they had rebuilt the country, both morally and materially, giving the people hope in the future and more faith in themselves. No nation—taking into consideration financial conditions and the semi-revolutionary state in which Italy had found herself immediately after the war—had ever recuperated so swiftly. Not only had Christian Democrats solved many recent problems, but centuries-old ones showed marked signs of improvement. A drive had started favouring domestic reforms intended to modernise the backward way of thinking still existing in certain regions. Above all, the country was now settling down to work, calm for the first time, after many years of agitation and turmoil. The task of creating a democratic trend of thought among people who had been governed by a dictator and over-run by foreign armies had not been easy. De Gasperi and his party had not only found material problems to be faced and solved; they had also had to convince citizens that Democracy, despite its simplicity, is the most effective way to rule a country.

Taking all this into consideration, it was most disappointing that in the general election of 1953 the alliance of the four democratic parties (Christian Democrats, Social Democrats, Liberals, and Republicans) should have been 50,000 votes short of the number required by the electoral law to get 65 per cent of the seats. Proportional representation was therefore applied. Christian Democrats got 262 seats in the Chamber of Deputies out of a total of 590. Although this made them the strongest group in Parliament, they were not strong enough to govern without support of the three small democratic parties. A new coalition was therefore necessary, and its formation in the beginning met with some difficulty. After an unsuccessful attempt by De Gasperi and a short period in which Giuseppe Pella, former Minister of the Treasury, was Italy's Premier, the four-party coalition was again formed in March, 1954, under Mario Scelba's leadership.

Italy's political situation after the 1953 elections is far from critical. It implies that the Government—formerly based on a party which held the absolute majority—has been replaced by another founded on a coalition and, therefore, on a certain amount of compromise. Christian Democracy, however, remains the leading factor. Besides, Italy's physical, moral, and economic strength is indeed greater than many observers would lead us to believe.

Chapter 9

Italy's Foreign Policy (1943–53)

A COUNTRY's foreign policy depends to a great extent on its internal strength and prestige. It was therefore understandable that after World War II Italy's position in the concert of nations was so weakened that her opinion no longer carried any weight in international affairs.

Among the clauses of the armistice signed by Marshal Badoglio on September 29, 1943, Article 25 showed that the Allies intended to prevent Italy from participating in foreign affairs, at least for the time being. Paragraph A of the article read as follows:

> 'Relations with countries at war with any of the United Nations, or occupied by any such country, will be broken off. Italian diplomatic, consular agents, and other officials and members of the Italian Land, Sea, and Air Forces accredited to or serving missions with any such country or in any other territory specified by the United Nations, will be recalled. Diplomatic and consular officials of such countries will be dealt with as the United Nations will prescribe.'

Less autonomy could hardly be left. Italy's only right was to comply with orders issued by the United Nations. Thus the terms of the declaration drawn up at the Casablanca Conference which called for unconditional surrender were applied in full to a State that was undergoing a most delicate phase of its history. The following month of October, in accordance with the provisions of the said article, Marshal Badoglio's Government declared war on Germany. This act created a most unusual situation. Italy was juridically at war with both sides, as the armistice had only suspended the use of arms, but had not re-established peace between her and the Allies.

The armistice terms were not limited to the control of relations with belligerent countries, they were extended to neutrals (Article 25, paragraph B), and provided as follows:

'The United Nations reserve the right to require the withdrawal of neutral diplomatic and consular officers from occupied Italian territory and to prescribe and lay down regulations governing the procedure for the methods of communication between the Italian Government and its representatives in neutral countries, and regarding communications emanating from or destined for the representatives of neutral countries in Italian territories.'

Italy's Government carried out its duties under the Allied Control Commission and the Advisory Council for Italy. The former—an agency of the Allied High Command—dealt with civil affairs and was divided into sub-commissions, each controlling a special section of the country's administration. The Advisory Council was a purely consultative body and dealt mainly with matters of policy, including foreign relations. While the Control Commission was chiefly an Anglo-American affair, the Advisory Council was formed of representatives of six States (the United States, Great Britain, France, the Soviet Union, Greece, and Yugoslavia), all of which were, at least theoretically, on the same footing. Under such conditions Italy's immediate task was that of re-obtaining her liberty and defending her possessions and prestige. Her only course of action was to stand firmly by the Allies and to contribute to their victory. These she did with loyalty and determination, and both were inspired by genuine enmity towards the Nazis. Her official position was not that of an ally, but of a co-belligerent. This term had been chosen to indicate that, although fighting on the Allied side, she was doing so under a very special status which did not imply any decision as to her future settlement.

The figures of casualties suffered during the period may provide a clear indication of how important the country's effort had been. After the armistice, 17,354 officers and men of the regular army were killed on the home front and in Corsica, while 55,976 were killed on other fronts. The partisans had 27,000 men killed and 17,000 wounded in action; 2,000 men were killed and 986 wounded by the Germans in acts of reprisal. The partisans, especially, deserved the highest recognition. Their ranks had been entirely formed of volunteers who did not receive any protection from international law. If captured, as we have already said, they could be put to death without a trial.

Partisan activity was one of the most important features of

World War II. It also took place in Yugoslavia, France, Poland, and nearly all occupied territories. Yet, while it was given due recognition everywhere, only in Italy's case was it of little help to the nation's recovery. Italy was, in fact, considered a defeated country, while Yugoslavia, which collapsed in little more than a week, collaborated through various governments with the Germans, and had two partisan movements, which spent more time fighting each other than the enemy, is generally considered a winning Power, owing to the notoriety with which Marshal Tito succeeded in surrounding his name and activities.

Relations had to be restored with the principal Allied countries. The first exchange of ambassadors took place with the Soviet Union before the liberation of Rome. This step was probably taken by the Soviets with the idea of impressing public opinion and of aiding Communism in its propaganda. On September 26, 1944, Roosevelt and Churchill issued a statement acknowledging that the Italians after their liberation had shown their will to be free and to fight on the side of democracy. As a consequence of this declaration some controls were relaxed and an exchange of diplomats decided on. Soon Great Britain and the United States accredited their representatives in Rome, while Italian ambassadors were appointed in London and Washington.

During the first months of 1945 relations were resumed with other former enemy countries, including France, Canada, South Africa, Czechoslovakia, Egypt, India, Iran, China, and the Philippines. These diplomatic advances were considerable, although their importance was somewhat lessened by the fact that contacts between the Foreign Ministry and its missions abroad were under supervision of the Allied Control Commission. During the Yalta Conference, President Bonomi sent the 'Big Three' a message requesting that all controls should be removed, and Italy allowed to deal directly with foreign States. This request was finally granted and Italy allowed to resume normal relations with other Governments. Alcide De Gasperi became Foreign Minister at the end of 1944. Until then the Ministry had simply been a liaison office with the occupation authorities, but after the new head took office it progressively became a policy-making body.

During 1945, hopes for a permanent world peace were high. Delegates from the so-called free countries met in San Francisco, where the United Nations Charter was signed. This organisation appealed greatly to the Italian mind and the Government officially asked to be admitted. The request was rejected. Later, after the signing of the peace treaty, it was repeated and constantly refused, because of Soviet opposition.[1]

Instead of an invitation to the San Francisco talks, Italy soon received news that at the Potsdam Conference the Big Three had recognised that a peace treaty was most urgent, and that a meeting would be held in London between the five principal Allied Powers (the United States, Great Britain, the Soviet Union, China, and France) with the aim of discussing the terms of Italy's treaty and of making recommendations. In the meanwhile the country's morale was seriously deteriorating. When Italy had begun fighting on the Allied side she had sincerely believed that a favourable peace would be the outcome of such a conference, at which only minor territorial changes would be discussed. She could not have been farther from the truth. During the last months of war it had become increasingly evident that the Allies intended to re-examine her entire position and that no political, military, or economic problem would be omitted. As time passed, the Allied Press became more hostile. The change was probably due to the fact that Italy's assistance, requested and obtained in 1943, when Germany's defeat was not yet sure, had become less necessary in 1945, when Hitler's downfall was a certainty. A sense of frustration spread over the country because problems which had seemed definitely solved were reopened by the Allies. One of them was the question of Alto Adige. Newspapers and politicians in Great Britain, France, and elsewhere were now pressing for the annexation of this region to Austria. A question which even Hitler had considered closed was therefore revived, bringing ill feeling between Italy and Austria.

On the eve of the London meeting, *Il Popolo*, official organ of the Christian Democrats, printed an article entitled 'Opinions that need correcting'. It listed some wrong impressions which were then spreading among the Allies. Included in these were that Italy had not respected the rights of minorities; that Austria had to be strengthened through the annexation of Alto Adige; that France was entitled to territorial concessions; that colonies were not necessary to Italy, and that her navy was to be included among the spoils of war. The Foreign Minister, De Gasperi,

[1] Italy was eventually admitted to the United Nations on December 14, 1955.

had probably influenced the article. During that period he in fact wrote to the United States Secretary of State, Byrnes, pointing out the problems on which Italy was willing to make concessions. His letter stressed that a centuries-old Christian heritage and an ancient tradition made of the Italian people a sure instrument of civilisation in the world. Italy was ready to consider the following changes: (1) The frontier with Yugoslavia could be fixed on the so-called Wilson Line. (2) The cities of Zara and Fiume were to be granted special statutes. (3) Trieste was to become an international port and Pola was to be demilitarised, on condition that the Yugoslav port of Cattaro should undergo the same limitations. (4) The Austrian frontier was to remain untouched. (5) As Italian rights in Tunisia had been given up to France in the agreement signed on February 28, 1945, it was believed that no other major question would divide the two countries. However, if the French were to ask for any corrections of the western frontier, the matter would be given attention. (6) Rhodes and the islands of the Dodecanese would be ceded to Greece. (7) The colonies of Libya, Eritrea, and Somaliland should be retained by Italy. De Gasperi's letter could hardly have been more moderate.

Would Italy's position have been stronger had she chosen a less compromising approach? Although it has now become a habit among Italy's nationalist parties to denigrate the democratic Government for not having defended the country's interests, we believe De Gasperi, first as Foreign Minister and later as Premier, achieved all he could. He has been charged by political adversaries with being too much in a hurry to conclude a treaty and it is contended that, had he postponed its signature, Italy would have benefited from the delay. Quite probably the truth of the matter lies in the opposite direction. If more time had elapsed, the gap between the western democracies and Russia would have widened, and there is no evidence that Italy would have got any advantage from it.

De Gasperi appreciated only too well the difficulties of negotiating a peace while the country was occupied by foreign troops. These difficulties emerged fully on September 18, 1945, when he spoke in London before the Council of Foreign Ministers, at whose request his speech was limited to the problem of the eastern frontier. Coming immediately after Kardely, the Yugoslav representative, who had attacked Italy, his arguments were less violent than those of his opponent, but clearer and more convincing in substance. Despite the hostile atmosphere, his words had effective results, because the Council rejected the Yugoslav plan of annexing the whole of Venezia Giulia up to the Austrian frontier existing in 1866, and accepted De Gasperi's proposal that the border should be fixed according to the ethnic line. It also decided that the problem would be investigated on the spot by a special commission formed by the Foreign Ministers' Deputies.

Investigations proved how entangled and complex border and minority questions are. The experts of four countries (Great Britain, the United States, France, and the Soviet Union), although using the same information, came to different conclusions, each representing, according to them, the perfect solution to the problem.

The Council of Foreign Ministers met again in Paris in April, 1946. All the problems linked to the peace treaty were on its agenda. De Gasperi was heard a second time, and spoke in his usual concise but firm manner. After accusing the investigation commission of having limited its work to certain areas of Venezia Giulia, he protested against the Russian solution to the problem, which, by giving Trieste to Yugoslavia, was opposed to the ethnic principle already approved of in London. If this solution was accepted, certainly no Yugoslavs would remain within Italian borders, but at least 600,000 Italians would be incorporated by Yugoslavia. He also rejected the French line as depriving Italy of south-western Istria, and the British one because it granted Yugoslavia the coal-producing basin of Arsa. The American solution was—he believed—nearest to the one suggested in 1919 by President Wilson, and the only one acceptable.

As Italy had not been admitted to the discussions, but only allowed to state her viewpoint, the treaty was being examined in the absence of the most interested party, by countries that were not favourably disposed to her. The United States, eager to withdraw from Europe, was willing to compromise. Great Britain, on the other hand, was not particularly interested in the matter, while the fact that the Italians had fought against her for over three years still rankled with the British public. The new Labour Government felt a certain solidarity with the regime of Belgrade and was favourably disposed to its requests. Even France did not support the Italian cause. Being the weakest among the great Powers and having co-operated largely with the Germans through the Vichy Government, she was suffering from an inferiority complex which gave her a more rigid and spiteful conception of the whole matter. She was on good terms with Russia—a recurrent phase of her foreign policy—and expected to gain from the Italian peace treaty. Russia was interested only in settlements from which Communist countries would profit. She therefore backed all Belgrade's requests.

Diplomatic initiative passed to the Russians and the French. Premier Bidault suggested that his line should be adopted, but with a notable change. An area carved round the city of Trieste was to be set up as an independent State under UNO's supervision. The Italians were stunned when they heard of this suggestion. It implied that the city of Pola would be annexed by Yugoslavia and that 140,000 compatriots would be completely sacrificed. This project would leave one of the danger spots of Europe in a permanent state of friction and unrest.

Other frontier problems were also examined in Paris. French claims on certain territories of the western Alps were acknowledged. France intended strengthening her strategic position and getting areas which are important for power production. The Council also decided that Italy should surrender her colonies and that discussion over their future should be deferred for one year. On the subject of reparations, Italy believed that in view of the great losses she had suffered during the period of co-belligerence and the contribution made to the Allied cause, she should not be called upon to make any. Yet, under the pressure of the Soviet Union, reparations were approved of in principle.

The full Peace Conference inaugurated in Paris on July 30, 1946, included not only the four great Powers, but also seventeen other States which had fought on the Allied side. The purpose of the meeting was to get the approval of the Allies to the draft treaty previously formulated by the Big Four. Participants in the conference could only make recommendations as to its clauses. This was indeed a queer procedure, for it placed before all the Allies the *fait accompli* of documents already drafted and worded.

The day before the Council met, the *New York Times* printed the text of the Italian treaty. When interviewed as to his reactions, De Gasperi said: 'Its hard terms are beyond all expectation. I share with all my compatriots the grief and hopes of these grave moments. I do not doubt that our delegation will fully interpret the sentiments and wishes of the Italian people.'

Italy's delegation was led by De Gasperi, and included the President of the Constituent Assembly, Saragat, and former Premier Ivanoe Bonomi. Again Italy was looked upon only as a defeated country and no consideration was given to her co-belligerence. Byrnes gave a most effective description of the way De Gasperi was received at the Luxembourg Palace on August 10, 1946. Nobody saluted him when he entered the hall, with the exception of Bidault, who acted as chairman. He spoke with quiet dignity and conviction, and after a few words the cold atmosphere in the hall gave way to a friendlier feeling. Everybody understood that this man, who had been imprisoned by the Fascists, was now receiving most unfair treatment.

De Gasperi explained Italy's point of view, protesting eloquently against the solution provided by the draft treaty to the Trieste problem by suggesting the setting up of a free Territory. He stressed that: (1) there was a substantial difference between the Atlantic Charter and the provisions of the treaty, the latter being of a vindictive nature; (2) Italy's efforts as a co-belligerent had been ignored; (3) her territorial problems had been settled without the slightest consideration of the rights of her people; (4) Italian minorities, under foreign sovereignty, were not guaranteed any protection; (5) no recognition was given to Italy's efforts in developing her colonies; (6) the military and economic clauses created an unbearable burden and undermined the country's independence.

In spite of his defence and of the good impression he created, De Gasperi did not change the course of events, as the Council had already agreed upon ratifying what had been decided on by the Big Four. However, his effort was not in vain. It put Italy in contact with foreign Powers and succeeded in creating a better understanding of her position. The country's success in regaining an active part in international affairs can probably be credited to these first contacts.

De Gasperi, faced with such a difficult situation, certainly proved himself a real statesman. His task was not easy, for he was opposed from all sides, and worked practically alone. Communists, although participating in the Government, were doing their utmost to obstruct him in every way. Their Press, instead of backing him, as the occasion warranted, went to the trouble of severely criticising him. To make matters worse, in August,

1946, Palmiro Togliatti went as a private citizen to Paris, where he made important contacts and was interviewed by the Press. At these conferences he discredited De Gasperi and backed the Russians in their policy of favouring Yugoslavia.

The Premier also had to face opposition from nationalist sections of public opinion that were not satisfied with his way of dealing with the whole issue. According to them, Italy should not have attended any of the meetings. De Gasperi was of the opinion that all responsibilities should be faced and all rights defended in an honest and straightforward manner. The more complicated the problem, the more determined he was to cope with it.

Alto Adige was at that period one of the chief topics of discussion, Austria having claimed that, owing to her large German-speaking population, she was entitled to annex it. Although occupied by four different armies, and practically in no position to exercise an independent foreign policy, Austria was permitted to send a delegation to Paris headed by Foreign Minister Grüber. In general, the delegates to the Conference favoured an Austrian annexation. Nevertheless De Gasperi succeeded in contacting Grüber and in signing with him what is known as the De Gasperi–Grüber agreement. Italy conceded certain rights to her German-speaking minority, but retained the whole of Alto Adige. It was undoubtedly a masterpiece of acumen and diplomacy on the Premier's part. Had it not been for his foresight and discernment, Italy might have been compelled to hand over certain territories also on this section of her frontier. De Gasperi was born in this region and had a firsthand knowledge of the problem. This may have been one of the reasons why he was so successful in clinching this awkward situation. The signing of the agreement was notified to the Secretary-General of the Paris Conference and to the Foreign Ministers of the Big Four. It was looked upon favourably by all delegations, and high hopes were held that a similar solution to the Trieste question might be reached. This unfortunately became more and more improbable.

Russia's animosity seemed to grow as time passed. When one of the delegates—former Premier Ivanoe Bonomi—asked that if the Free Territory of Trieste was to be set up, it should at least include the city of Pola, which the French line left within Yugoslav territory, Vyshinsky, the Russian delegate, not only accused Bonomi of having imperialistic aims, but added that it was general knowledge that Italians are more competent in the art of running away than in the art of fighting. This direct insult had immediate repercussions in Italy. Partisans, above all, were deeply offended and sent many telegrams of protest to Vyshinsky. The only people to ignore the insult were the Communists.

The Paris Peace Conference ended on October 15, 1946. The project of the treaty remained as drafted by the Big Four. Decision as to the fate of the eastern border was made in favour of the French line, and Trieste became a Free Territory under United Nations control. For the time being, and until a Governor could be appointed, the Territory was to be divided into two zones, of which the Western (Zone A) was to be administered by the Anglo–Americans and the Eastern (Zone B) by the Yugoslavs.

The Council of Foreign Ministers of the Big Four met in New York during the following month of November to consider the final drafting of the treaties. Again no changes were made in its decisions concerning Italy, in spite of the protest forwarded through the Italian Ambassador in Washington, wherein the usual reservations were formulated and the Allies were reminded of their past promises.

The treaty was in fact signed in Paris on February 10, 1947, a very sad day for the Italian people. Foreign Minister Sforza protested again in a note in which he pointed out that the expiation the Italians had been called upon to make for past mistakes was too harsh, and the people had a right to ask for a radical revision of a document which could either paralyse or poison their life. The treaty was ratified by the Constituent Assembly, and before the end of the year all Allied troops had left Italian soil. This was the end of the military occupation which had started on the beaches of Sicily in 1943.

The worst provisions imposed on Italy concerned the eastern border. They proved unpractical and could not possibly last. Frontier corrections were also made in favour of France. The other clauses were equally harsh and their effects were deeply felt. Military and naval restrictions resulted in the practical disarming of the country. Permanent fortifications and military installations along the French and Yugoslav frontiers were to be destroyed. Demilitarisation of certain strategic spots was ordered. The islands of Sardinia and Sicily were subjected to grave restrictions. Italy was prohibited from manufacturing arms in excess of the bare needs of her armed forces, which were limited in power and efficiency. The greater part of her navy was to be divided among the Allies, while naval personnel was fixed at a maximum number of 25,000 men. The army was reduced to 185,000 men and 65,000 military police (*carabinieri*). The total air force was limited to 200 fighter and reconnaissance planes and 150 auxiliary aircraft. She was forbidden to construct battleships, aircraft carriers, or submarines. Reparations were fixed as follows: 100 million dollars was granted to the Soviet Union, 5 million to Albania, 25 million to Ethiopia, 105 million to Greece, and 125 million to Yugoslavia, the payment of which was to be drawn from various sources, including assets abroad and current industrial production.

Some of these provisions were so inconsistent with the world situation that not many years were to elapse before they were declared void by the majority of the Powers concerned. The United States and Great Britain were the first to renounce their quota of navy units, while France made certain concessions. The Soviet Government, however, insisted on getting everything to which it was entitled. Revision of the peace treaty became one of the principal aims of Italy's foreign policy.

From February, 1947 until July, 1951, Italy's Foreign Minister was Carlo Sforza (1873–1952). A man of international reputation, he had been Minister in Peking, Foreign Minister in 1920–21, Ambassador in Paris until his resignation after the march on Rome. During the Fascist regime he lived in exile abroad, where he was considered one of the outstanding members of anti-fascism.

When De Gasperi broke away from the Communists and Socialists he decided to hand over the Foreign Ministry to a man of experience and ability. This man was Sforza. In addressing him De Gasperi said: 'Your task is a great one. I need a man with great prestige abroad who can make the voice of Italy heard.' For five years Sforza shouldered this responsibility skilfully. His influence was especially prominent in the movement for European integration. Like De Gasperi, he believed in continental unity and was anxious that it should abandon theoretical schemes and become something practical and concrete.

At the beginning of 1947 De Gasperi accepted an invitation to go to the United States. Politically the journey was a risk, as the Communists would be only too pleased to stress any failure. The Premier, however, did not waver, but took the chance. The outcome was a personal success owing to his ability and firmness in handling matters. Washington confirmed her intention to renounce reparations and her quota of the Fleet. These direct contacts with the United States were the beginning of new and more intimate relations destined to become closer during the following years. The number of Italians and Americans of Italian descent living in the United States has been high since the beginning of the century. Friendship between the two countries had been tested before and during World War I and had stood the strain of Mussolini's absurd declaration of war. The United States were now following the far-sighted and broad-minded policy of assisting countries ravaged by war, and Italy was being shown special attention and goodwill.

While the Government was engaged in the task of regaining the confidence of former enemy nations it was being again hard pressed by Communists, who were taking initiatives definitely contrasting with its official policies. On November, 1946, their daily paper *Unità* carried the text of an interview in which Palmiro Togliatti declared that on a recent visit to Belgrade he had met Marshal Tito, who had announced his willingness to give up any claim on Trieste, provided the city of Gorizia, which had been left to Italy by the Peace Treaty, were given to Yugoslavia. Public opinion was taken aback by this unexpected news. It implied that the Government had not acted wisely in its dealings with the Allies and had lost the favourable opportunity of reaching a settlement of that delicate issue. The Press lost no time in opening a discussion on the matter, while De Gasperi strongly protested against Togliatti's unethical action. He had travelled to Yugoslavia as a private individual who held no official position. It was therefore his duty, before publicising the news, to report his interview with Tito to the Foreign Minister. Tito's goodwill gesture turned out to be pure propaganda. When contacts were made with the Yugoslav delegate in New York, the Italian plenipotentiary found a very unco-operative attitude. Togliatti had tried to demonstrate that he enjoyed great influence and could secure the repatriation of prisoners-of-war held in Yugoslavia, which the Government had failed to do. He proved his point in a doubtful manner, as an agreement—even if reached—with Tito would have resulted in little gain and would have sacrificed thousands of Italians.

This episode and later Communist interference of a similar kind did not prevent Italy from participating in one of the greatest economic schemes of all times. On June 5, 1947, General George Marshall delivered his famous speech at Harvard University outlining a plan for world recovery. Never before in history had a winning country set apart funds and resources to assist the rebirth of former enemies. The approach of the United States to the problem was a generous and friendly one. Economic recovery was to be handled through an organised distribution of supplies, so that industry and trade could regain their feet. No discrimination was made, but help was offered to all European nations with the exception of Germany and Spain. In spite of this good will, it was then that Europe definitely split into two groups. When countries were invited to take part in a conference to arrange the future of the plan, they all accepted with the exception of Russia and her satellites. The conference convened in Paris on July 12, 1947. Here Foreign Minister Sforza declared that Italy was ready to give full support to all forms of co-operation that would strengthen Europe's economic structure. He also emphasised the importance of the plan, stating that should it fail Europe would again become what it had been 10,000 years ago: an insignificant peninsula of the Asian continent.

Communists rigorously opposed the Marshall Plan by accusing the United States of unnecessary meddling in the domestic affairs of other nations. Russia, being in no position to set up a plan to match the American one, but foreseeing its vast propaganda effects, hastily ordered Communists to oppose the scheme regardless as to whether or not their countries would benefit from it. When we consider the importance of Marshall aid on Italy's rehabilitation and reconstruction, it is difficult to understand what logical grounds the Communists had for opposing it. The only explanation is that they were so influenced by their Soviet masters that they had lost all initiative to judge events of national interest independently and wisely.

The Paris Conference prepared a report signed by sixteen Powers. The document, divided into various sections dealing with the economy and necessities of every single State, was forwarded to the American Government. During the spring of 1948 a second conference was convened in Paris which ended with the signing of a treaty setting up the Organisation for European Economic Co-operation (O.E.E.C.). During that same period the Italian general elections took place, and the world in general was waiting to see whether Italy would veer towards the

West or the East. Foreign affairs were among the principal issues of the campaign, and this meant the Marshall Plan in its full significance. Fortunately things went according to general expectation.

A treaty between Italy and the United States regarding American aid was soon settled in Rome. Ratification of the Paris Agreement for Economic Co-operation was immediately discussed in Parliament and approved, after much Communist opposition. The plan also had great bearing on the nation's political standing abroad. Until then Italy had never been received on an equal footing with the winners of the war. At the Peace Conference she had been heard as a matter of routine, but had not been allowed to discuss the terms imposed on her by the treaty. Now things were different. She was backed by the United States in the same way as Great Britain and France, and could examine her own problems without simply having to abide by the decisions of other countries. In answer to a letter sent to him by De Gasperi, President Truman wrote that he was confident that Italy's political maturity and working capacities would be among the basic factors on which the success of the Plan depended. So it was, indeed.

A matter which caused much controversy was the Three-Power declaration on Trieste. On March 20, 1948 (less than a month before the general election), France, Great Britain, and the United States put forward a new proposal on this grave problem. They started by acknowledging that the Security Council of the United Nations had not succeeded in selecting a Governor for the Free Territory, and that Zone B had virtually been annexed by Yugoslavia through anti-democratic procedures. In view of the existing conditions, they promised to recommend the return of the Free Territory to Italian sovereignty, as this seemed the best way to ease unrest among the population and stabilise the entire region. Necessary arrangements to this effect would be submitted to the Security Council. These ideas were embodied in three official notes forwarded to the Government in Rome. The American note stated:

> 'It is necessary to recall that the Government of the United States has always consistently maintained that the entire zone of the Free Territory is ethnically and historically Italian territory and that this Government agreed that it should be separated from Italy only on condition that it

was really independent and that the human rights of the population were completely protected and guaranteed against any possibility of being suppressed or violated. It is evident that this condition cannot now be reached and therefore this Government has decided that the rights and interests of the very large Italian majority of the zone can be safeguarded only by restoring the Free Territory to Italian sovereignty.'

What was the purpose of the declaration? The simplest explanation is probably the nearest the truth. The three Powers wanted to assist Italy's democratic Government in its electoral campaign, and believed this move would help it. Trieste had always been a delicate subject with the Italians, and this promise of its return to the motherland was the cause of great elation. It is difficult to say, however, to exactly what extent it influenced the voters. A closer study of the document showed that no indications were given as to when the Free Territory would be handed over to Italy, for the three Powers only promised to refer the matter to the Security Council, where the Soviet Union would probably have vetoed the issue.

On March 22, 1948, Italy answered the Western Powers, and voiced 'the joy of the people of the Free Territory and of the whole Italian nation'. The same day the Yugoslav Government protested against the decision, stating that it violated the Peace Treaty. It has been rumoured that the declaration was made because information that Russia intended to make the same offer had reached the Western Powers. That this move was well advised is open to doubt. The fact that the declaration was never enforced certainly did not strengthen Italy's confidence in western solidarity, and kept her in an unsettled state of agitation. After that the problem of Trieste came forward many times —often in the form of riots and disturbances. This embittered Italy, although it did not weaken her trust in European cooperation nor prevent her from taking part in several schemes aimed at the strengthening of democracy.

With the passing of time divisions between East and West became more pronounced. During the war the United States and Soviet Union had put aside their feuds in order to defeat the Axis. Now that danger was over, basic differences were emerging. A deep feeling of weakness and insecurity and a dangerous atmosphere of defeatism were spreading over Europe. The

Western Allies, and especially the United States, had in fact demobilised their armed forces as soon as possible. That America had no wish to become entangled in European affairs has already been proved by the way she dealt with the Trieste question. Yet, despite demobilisation, sometimes carried beyond the safety line, Communist propaganda continued to spread the absurd story that the United States and their associates wanted war.

Democratic Powers soon felt that a strong arm and closer cooperation were urgently needed to maintain peace. This could only mean a military alliance. The Communist parties, both in Italy and France, had already realised that this was bound to happen sooner or later, and for this reason had opposed the Marshall Plan. Their opposition was not caused by the belief that material aid was unnecessary, but because they saw that a treaty of economic assistance could easily lead to a political and military pact. Yet this turn of affairs would not have been so rapid had Soviet propaganda not become so virulent. People in Europe and North America, awakened to new dangers, realised that demobilisation had to be halted. Post-war experience had removed illusions that controversies could be solved by fireside discussions among statesmen. Strong action was necessary. The dream of an efficient United Nations was fading away under the blows of Soviet policies and propaganda. Yet even this change from a peaceful to a defensive approach on the part of the Western world did not take place easily. It did not seem possible to people who had just fought a war of long duration that military preparedness was again necessary, and that the international bodies set up under the illusion that they would guarantee peace had turned out to be failures.

No Italian could willingly advocate rearmament even if of a defensive nature. This approach might have strengthened neutralistic tendencies had not the public realised that the country could not remain isolated. Neutrality in international affairs is not a consequence of a state of mind but of concomitant factors, few of which depend on the neutral himself. These factors are non-existent in Italy, where events taking place in other parts of Europe always have immediate repercussions. The illusion that neutrality was still possible was being spread by Communists, who used it as the easiest line of resistance against the ever-tightening bond between Italy and the Western democracies. There were, however, also less extreme people who believed Italy's best course would be to maintain a neutral attitude towards the Western and Eastern blocks. At the time of the general election propaganda in favour of a neutral Italy was at its height, but with the intensification of Soviet policies and the imminent danger of aggression it rapidly diminished.

De Gasperi was quick to note this, and acted accordingly. Together with Sforza, a line of action was worked out. Italy, they felt, was 'the front line' of diplomatic relations and military events. It was a waste of time talking of neutrality when her territory was vulnerable to attacks from the east, and any conflict would most certainly, from the beginning, be fought on her soil. The Premier's policy aimed at collective security among democratic countries.

The preparatory phase of Italian participation in the Atlantic Pact began after the 1948 election. Italian diplomats abroad were instructed to follow events very carefully, as the country would find it impossible to remain out of a future Western Alliance. Later the Berlin blockade proved the ever-growing danger of Russian expansion in Europe. Information reaching Rome convinced the Government that the signing of a military pact would probably take place sooner than expected and that, if Italy wished to take part in it from the beginning, she would have to make up her mind quickly. The meetings for the drawing up of the Atlantic Pact started in Washington on December 10, 1948. A month later Italy forwarded a memorandum to the American Government asking what guarantees she could count on in case of aggression and if the United States would pledge themselves to assist her militarily and financially. After having been given these assurances, she was officially invited to become a signatory of the Pact.

Before committing itself, however, the Government called for a vote to be taken in Parliament, where Foreign Minister Sforza emphasised that the treaty in the making was in no way aggressive and that all participants were moved by a sincere and common desire to maintain peace. 'Hostility towards the Atlantic Pact,' he said, 'comes from those who have opposed the Marshall Plan, the European Union, who detest Federalism, who, in conclusion, wish to check all the roads that we and the other countries of Western Europe want to follow in order to reach real prosperity and real peace.' He went on to say: 'We do not possess the instruments for a policy of power, neither do we wish to have them. Our aim, we must repeat, is to be in a position to contribute to a policy of co-operation among all countries, with the exclusion of none.'

On April 4, 1949, after a series of conferences between the Foreign Ministers, the Pact was finally signed in Washington. Parliament's ratification was not easy to obtain, for Communists and Socialists tried to delay it by filibustering tactics. They were not successful, and Italy thus became a partner in one of the most powerful alliances of all time. Her entry into the pact was a great feat of Italian diplomacy. The treaty's provisions followed the statute of the United Nations. Its members pledged themselves to solve international disputes by peaceful means and not by threats or the use of force. Armed attack on any one member would be regarded as an attack on all. In obtaining military and political security Italy had strengthened the foundation of her economic and moral rebirth. This was a great reward for those men who had worked so devotedly for their country's welfare during the post-war years. Until then reconstruction had been carried on in an atmosphere of uncertainty and distrust, but now, with the success of the 1948 election and the signing of the pact, hope and confidence in the future had spread among all.

The pact hampered relations between the two blocks. The Soviet policy, although constantly designed to divide democratic countries, had had the reverse effect, by making them rely more and more on the United States. Europeans had learned that cold war was not merely a question of differences of opinion, but something far more dangerous, involving their future existence. If at times they had cherished the idea that the continent could in case of war remain neutral, they now realised the absurdity of that illusion. Thus the measures adopted in the pact were most necessary from a practical point of view, even if they proved that the U.N.O. had been in many ways a failure.

At the Peace Conference no agreement had been reached on the important question of Italy's colonies (Libya, Eritrea, and Somaliland). Italy having surrendered her sovereignty on those territories, the problem was referred for solution to the Foreign Ministers' Deputies, who decided that a special commission should visit the colonies and make its recommendations. As in the case of Trieste, all delegates made conflicting reports and suggested different solutions.

At the beginning of 1948 a tragic event occurred in Mogadishu, the capital of Italian Somaliland. Although British military authorities were still responsible for the country's administration, a mob formed by natives and led by the sect of 'Young Somalis', attacked the Italian inhabitants, several of whom were killed. This regrettable incident, which the British did not succeed in preventing, did not help to make the solution of the colonial problem easier. The British military authorities were accused of having shown 'a distinct lack of understanding', by not enforcing order.

At the meeting of the Foreign Ministers' Deputies held in London on July 30, 1948, Italy officially asked that her colonies be returned to her under the form of United Nations trusteeships. But the Deputies did not approve this request, and being unable to reach an agreement, referred the whole question to the General Assembly of the United Nations.

What was the foundation of Italy's request? Italians had arrived late in the colonial competition, obtaining only territories of little importance to others. They had at times even refused offers, especially on the part of Great Britain, to take part in ventures (for example, in Egypt) of greater economic value. Francesco Crispi, the Premier who believed in the colonial future of his country, had never been very popular. His policies were abandoned almost immediately after his fall, only to be resumed by Mussolini. Even then they were received with a feeling of distrust. The spurts of enthusiasm shown at the time of the Libyan (1911–12) and the Ethiopian (1935–36) conquests were mostly outbursts of public exuberance.

Yet Italians also thought the pioneering they had started deserved to be carried on. They had found backward people and had developed in them a certain amount of civic maturity, which, they felt, would soon give results if they were allowed to carry on with the task unhindered. Their work and capital had started the colonisation of the Libyan desert, which can only be compared to that of the Palestine desert accomplished later by the Israelis. Before Fascism parliamentary representation had been granted to the Libyans, who had later been given full Italian citizenship. In the three colonies cities had been constructed and small villages had become prosperous centres of trade and industry. With such a fine record, the Italians never doubted that they were entitled to finish the task they had begun. Hence their request to be granted trusteeship. In this way the three colonies would be guaranteed full independence, but their evolution would be sponsored and expedited by the nation through which they had come into contact with European civilisation.

Three memoranda were sent to the Conference of the Foreign Ministers' Deputies, all of them explaining the reasons for Italy's request that she should receive the trusteeship of her colonies. This was again voiced by Foreign Minister Sforza in his speech at the United Nations on April 11, 1949, when he stressed that Italy could not be judged according to opinions biased by war propaganda. This request, however, was not granted by the General Assembly.

A month later it was hoped that a compromise might be reached with Great Britain and France. A plan was laid down in London by Foreign Ministers Bevin and Sforza whereby Libya was split into three regions, of which Cyrenaica was given to Great Britain under trusteeship, Tripolitania to Italy, and Fezzan—the south-western part of Tripolitania—to France. The western provinces of Eritrea would be annexed by the Sudan, while the rest of the territory was to become part of Ethiopia. The cities of Asmara and Massawa would be granted a special statute as a protective measure for the vast Italian colony domiciled there. Somaliland was to be administered by Italy under trusteeship. Unfortunately even this compromise was rejected by the United Nations Assembly.

This rejection brought about important changes in Italy's policy. Up to then she had firmly believed that she was entitled to lead her colonies on the path of home rule. When this proved impossible, she decided to insist on complete independence. This formula was put forward on October 1, 1949, at Lake Success by Foreign Minister Sforza, who delivered a memorable speech. He again stressed the fact that if Italy had formerly asked for the trusteeship and was now sponsoring independence, this did not imply any change or contradiction in her policy, but was simply the consequence of events. The formula of immediate independence, however, did not completely prevail. The General Assembly of the United Nations in fact approved a scheme, by which—

(1) Libya was to become an independent and sovereign State by January 1, 1952.

(2) A commission of inquiry was to be sent to Eritrea to ascertain the wishes of the inhabitants.

(3) Italy was to be granted a ten-year trusteeship of Somaliland.

Thus the problem of Eritrea remained unsolved until a year later, when the General Assembly approved a plan by which it was to be federated with Ethiopia.

Since these events took place Libya has become a monarchy under King Idris, a political *émigré*, and the recognised leader of a religious sect. The federation of Eritrea with Ethiopia should have been a loose one, and more political independence should have been guaranteed the population, especially the Italians. This unfortunately was not the case, for the Addis Ababa Government always regarded Eritrea as a permanent territorial acquisition. Following the United Nations decisions, Ethiopia's position was greatly strengthened, as she became a pivotal point of British and American policies in eastern Africa. Relations with Italy were at times influenced by past enmities, although every effort was made to reach a permanent agreement. In Somaliland, Italy is carrying on the task of educating the natives with all possible speed, so that when the ten-year period is over they may be in a position to administer their country in a modern and efficient way.

Italians are often accused of feeling too strongly the heritage of Machiavelli and of being too inclined to consider problems according to their interests, without respecting commitments. This frequently repeated accusation is entirely unwarranted. From the time they signed the Peace Treaty, for example, they could easily have taken advantage of the cold war and readjusted their policies to suit their interests. They did nothing of the kind, but took their place alongside the other free nations in European and world affairs, making it always a point to back the Western world. While acknowledging that this staunch fidelity to democratic principles has not always brought the results one might have expected, we must add that it was the only policy adapted to the nation's beliefs and to her moral standards. As a direct consequence, the atmosphere existing when the Peace Treaty was signed has given way to a more serene outlook.

This has made the revision of the treaty feasible. It has, of course, been impossible to change its territorial clauses, these being tied to the sovereignty of other States. Yet the Three-Power declaration of March 20, 1948, can be considered a first attempt to find a *modus vivendi* in this field. By acknowledging that the provisions of the treaty had not been fulfilled by Yugoslavia and suggesting that the whole territory should be returned to Italy, the Three Powers were openly admitting that a mistake had been made. Agreements were also signed with several States regarding the treaty's economic clauses. Italian properties have often been derequisitioned, and satisfactory settlements were reached.

The greatest results, however, were achieved in the military field. Having entered the Atlantic Pact, which placed on its members certain obligations, it was absurd that Italy should be tied by a treaty imposed on her by her present allies. At NATO meetings she always stressed the absurdity of her situation and the necessity of immediate changes. France showed exceptional goodwill over this matter, and if the problem reached a conclusion, it was largely due to her influence. Although during the Peace Treaty negotiations France had not always backed Italy's cause, her subsequent attitude became progressively more favourable. Sforza's diplomacy contributed to the change.

The first example of a friendly approach had been the signing of a Customs Union which, although never ratified, had proved that the two Latin nations were once again on the path to fruitful co-operation. A conference between the two Premiers—De Gasperi and Pleven—with the assistance of Foreign Ministers Sforza and Schuman, was held at Santa Margherita, on the Italian Riviera, during the month of February, 1951. The meeting turned out to be an important event. Talks dealing with problems of the day, such as the European Army, the Schuman Plan for the pooling of coal and steel, and the emigration of Italian labour, were carried on in an atmosphere of mutual understanding.

As an outcome of the conference, and following an official Italian request, a declaration was issued in Paris on August 22, 1951, stating that the peace treaty with Italy needed to be revised. The document, couched in friendly terms, placed this vital problem before the original signatories. News of it was received in Italy with general satisfaction. The declaration was not made with the intention of enforcing an immediate revision, but as a reminder to governments, especially to Washington and London, that the situation had sooner or later to be faced. If results were obtained and the treaty was revised within a few weeks of the French declaration, it was due to De Gasperi, who had now assumed Sforza's responsibilities as Foreign Minister. The NATO Council was in fact to meet in Ottawa, and he decided to attend.

On September 17, 1951, the Premier spoke before the Council. He described Italy's most urgent problems in connection with the defence of the Free World, especially stressing her obligations, which, he said, were entirely inconsistent with the limitations imposed by the treaty. His appeal had immediate results. On September 26, 1951, the United States, Great Britain, and France issued a common declaration acknowledging that restrictions and limitations on Italy's liberty of rearmament were now obsolete. They declared themselves ready to give favourable consideration to any request for revision made by Rome. On December 8, 1951, a note was addressed to the signatories of the Peace Treaty asking that certain provisions be revised. They concerned the treaty's foreword on Italy's responsibility in undertaking a war of aggression, the general clauses (Articles 15 to 18), and the naval, military, and air-force clauses (Articles 46 to 72) limiting the country's right to rearm. All signatories who had become members of NATO, together with other Powers, agreed to Italy's request. Of course, Russia, Poland, and Czechoslovakia opposed it, stating that it was a unilateral denunciation of the Peace Treaty. But as the overwhelming majority had accepted her point of view, Italy considered the treaty revised, in accordance with her proposals.

Since 1950 Trieste has always been prominent in the public's mind. For Italy, in fact, the Three-Power declaration still remained the basic document which had to be enforced by its signatories. That it would ever be carried out in full was, however, doubtful. With the passing of years Yugoslavia had found herself on friendly terms with the Western Powers, from whom she was receiving more and more aid. In 1951—following a wave of demonstrations—Great Britain and the United States agreed to hand over to Italy some of the authority they held in Zone A. This hardly changed the situation at all, as real power still remained in the hands of the Anglo-American Military Government. Trieste was on De Gasperi's agenda when he visited North America in September, 1951, but this problem met with less success than the revision of the Peace Treaty. It was decided, in fact, that no change would be made for the moment and the *status quo* would be maintained. This was an especially unpleasant decision for the Italians, who claimed that the Yugoslav authorities were carrying on a policy of denationalisation of Zone B, bound in the long run to change its ethnical picture. Italy's approach to the problem, although firm in the defence of her recognised rights, was not uncompromising. She constantly maintained that some agreement could be found so long as goodwill on the part of all States concerned existed.

As time passed, a solution became urgent, because practically every year the question was the reason for a crisis between Italy, Yugoslavia, and the Western Powers. The most serious was that of 1953, when the Italian Government was compelled to take military measures on the border of the Free Territory in order to prevent any surprise action from Belgrade. A dangerous phase followed, because Yugoslavia answered these protective measures by mobilising even stronger forces. It seemed as if the crisis might lead to a conflict. On October 8, 1953, the British and American Governments announced that they were seriously concerned and had decided to withdraw their troops from Zone A, relinquishing its administration to Italy. Belgrade's reaction was unfortunately so violent, and resulted in such demonstrations, that Great Britain and the United States did not carry out their decision, as they were apprehensive of its consequences were it to be enforced in such an atmosphere of tension.

Yet everybody felt it imperative that the matter should be settled through some kind of compromise. Negotiations took place in London, sponsored by Anglo-American diplomacy. They led to the signing on October 5, 1954, of an agreement by which the Free Territory was partitioned between Italy and Yugoslavia, practically along the previous demarcation line between Zones A and B, but with a minor frontier rectification in favour of Yugoslavia. The agreement also enabled the inhabitants of both zones to leave freely for Italy and Yugoslavia and to transfer their assets without restriction; it provided for guarantees of human rights and of cultural facilities for racial minorities.

This agreement was undoubtedly a sacrifice for Italy, because it left many of her nationals within the territory of a foreign State. Yet we believe the settlement was worth the effort. Italy and Yugoslavia have in fact complementary interests and economies, and now that the way has been cleared of this main obstacle, they are bound to reach a larger and more comprehensive understanding.

From 1951 onward Italy has contributed her share to the common defence effort of the Western World. After his journey to North America, De Gasperi, having been assured once again as to American goodwill, was more than ever determined to carry out a policy of strict co-operation with the West. This he stressed before Parliament when he declared that only by strengthening the already firm alliance would Italy free herself from the state of inferiority in which the Peace Treaty had left her.

At the end of 1951 the Atlantic Council was convened in Rome. De Gasperi chose this opportunity to emphasise his attachment to the ideal of Western co-operation. The Council was to examine the problem of German rearmament. Although from this point of view the talks were almost a failure, they nevertheless afforded Italy the opportunity for stressing the aims of her policy. De Gasperi delivered the opening speech. 'The North Atlantic Pact,' he stated, 'is a treaty of peace within liberty, freely developing towards justice among classes and nations. The means of defence that we are searching for have been set up in order to enforce active peace, and not to cause war.'

During 1952 and up to July, 1953, De Gasperi's activity was dedicated to fostering schemes of international co-operation. We will examine in the following chapter Italy's participation in those schemes. Here we wish to point out how the Premier made them the central pivot of his policy, and to this purpose took part in several international meetings. His activity was backed by all democratic parties and opposed only by Communists and Socialists, who denounced it as a form of servitude to foreign Powers—namely, to the United States. On the contrary, this approach gave the nation a friendlier and more co-operative outlook on European problems. A closer understanding between countries became the common objective both of the Government and the people.

This proves that Italy has accepted her full share of responsibility. She has regained a premier position in the framework of European relations, especially in areas where she once played an important role. Although her industrial and financial capacities cannot compare with those of some other countries, she is nevertheless expanding in the economic and political fields, and her presence is bound to be felt more and more. Several factors remain basic in her conduct, and are unlikely to change in the near future. First, her friendship with the United States, which has passed through heavy tests, always emerging undamaged. Good relations with France in what is known as the 'spirit of Santa Margherita' also remain a foundation of present and future policies. Equal disposition of mind, moral experience, and historic ties link the two countries closely, so that the famous expression 'Latin sisters' still does not appear outmoded or in any way obsolete. Relations with Germany are also good, and destined to improve, for the two countries have common interests and aims, together with a belief in the supranational future of the Continent. If at times relations with Great Britain have been strained and somewhat unfriendly, they have improved since the Trieste question has been, at least partially, solved. During the nineteenth century, and up to World War I, a policy of friendship with Great Britain was one of the principles of Italy's foreign policy. It will be in everybody's interest, and especially of the two parties concerned, if mutual understanding again becomes as complete as it used to be.

Italy owes her increasing authority to the determined leadership she has enjoyed in recent years. Above all, what has put her on the road to recovery and restored her prestige has been her attachment to moral principles and to plans of collective security. For centuries supreme in the fields of culture and civilisation, she inherits a tradition which belongs to the unconquerable and constantly progressing spirit of man. By relying on it, and by retaining her high standards of integrity and fidelity to commitments, she is bound to hold and strengthen her position in world affairs.

Chapter 10

Italy and European Unity

DESPITE the confusion and upheaval of Europe's life during recent years, despite the social and moral unrest, one element has been highly encouraging, and that has been progress towards European unity. The importance of this ideal, which, although a dream until a few years ago, may eventually come true, cannot be sufficiently stressed. This great enterprise must overcome many difficulties, but it does represent the ultimate goal at which Europeans must aim.

Italy has given much impulse to the plan for welding Europe into one, and at times, had it not been for De Gasperi's dynamic approach, plans for continental unity would certainly have moved at a slower pace. The futility of war is often clearer to the vanquished than to the victors. After the sad events of World War II and the strife witnessed by all, Italians feel that the era of Nationalism and Chauvinism is over, and that everybody must tend towards continental unification. They have attained on this point a unity of feeling and purpose which is rarely met with in a democratic country. If certain parties oppose it this is only because they do not faithfully express the feelings of the people they are supposed to represent.

Apart from sentimental values (which are, nevertheless, of great importance to the success of any cause), strong rational factors are also moving the most enlightened Italians. Everybody knows, for instance, that the old diplomatic formula based on 'balance of power' is practically dead in a continent where no State is any longer independent in the sense that the term conveyed a quarter of a century ago. Thus in a strictly political sense the trend towards unity has never been as strong as now.

Italy's history has always been dominated by universal values, and it is not without reason that the Roman Empire and Catholicism developed on her soil. Both of them were the widest and most successful attempts at organising the material and moral existence of mankind. Italians have often been accused of spurning details and displaying interest only in general ideas. If this does at times make them appear unpractical, it does, however, show a readiness to co-operate with others and to see problems in a universal way. It is therefore not a coincidence that their foreign policy has been formulated for several years by such men as De Gasperi and Sforza, who recognised that the right approach to the problem of unity was not one of impatience, but of constant and careful dedication. If these men were able to act as they did, it was only because they could count on the nation's backing.

As far back as 1947, Luigi Einaudi, later President of the Republic, told the Constituent Assembly that the first World War had been fought in vain because in its wake Nationalism had flourished, while Europe's problems had remained unsolved. The following were his words: 'If Europeans wish to avoid a third World War they must raise the sword of God by allowing the idea of voluntary co-operation to prevail for the common cause. The sort of Europe that Italy advocates, and for which she must fight, does not exclude anybody, but is open to all. It is a Europe in which men may freely express their ideas and where majorities respect minorities and support their aims as far as they are compatible with the continuity of community life. For the purpose of creating this Europe, Italy must be ready to sacrifice part of her sovereignty.'

The first attempt to put these principles into practice was made by O.E.E.C. (Organisation for European Economic Co-operation), set up in Paris to co-ordinate European economies and distribute Marshall Aid. A body of that kind could remain either a temporary expedient or develop into something more solid and permanent. In the sixteen-Power convention, signed in Paris on April 16, 1948, the necessity of co-operating was particularly stressed, as being the only way to reconstruct the Continent and regain lost prosperity.

Great ideas often require impulse to set them into motion. There are also men who during the course of history feel the impact of these ideas and the urge to bring about their enforcement. Sforza was one of them. In August, 1948, he forwarded a memorandum to the Quai d'Orsay explaining Italy's point of view. The following are some excerpts from the document:

> 'Italy's Government is convinced that the realisation of a European union or federation must be reached by degrees,

> starting with an economic platform (already partially existing and only awaiting to be perfected), so as gradually to reach forms of political, economic, and social co-operation.'
>
> 'According to Italy's Government, it will soon be realised that the safest and historically most pertinent road places Europe's final union within the reach of sixteen States, now co-operating in O.E.E.C. in the economic field for European reconstruction.'

The memorandum indicated that immediate decisions were to be taken on the following lines: (1) O.E.E.C. was to become a permanent body and co-ordinate European economies independently of American aid; (2) new forms of social and cultural co-operation were to be carried out; (3) a political committee should be formed for the purpose of examining and solving international problems; (4) a court of European justice was to be created.

Similar ideas were disclosed in another Italian memorandum, forwarded in October, 1948, to O.E.E.C. members. The document stated that governments receiving Marshall Aid were to make every effort to set up a society of nations and develop mutual trade so as to achieve a reduction of costs, more employment, and an improvement in the general standard of living. The document stressed that O.E.E.C. should become the backbone of continental unity and that Italy was prepared to accept any limitation of sovereignty. These suggestions were partly accepted. In February, 1949, a Ministerial Committee of O.E.E.C. was established, having jurisdiction upon common matters of policy.

Another event was received in Europe, and especially in Italy, as a decisive move towards unity. That was the Western Union, signed in Brussels on March 17, 1948. The purpose of this agreement was to strengthen Western defences against a possible revival of German militarism. Three years had not yet elapsed since the end of hostilities, and it was therefore understandable that five countries (Great Britain, France, Belgium, the Netherlands, and Luxembourg), with German aggression still fresh in their minds, should want a guarantee against future attack. This alliance was looked upon by Italy as the first effort towards union among the five nations. Bevin's words, calling for more co-operation, were understood to mean that Great

Britain had become the crusader of an association between European countries.

Optimism increased with the formation of a Consultative Council that was to meet at regular intervals. Its importance was particularly stressed by European federalists. They shared the opinion that international organisms were necessary because in due course their powers would expand and reduce State sovereignty. Although formed only by the five Foreign Ministers, this body of a somewhat parliamentarian nature seemed to justify this opinion.

In October, 1948, the Consultative Council decided to set up a committee that would report on the steps to take in order to secure more unity among European nations. As a result of this committee's work, the decision was reached to set up a European Assembly, known as the Council of Europe.

During discussions, two conflicting opinions were brought forward. France and Belgium advocated that the new Assembly should be formed of parliamentary representatives; Great Britain thought instead that it should consist of Government delegates. Public opinion was also beginning to influence the matter. In all countries the urge for unity was in fact getting stronger daily, and could not be ignored. The congress of movements favouring European unity which had met at The Hague had recommended that the five Powers of the Western Union should prepare a conference for the setting up of an assembly. A compromise solution was therefore reached by which the new body would be governed by a Committee of Ministers, but would also have a Consultative Assembly formed by representatives of member-States. Italy was associated with these works and contributed to the drafting of the statute, signed in London on May 5, 1949, by the Foreign Ministers of ten countries. She was represented by Count Sforza. The statute was ratified by Parliament in July, 1949.

Federalists were disappointed with the Council of Europe. According to the statute, the Consultative Assembly could only discuss matters referred or approved by the Council of Ministers, yet many Italians hoped that it would succeed in freeing itself from this limitation. No concrete result was, however, reached. Some national delegations were elected by Parliament (the Italian, for instance), whilst others were appointed by governments. The former were anxious to extend the powers of the Assembly, but the latter had no intention of widening the sphere of action laid down by the statute. A psychological obstacle was also the 'cold-war' atmosphere. Soviet propaganda was extremely active at the time and the war in Korea was imminent. Delegates were understandably influenced by events, which naturally made them more sensitive to national issues.

Italy's first delegation to the Council of Europe consisted of deputies and senators from the four democratic parties (Christian Democrats, Social Democrats, Liberals, and Republicans), excluding extreme left and right. All of them were favourable to a federal programme. Despite disillusionment caused by several delays and the general approach of the Council of Europe, Italian Federalists advocated certain developments, which they believed might be the prelude to an enforcement of more concrete schemes. Hence the importance they placed on the Assembly's session of August, 1950, which dealt with the creation of a European army and of a common Ministry of Defence. Although neither of these materialised, the fact that they had been discussed was in itself a success.

The impossibility, at least for the moment, that the Council of Europe should become the channel for continental unity soon became evident. This did not imply that in Italy or elsewhere all hope was lost. Although the Council of Europe had proved that the Continent was still not prepared for unity and that certain countries did not intend to renounce their sovereignty, some results had been obtained. Six nations (Italy, France, West Germany, Belgium, the Netherlands, and Luxembourg) reacted more than others to the impact of new ideas. At all times they had been more closely associated politically, economically and culturally, and there were indications that they could also find some common platform whereby they could cooperate more intimately. Federal ideas had penetrated their governmental circles through men who firmly believed in them. Italy had De Gasperi and Sforza, France Schuman and Bidault, Germany Adenauer, Belgium Spaak and Van Zeeland. These countries could begin by forming some supranational organisation capable of future development on a wider scale. Thus plans for the creation of Little Europe came into existence.

For several reasons, continental unity has been among the main concerns of these six Powers. Among them were Germany's rearmament, the 'cold war', the conflict in the East, and the feeling that something concrete had to be done at a moment when traditional diplomacy was crumbling under the impact of events and new answers were urgently required to old problems.

Some of these problems—such as Germany's rearmament and the question of the Saar—were of an international nature, and could be solved better within a continental frame founded on unity. The Schuman Plan was the first experiment in this direction. It dealt with one of the great questions of our age: control of coal and steel. It was generally felt that if French and German heavy industry could be pooled, and production could be placed within a single market, one of the greatest dangers of modern times could be eliminated. On May 9, 1950, France's Foreign Minister proposed the creation of a single supranational authority for the control of the entire French and German production of coal and steel. When invited to take part in it, Italy's reaction to the plan was a favourable one. Public opinion understood in fact that it meant a further step towards the Continent's unity. The Government agreed immediately in principle to the plan and dispatched a delegation to Paris. In his instructions to Mr. Taviani, the delegation's president, Foreign Minister Sforza wrote: 'We must follow a real European approach. If other countries wish to misconstrue this plan in a national sense, our approach will have to change. It is, however, essential that we do not take any initiative in this direction.'

On July 11, 1950, speaking before Parliament, Sforza stressed that Italy would benefit economically from the Schuman Plan and that any relinquishing of sovereignty in favour of a supranational authority would be rewarded by multiple benefits. 'Our answer to Schuman's appeal,' he said, 'could only be in the affirmative. Italy's entrance into the Franco-German system is unquestionably advantageous also from an international point of view. If she were to abstain, it would mean her exclusion from the European community in which she has already participated in many ways.'

Implications of the plan were again expressed by Sforza in a speech delivered on November 10, 1950, when he said: 'We always retain that same spirit which led us to be the first nation to accept the courageous project launched by Minister Schuman. We want it to succeed, because we regard it as the first sign of reconciliation between France and Germany, so necessary to European peace.'

The treaty was signed by the Foreign Ministers of the six countries on April 18, 1951. On this occasion Sforza granted a Press interview to the daily newspaper *Il Corriere della Sera*. He said: 'You know how long I have been fighting for the realisation of a united Europe. I am very happy at the results achieved with the O.E.E.C. and the Council of Strasbourg. But never, as now, have I felt that Europe is really marching on. As an Italian I may stress that our country, with the strength of a free nation which has again acquired an important place in the international community, has been a decisive factor in the conclusion of the agreement.'

Before the plan could be put into effect both Communist and industrial opposition had to be fought. Discussions before Parliament started a year after the signature, and were preceded by a statement on the part of the National Confederation of Industry, which predicted that Italy's production would definitely suffer from the formation of the coal and steel pool. Communist opposition was based on the usual propaganda theme, according to which the Schuman Plan was a new expression of American capitalism which would enslave Italian labour to foreign monopolies. During the debate De Gasperi, together with all speakers favouring the scheme, pointed out that it would be the first step towards a unified Europe. According to him the treaty would oppose the revival of German militarism and would avoid the errors made after World War I. Special emphasis was placed on the economic consequences of the agreement, which would put an end to dumping and would guarantee a freer circulation of labour. The steel industry could not suffer, while the steel-using industry was bound to benefit from it. Despite opposition, the treaty was ratified by the Senate and the Chamber of Deputies. De Gasperi's prediction has proved completely true, for all the six countries have benefited from the Schuman Plan.

It appeared as if European unity was to receive more impetus from factors which seemed to be scarcely related with it. German rearmament, for example. Under pressure of events, especially after the beginning of the Korean war, Germany's contribution to Western defence became an urgent necessity. It appeared impossible to everybody, and above all to the United States, that while westerners were making strenuous efforts to increase their defences, one of the world's greatest military powers should still be kept out of existing schemes of collective security. On the other hand, old problems had to be taken into account. First, the centuries-old antagonism between France and Germany. Here was an opportunity of placing rearmament on a collective basis and of turning it into a continental issue. France again took the initiative, probably fearing that in the absence of other programmes the United States, confronted with the necessity of defending the continent, would insist on forming independent German armed forces.

On October 24, 1950, Premier Pleven made a declaration to the French National Assembly in Paris suggesting the formation of a European Army, which would include German units. He emphasised that this army should in no way be a coalition of the old type. Common organs would be set up, while man-power and war material would come under the direction of a single military and political authority. A common Defence Minister would be appointed by governments taking part in the plan, who would have to be responsible to a European Assembly which—Pleven suggested—could either be the Council of Europe or a new assembly formed of elected delegates. Pleven implied that this project would mean a new step towards political union.

Not until the beginning of the following year (1951) did the French Government announce its decision to call a special conference in Paris wherein the project could be discussed along the lines of the Pleven resolution. Among the countries invited (all the members of NATO and the Government of Bonn), the only ones to accept were Italy, Belgium, Luxembourg, and Western Germany. The Netherlands accepted the invitation with the reservation that the status of their delegates (whether observers or participants) would be decided after a plan had been put forward.

The inauguration of the conference took place on February 15, 1951, at the Quai d'Orsay, with an opening speech by Foreign Minister Schuman. The outline of the European Army was discussed extensively by the five delegations, and after several adjournments an interim report was signed. Soon the Netherlands announced that she would participate as a full member. Negotiations lasted until May, 1952. De Gasperi represented Italy when, on May 27, the European Defence Community Treaty (E.D.C.) was finally signed.

E.D.C. should have been a supranational community governed by four supranational institutions such as a Council of Ministers, a Board of Commissioners, an Assembly, and a Court of Justice. It was anticipated from the beginning that these bodies would be the channels through which a political union might come into being.

Two tendencies had by now developed in Europe, both of which could count on strong support. One that favoured a loose co-operation among countries outside the Iron Curtain did not advocate the abandonment of national sovereignty, but only the co-ordination of common policies. The other supported instead the partial abrogation of sovereignty and the formation of a political community with jurisdiction over member States. This was the attitude generally adopted by countries taking part in the Coal and Steel Pool.

Which side should Italy take? Should she insist on integration, or was it preferable that a continental union should be something like the British Commonwealth, in which self-governing dominions are practically independent? Should her ultimate aim be the formation of a new State in which national sovereignties would gradually disappear? These questions of a doctrinal nature may appear strange to an English mind, traditionally concerned with positive problems, that would rather leave such generalities to university professors. But Italians love theoretical issues. The problem of what line should be followed became therefore the subject of many discussions in Parliament, in the Press, and among the people. The general conclusion was that one should aim towards a closer union between the six members of the Schuman Plan. This feeling naturally had repercussions on the Government's attitude.

The signing of E.D.C. was undoubtedly an important achievement. Some difficulties existed, however, because certain leading circles of France and Germany were still under the spell of nationalistic ideas. They felt that things had been carried too far and important issues had been overlooked. In fact there were more doubts expressed and more reservations made after the signing of the treaty than before. The Saar, in particular, seemed to be a crucial point of discussion, while the rebirth of German strength was an incubus for the French. E.D.C. intended to bring German units within the Western Defence System, yet when all had been concluded and only ratification was needed, some French circles began thinking that the best solution to the problem of Germany's rearmament was not to rearm her at all.

Soviet influence was of course strong, for Moscow understood that all schemes which would bring the Western world together would impair its programme. In an attempt to silence all voices calling for a united Europe, it started an offensive against E.D.C. stating that it could only lead to war.

Neutral tendencies, germanophobia, desire for revenge, and Communist propaganda, all contributed to the weakening of France's enthusiasm for E.D.C. It was easy for politicians who mistrusted the plan to convince their countrymen that it would bring in its wake dangerous commitments. They emphasised, for instance, that Germany would not want to remain split into two zones, each independently governed, nor could she allow some of her more important territories to be in either Polish or Russian hands. Sooner or later she would demand them back, thus endangering the world's peace. Their fear also was that if France identified herself with E.D.C., she would probably be inveigled into diplomatic and military engagements that would solely benefit other Powers. Such psychological obstacles also arose among Germans, who believed that E.D.C. would impair the chances of reuniting their country.

The opinion of German Socialists was that by becoming part of a supranational community they would provide Russia with a reason for delaying the Peace Treaty and of insisting indefinitely in her partition policy. Rearmament was opposed by others from an economic viewpoint. Having no military obligations to comply with, Germany's industry, concentrating on peace-time production, had achieved important results with increased exports. Should this industry be reconverted to military production? Would it be equally easy to compete so successfully in world markets?

Despite these doubts, Germany finally ratified the treaty, together with Belgium, the Netherlands, and Luxembourg. France, however, remained adamant. At first she insisted on additional protocols which would protect her interests more securely. After these were signed and negotiations completed, she still hesitated, thus losing valuable time. Finally when, in 1954, Mendès-France was appointed to the premiership, forces opposing E.D.C. became more pugnacious and were eventually successful in voting the treaty down.

Italy's Parliament had consequently no chance of approving the agreement, in spite of the fact that four of its commissions, the opinions of which were to be heard before the project could be brought before the full Assembly of the Chamber of Deputies, had declared themselves in favour of ratification. This was among the primary problems on the agenda of the Scelba Cabinet, and considering the number of members forming its majority, there is little doubt that it would have been approved.

At present the attitude of the eight parties regarding European unity remains the following: Christian Democrats definitely back it. Not only does the Catholic doctrine favour continental integration because of the Christian principle of universal brotherhood, but De Gasperi's teachings have left a permanent mark and impression on all members of the movement. The three smaller democratic parties forming the Government's coalition (Social Democrats, Liberals, and Republicans) are also strongly in favour. Their political philosophy on this issue differs in fact little from that of the Catholics.

Communists, however, have opposed all projects of integration. They fought against Marshall Aid, the Council of Europe, NATO, and the Coal and Steel Pool. Their vehemence and their filibustering tactics reached such extremes that at times they gave people cause to doubt their sanity. During the debate on the ratification of NATO all Communist members of Parliament made lengthy speeches in order to break down the Assembly's resistance. Their attitude towards E.D.C. could not have been different if a vote had been taken, as among all plans this was for them probably the least acceptable. Communists would in fact advocate the Continent's unity only if it took place under the banner of Marxist totalitarianism. To them unity between democratic countries spells danger and a collapse of their hopes of reaching power, for they realise that a supranational formation, such as Little Europe, would probably be led by Catholic-inspired parties. Besides, the security and prosperity which would most certainly follow would not fit in with their programmes, which have always thrived on misery and unrest.

The same may be said of their Socialist fellow-travellers, who also opposed E.D.C. Yet it is puzzling that these two movements should follow the same line, as world unity has always been one of the basic points of the Socialist programme. Why Socialism should have abandoned its past creed at the very moment when at least a part of it was on the point of materialising, is truly a source of wonder.

That the Italian Social Movement should oppose unity is, on the other hand, quite comprehensible. Like their predecessors,

Neo-Fascists are incapable of accepting any surrender of sovereignty, and see nothing outside the circle of national interests.

The Monarchists' attitude is less determined. As bitter anti-Communists, some of them approved of E.D.C. as a means by which to oppose the expansion of Communism; others realise that any such plan would not be favourable to their cause, as it would diminish the likelihood of the King's return.

Although France's failure to ratify has delayed the Continent's unity, the ideal is certainly still much alive. Europe is passing through a highly critical period, comparable in importance to those of the formation of the Carolingian Empire or of the rise of national States. The Continent has reached a turning point, and the next few years should prove highly eventful. Such schemes as the Coal and Steel Pool and E.D.C., even if this last one was not ratified, are not just diplomatic events similar to the many which have preceded them. They give a fresh approach to old problems and form a springboard for a supranational community, which is bound to guarantee the Continent the stability which it has hitherto lacked. This is why, before concluding this chapter, we wish to speak briefly of a highly interesting project which has been discussed by the six countries forming Little Europe, known as the European Political Community.

Economic and military schemes (Coal and Steel Pool and E.D.C.) rotated in the wrong order. They should have followed, not preceded, the setting up of political structures. Italy was the first to point out that E.D.C. would be meaningless unless based on a wider political scheme. This was stressed in an Italian memorandum and also emphasised by De Gasperi at the Rome meeting of NATO in November, 1951, when, referring to a European army, he said: 'We must keep in mind that it is impossible to create a collective instrument without a collective constitutional body to direct this army's activity.'

Doubts were expressed by some statesmen as to the advisability of starting on programmes of political integration. The Belgians and Dutch seemed especially uncertain. Others shared De Gasperi's opinion that a military agreement without a political foundation would not be vital. The latter point of view prevailed at the Paris meeting of December, 1951, when the six ministers decided in principle that the E.D.C. Assembly should study the creation of a European organisation 'of a federal or confederal nature'. This principle was embodied in Article 38 of the statute, which stated that within six months of its first meeting the Assembly would submit to the Council a proposal for a permanent assembly so devised as to become 'one of the elements of an ultimate federal or confederal structure founded on the principle of separation of powers and entailing a system of bicameral representation'.

Thus E.D.C., even before being ratified, had already prepared the groundwork of its own revision by becoming the vehicle for larger schemes. Article 38 was far from perfect, as it did not specify, for example, the powers or the legislative functions of the future Assembly. It nevertheless created much joy among people advocating the Continent's union. Under the moral impact of enthusiasm, felt in all federalistic circles, and in order to expedite events, the new scheme was also examined in May, 1952, by the Council of Europe in Strasbourg, where a motion was adopted recommending that a European Political Community should be set up.

The difficulty of building a military community without the necessary political foundation worried the six countries, and they seriously considered the possibility of putting Article 38 into effect even before ratifying E.D.C. It was thus suggested that the Coal and Steel Community should be given the task of drafting the project for a political authority. The Council of Ministers of the Coal and Steel Community approved the proposal and entrusted its Assembly with the duties of a preconstituent organism. Thus the *ad hoc* Assembly was set up in September, 1952, to frame a draft treaty of a European Political Community. On March 9, 1953, the draft constitution was solemnly handed to Bidault in his capacity of president of the Council of Ministers. The statute of 117 articles was a complete plan for a supranational authority, founded on a democratic and parliamentary basis, although, of course, the voting down of E.D.C. made even this scheme null and void.

Speaking at the Council of Europe in September, 1952, De Gasperi said:

> 'The first and most important question to be faced is the following: Which are the fields of life of our countries that, above all others, should be placed under the authority of a central political body in order to guarantee and operate a common defence? We must act in such a manner that E.D.C., which should come into force next spring, will be

founded from the very beginning on a common constitutional basis covering the fields within its competence.

'I am also of the opinion that one cannot ensure solidarity among military forces in war and peace unless there is a minimum of solidarity in the fields of economy and labour. This mutual economic interest presents a number of possibilities: a customs union for the reduction of tariffs, a confederal bank founded on a convention similar to that of several other international banks, a common currency, and the creation of a common market. Whilst studying the constitution, it will be necessary, in my opinion, to keep the following principles in mind: first of all we must limit, as far as possible, all general statements such as those already existing in our national constitutions, and we must make a distinction between structural changes compatible with our present constitutions and those for which constitutional revision will be necessary.

'We must also pool only what is indispensable to the immediate aim we have in mind and use those means that will reconcile the juridical Latin spirit to British pragmatism. A propulsive force—that is, the political desire to create unity in Europe—must be the deciding factor of our work. Economic co-operation is, of course, a compromise between autonomous, natural requirements of each participant and a mature political understanding. These ideas might be of some use to the "ad hoc" Assembly in its task, and I am sure that these proposals will represent a solid basis for the final decision of member states. You therefore see that we can already speak of final decisions as to the creating of a political authority, without being accused of following utopian dreams.'

A considerable time has elapsed since that speech was delivered and—unfortunately—what has happened during this period has been, not the signing of a treaty in which the statute of a political authority has been embodied, but the vote taken by the French National Assembly.

Although delayed by this last event, the project of a Political Community is still alive, because our Continent is beginning to realise that unity is the only way to preserve liberty.

Italy should be proud of having been one of the pioneers of this cause; proud also that the enthusiasm of her people and the statesmanship of her leaders have contributed to the forming of an approach which is bound to result in permanent structures.

Europe still has a message to deliver which is the heritage of her civilisation and culture. In the ideological conflict of our times she retains her moral standards undamaged. These characters can be saved only through unity, and to reach this goal Italy is eager to give her full support.

Chapter 11

Church and State (1870–1948)

ITALY'S history during the last hundred years has been a very colourful one. Seldom has a country been confronted with so many obstacles. Foreign hostility and domestic incomprehension, added to lack of experience in industrial and economic affairs, plus ignorance and bigotry, were among the chief difficulties she had to deal with and master in her struggle for independence. Still, the main obstacle on her path had been that Rome was the centre of Catholicism and of the Pope's temporal domains. Clashes between Church and State were therefore destined to become sharper when the forces which for decades had advocated unity became the nation's ruling class. Had it not been for the presence of the Roman Pontiff on Italian soil, Catholicism might have helped in the battle for independence, exactly as it had done in other countries.

Relations between Church and State were also difficult because each side believed itself entitled to play a leading role in the nation's affairs. The Church, for instance, claimed that she could talk with laudable pride of eighteen centuries of history, during which time she had preserved much of that Roman tradition which the State had placed at the foundation of its existence. Had it not been the Church that had resisted German invasion, during the last centuries of the Roman Empire? Had not the barbarians invading the west found in the Church the spiritual power that had brought about their conversion? Had it not been Pope Leo I who had induced Attila, leader of the Huns, to withdraw from Italian soil? Had not the spread of Christianity also meant the expansion of Roman ideas? After the turn of the millennium had not the Church contained the power of the Empire, enabling the Communes to obtain unprecedented conditions of liberty and prosperity? Humanism and the Renaissance, which had revived Latin culture, Roman traditions, and the Italian love of beauty, had they not been nurtured by the Church? Had not Pope Julius II headed a coalition of Italian princes for the purpose of ending foreign domination? In fact the Church's claim to having kept alive the tradition on which the Italian State was founded was not unwarranted.

The State was equally firm in defending the part it had played in upholding the nation's continuity. It maintained that at all times a long succession of statesmen and philosophers had stressed the relations between the Italian nation and the lasting structures of the Empire. This trend of thought accused the Church of ignoring the State. Machiavelli had written: 'The Church has been the sole reason why Italy has never been able to unite under one leader, but has remained under many princes and lords. From this so much weakness has derived that she is the prey of the first person who attacks her.' Guicciardini, the historian and diplomat of Machiavelli's times, had stated that before his death he hoped to see Italy free from all barbarians and 'wicked priests'.

During the first years of the nineteenth century, however, there had been a certain co-operation between Catholicism and the renascent ideal of an Italian State. None of the patriots who was sent to the scaffold after the revolutions of 1821 and 1831 had ever been an atheist or a heretic. But Catholic acceptance of the movement for independence could last only so long as the issue remained uncertain and on an irrational level. This approach was bound to change as soon as progress towards unity took on a more practical form, endangering the Church's temporal power. How could the Church possibly accept a movement which advocated violence in an area that was so near to St. Peter's See? Gioberti's idea of bringing it under Catholic control was a noble and popular one, but it did not have much success and completely faded away when war broke out in 1848 between Austria and Piedmont. How could the Pope side with the Italians against the Austrians? Here were two nations fighting against each other on temporal issues which did not directly concern the Church. What did interest her, however, was that the subjects of the Apostolic Emperor of Austria should remain within orthodoxy and that a minor conflict should not be used as a pretext to break Catholic unity. In 1849, when revolution broke out in Rome, the already existing gap widened even more.

All possibilities of co-operation between the Church and the Risorgimento were by now out of the question. The Roman Republic, for instance, although inspired by Mazzini, a man of sound religious sentiments, had been a period of violence and had aimed at the destruction of the Church's temporal power.

Was this power really indispensable? Opinions were divided. Some of the clergy believed that its disappearance would free the Church of a great burden and enable her to dedicate herself entirely to spiritual matters. The majority maintained, on the contrary, that only a temporal domain could guarantee complete independence to the Papal See.

Something more than politics caused the Church's opposition to the Risorgimento. Unity and independence of the peninsula were being fostered by a newly formed class, the *bourgeoisie*. This class, enriching itself by commerce and industry, was influenced by practical and materialistic ideas. Its philosophy was that happiness is attainable and that the purpose of life is to attain it. Principles of this kind were opposed to the traditional doctrine of the Church The approach of the middle class was an optimistic one, and Liberalism was the political expression of its social and economic doctrines. It claimed that individuals should have a government of their own choice and act freely, provided they accepted equal rights of others to freedom. With a liberal State the Church was bound to lose much of her importance and to become just one of the many organisations that were influencing the minds and hearts of the people.

Before the Industrial Revolution began the Church had only had to compete with the State. Sometimes she had been successful, sometimes not. She had, in fact, been challenged most dangerously by the Empire during the investiture contest. But the fight against the *bourgeoisie* was something entirely different. Here she had to deal with a class of people who believed that making and investing money were commendable things. The *bourgeoisie* based its activity on the physiocratic principle '*Laissez faire, laissez passer!*' But what had to freely pass? Did the principle only concern goods, labour, or even heretic and unorthodox theories on religion?

Italy's Risorgimento was founded on liberal principles. Although it had started as a movement of a few idealists, it had soon been sponsored by the middle class, to which the Savoy monarchy had given its support. The Church could not back such a movement, as it would have called for radical changes in the very heart of her tradition and refused to contemplate any agreement with the State of Piedmont. When Cavour, for instance, tried to reach a conciliation based on the famous principle: 'A free Church in a free State', he was unsuccessful. It would have simplified things too much, because it prevented the Church from intervening in certain matters which she believed to belong to her domain. That is the reason why she soon condemned the theory of complete separation between religious and civil powers as contrary to her doctrine.

After Cavour's death laicism and anti-clericalism over-ran the country, greatly influencing its life and mode of thought. In its endeavours to create a modern and progressive structure, the State aimed at crushing all opposing forces, among which the Church came first. Intolerance became more open. Catholic schools and seminaries were forcibly closed, convents and properties belonging to religious communities were confiscated, bishops were compelled to abandon their dioceses, and parish priests were obliged to officiate in civic events.

Annexation of the Papal States ended in 1870 with the occupation of Rome, an event which caused deep consternation in papal circles, as if the Reformation had reached the banks of the Tiber. This, indeed, was an exaggeration, for no Italian statesman had any intention of reforming the Church or of interfering in her affairs. If this had been their purpose they could have chosen no better moment. The recent approval of the dogma of papal infallibility on the part of the Vatican Council had not been unanimous. In Germany and Switzerland, for instance, it had been the cause of much controversy and had given rise to the movement of the so-called 'old Catholics'. In Italy also some bishops had opposed it. Had the State wished to start a heresy so as to separate the Italian Church from the Papacy, this was the time to act. But nothing of the kind was ever thought of.

Although the State's victory had been political, it was sorely felt by the Church, whose diplomacy had been heavily defeated. The fact that in 1870 not one Catholic Power had lifted a finger to assist him was considered by Pius IX a serious insult to his prerogatives, perhaps even more serious than the imprisonment of his predecessor, Pius VI, by the French. He retired into voluntary exile in the Vatican Palaces, an act which created a wave of filial emotion among Catholics all over the world.

The situation in no way changed when, a few months later, Parliament approved the Law of the Guarantees, by which the Papacy was allowed vast immunities and full liberty in carrying out its missions. The Church refused to accept this law or the compensations which accompanied it, such as a yearly allowance. Acceptance would have meant compliance with everything to which the Holy See had been so violently opposed during the preceding years.

Yet, had the Church really suffered from these events? That the annexation of her domains had been an act of aggression, carried out without respect for international obligations, was undoubtedly true. But even taking this into consideration, how could the Church stop the trend towards national unity? How could the Pope, who was also Bishop of Rome and Primate of Italy, obstruct or delay the aspirations of people who depended on him for spiritual guidance? Besides, it was untrue that he had previously enjoyed complete political independence. The dual position of being head of the Church and sovereign of a State had often proved more a liability than an asset. Defence of temporal rights had obliged him to yield in important religious fields. As head of the greatest religion on earth, he had an outstanding position, but as chief of a State he had very little power and was constantly at the mercy of other countries. It has been said that during the Conference of Yalta in 1945, when reference was made to the views of the Pope, Stalin sarcastically inquired how many were the Pope's divisions. The samc sort of appraisal was made ninety years ago in international affairs. When the Papacy disposed of temporal domains, it was considered not for the high moral values it represented, but for the size of its army and the number of divisions it could put in the field. And this was nil. With the loss of her domains the Church could devote herself entirely to the spiritual welfare of the faithful.

Pius IX remained in voluntary exile in the Vatican up to his death in 1878, when he was succeeded by Leo XIII. The Church counted on some international crisis that might break up the Italian nation and thus restore her to her previous position. So little reliance, in fact, was placed on the new State, that the Church ordered her faithful to abstain from taking any part in public affairs, especially in elections. This policy, generally known as the *Non expedit*, from the name of the encyclical in which it was embodied, left the State almost entirely in the hands of the Liberals.

The year 1876 saw the fall of the moderate right and the rise to power of the more extreme left. Thus the policy inspired by

Cavour came to an end, because the new men were far more inclined to favour extreme ideological issues, especially anti-clericalism. Several among them were not prepared to bring about a conciliation between Church and State, even if it had been possible.

Only a few years had elapsed since the day Italian troops had entered Rome; resentment and the desire for revenge were still high on both sides. Life during this period became extremely difficult for Catholics. Their ideals were persecuted and their activities limited, while political circles and clubs were rapidly increasing in number with the sole purpose of spreading doctrines which opposed the Church.

Yet, in spite of this general animosity, it was felt that some change would take place sooner or later. There had been no public disturbances or official interference when Pope Leo XIII had been elected. The Pontiff was a man of extreme tact and great intelligence, and the first years of his pontificate brought about a succession of diplomatic victories for the Vatican. He succeeded, in fact, in re-establishing relations with several Powers and in putting an end to the conflict between the Church and the German State generally known as the *Kulturkampf*. A fruitful policy was also carried out towards France, where the Catholic party was strong but tied to the ideal of a royalist restoration. Here the Pope maintained that the clergy should follow a more moderate line towards the new republican regime.

What was Italy's position? Was Catholicism to continue along the same uncompromising line taken by Pius IX, with the Pope considering himself in a state of captivity, or could some solution be reached? The Church, well experienced in this sort of trouble, knows that, no matter how critical a situation may appear, it is always bound to find a way out in the end. Much more difficult, and sometimes impossible, is the solution of theological and dogmatic differences. Politics, however, being linked to human interests, may easily change. Above all, passions need to be decanted. Unfortunately, passions were still too violent and events too recent for a reconciliation to take place.

Italian political leaders as has already been stated represented the liberal middle class. But were they qualified to lead in a country where industry was expanding and social ideas were finding their way into the minds of the people? Parliament was elected by an insignificant minority of the electorate. What would happen if political suffrage were granted to all citizens? If numbers were to be the only determining factor of future politics, then Liberalism and the middle class which it represented would crumble under the increasing number of people who were becoming aware of their rights.

From 1870 on history has shown that Italy's lower class has slowly raised itself from misery to a higher standard of living. What attitude could the Church adopt in face of this progress? The answer was not difficult to find. In fact she intended favouring the working class and the victims of industrial revolution because by doing so she would be acting in complete accordance with her principles.

The birth of capitalism did not come as a surprise. The Church had prophesied it since the Reformation, when not only had she seen her supremacy wane, but had also witnessed the beginning of an economic world which did not fit in with her schemes, either spiritually or materially. According to her views, capitalism lacked all Christian approach, because it was the philosophy of the few who had achieved success and had come out victorious in the gigantic but pitiless battle for 'the survival of the fittest'. The Church instinctively sided with the worker. As far as she was concerned, liberalism could disappear and the middle class could once again be absorbed in the mighty vortex of the proletariat, from which it had emerged. If the workers wanted to organise into a common front, the Church was ready to offer them all the means in her power to do so. For her the social question was chiefly a moral one, and there was no need for warfare among classes when co-operation was possible. Only strong faith and the knowledge that 'everything comes from our Saviour' were necessary. Once this principle had been accepted by the working man, social struggles could be faced more confidently and would certainly be successful. This attitude was so effective that people began to talk of 'Catholic Socialism'.

The Catholic social movement spread immediately all over Europe. In Italy it was led by Giuseppe Toniolo (1845–1918), a professor of economics in the University of Pisa. His programme of reforms was considered revolutionary. Together with the works of other Italian and foreign sociologists, it formed the background to Leo XIII's famous encyclical *Rerum Novarum*, published in 1891, the most advanced part of which dealt with the forming of Catholic trade unions.

The birth of these unions was destined to impress Italy's public opinion, because in no other European country was there such strong contrast between Church and State. As these unions, together with other Catholic organisations, were quickly gaining political influence, the Liberal Government could not remain indifferent to what it believed to be the Church's revenge on those who had deprived her of temporal power. She had found —the Liberals thought—a virgin soil (the proletariat) to exploit and was bound to take advantage of it by advocating such reforms as factory laws for children, old-age pensions, minimum wages, and an eight-hour day. While the Government had never tried interfering in dogmatic questions, it was now anxious to curb the developing Catholic influence on politics. In 1888, for instance, the mayor of Rome was dismissed from his post simply because he paid a courtesy visit to the cardinal who administered the diocese of Rome. Aid was given to Freemasonry, which in Italy, as in France, was violently anti-clerical. This support seemed to reach its peak in 1889 when, under Government patronage, a monument was unveiled in Rome in honour of Giordano Bruno, the sixteenth-century philosopher, who was burned at the stake as a heretic.

Yet these and other Government actions did not seem sufficient to arrest the growing strength of the Church. At the 15th Catholic Congress, held in Milan in 1897, the number of organisations represented was unprecedented. There were at that time in Italy 921 labour societies (trade unions), 705 rural co-operatives, and twenty-four Catholic banks.

Serious social unrest troubled Sicily in 1893. It was caused by the economic condition of the working class, which had been neglected by the Government. All power on the island was in the hands of a few landowners, whose ideas, supposedly liberal, were as old as their ancient land. The clergy were not inactive during these grave agitations and often sided with the revolutionaries, while the Catholic Press held that only misery, hunger and distress were responsible for the revolt. Sicilian events enhanced the general feeling that the Church was gaining power and that she was quite different from the religious body which had been defeated by the State a few years before. She was now capable of influencing the masses, as she had rarely been in a position to do before. Sooner or later the State might want to reach an understanding. This hope must have inspired Francesco Crispi in 1894, when he made the following unexpected statement: 'More than ever we feel that civil and religious authorities should agree, so as to bring the ill-advised multitudes back to the road of justice and love.' The suggestion was certainly an interesting one and destined to have success in the future. Yet at that time it was premature and was rejected by the Church. In 1895, in fact, the Pope reminded Catholics of their duty to abstain from taking part in general elections, recalling the *Non expedit* of a few years earlier.

In 1898 revolution broke out in Milan. The reason for the trouble was again economic, and the Church was once more on the side of the poor. A Catholic paper wrote: 'There is shortage of bread. Its lack is not felt by those who eat and drink in peace and need quiet to digest. . . . These people are satisfied with their villas and horses and look with contempt on the crowds of destitutes who beg for work and bread.' Liberal reaction was directed against Socialists and Catholics alike. Several religious associations were dissolved and some of their leaders arrested.

In spite of persecution, the conflict between Church and State was destined to end, and acts of intolerance such as those which followed the revolt of Milan were among the last.

The year 1900 was a memorable one. A new Holy Year was proclaimed and celebrated with great solemnity. At the inauguration the bells of Rome pealed loudly, as if announcing the beginning of a new era in which States, social classes, and citizens alike could look forward to better relations, with more justice and understanding. The atmosphere was one of optimism. If the eighteenth century had been one of enlightenment, and the nineteenth one of national independence, why should not the twentieth lead to new achievements in terms of prosperity? If this was to be, the Church had certainly kept up with the times. A quite modern approach was penetrating her institutions and inspiring her religious, social, and economic programmes.

A different spirit was pervading relations with the State. Thirty years had passed and a new generation of younger men, who had known only a united Italy, now ruled the Church. To many of these men the Pope's temporal power had more a historic value than a political meaning. Statesmen and politicians, although claiming to be Liberal in the traditional meaning of the word, which is together political and economic, no longer harboured the same anti-clerical animosity as their predecessors. People were beginning to realise that too much emphasis had been placed on abstract problems and too little on the solution of concrete questions, the most important of which was that Italy could not indefinitely be divided between religious and civic powers. Both Catholic and Liberal circles were feeling the impact of this new trend.

A priest—Romolo Murri—had founded a newspaper in which he stressed the necessity of an agreement. He believed Catholics should take part in politics and form their own party. To attain this aim he also set up an organised movement. In the fourth chapter of this book, which deals with political parties between 1890 and 1915, we discuss Murri's movement, and how it met with the opposition of the ecclesiastical hierarchy and was finally condemned by Pope Pius X.

The death of Leo XIII in 1903 and the succession of Pius X brought a new approach to political problems, that was destined to favour the rising of Catholics and their progressive participation in public life. That such a change could take place immediately, as advocated by Murri and his followers, was doubtful. Continuity has always been the foundation of the Church. No pope immediately after his succession to the papal throne will ever take a decision which is in conflict with the policies of his predecessor. For this reason Pius X, although thirty years younger than Leo XIII and less influenced by the memories of temporal power, protested to the Italian Government, as his predecessor had done, against the occupation of the Papal States. Leo XIII had never allowed Catholics, at least officially, to run for Parliament or even to vote. Anyone who thought that this ban would be raised through an open rejection of the past was doomed to disappointment. The *Non expedit* was cancelled in 1904 in a indirect way when a group of Catholic leaders who had asked if they were to abstain in the coming election were simply told to act 'according to conscience'.

From the beginning of the century until 1914 politics were dominated by Giovanni Giolitti, who believed in a line of compromise and progressive understanding with the new popular forces. Under him Catholics were to increase their influence and start a process of integration in the State. The Gentiloni Pact of 1913 was the outcome of this approach. This official agreement between Catholics and Liberals favoured the running of common candidates. It was especially advantageous to the first, who enjoyed the favour of the new electorate. Although the Church had not signed the agreement, she certainly approved it. Catholics had in fact demanded that Liberal candidates elected through their support should respect certain conditions (prohibition of divorce and freedom of teaching for Catholic schools among them) that were undoubtedly inspired by the Church.

There was also a strong religious revival among Italians. The power of Laicism, as a doctrine, was gradually decreasing, even if it could always count on strong and uncompromising supporters. There were, of course, anti-clerical outbursts in certain papers and parties, but they could hardly be compared with the intolerance and verbal onslaughts of previous decades.

During those years the Church fought a spiritual battle against modernism, a doctrine which was eventually condemned. The State might have been tempted to intervene in the crisis by siding with those who were trying to innovate religion, often without any respect for orthodoxy. Giolitti was, however, a far-sighted man, and realised that if Catholics were to enter public life the State must in no way interfere in their religious affairs. Under his influence the Church was neither ignored nor intentionally slighted. By granting universal suffrage, he greatly increased the number of electors, among whom Catholics were most numerous. What was the situation destined to be if they decided to set up their own party and to convey in one direction—strictly in accordance with their principles—the social, economic, and political strength upon which they could count?

Pius X was succeeded in 1914 by Benedict XV. For the third time since the occupation of Rome a conclave was held in Italy's capital, and this time it was during a major war. Everything took place with calm and order. It was again proved beyond doubt that the Church was as free as she had ever been and that the Government had not interfered in any way. The new Pope was confronted with a war-torn world. Catholics were to be found on all sides and therefore he could not openly favour any of the contestants. The Church, however, could not ignore the fact that Austria and Hungary were probably the most faithful among Catholic Powers, while Germany, although a Protestant nation, had a large Catholic population. The Entente, on the other hand, included Great Britain, Serbia, and Russia, notoriously non-Catholic Powers, and France, ruled by anti-clerical governments. If the Church was neutral, Italian Catholics who lived and operated so near to her could not be favourable to the war. Besides, Giolitti, a convinced neutralist, believed that no material or moral advantage was worth the lives and suffering of his countrymen. Had he been in power in 1914, the nation's history would certainly have taken a different course.

Italy's intervention in World War I, although opposed by all major parties, was imposed upon the country by a minority who succeeded in stirring the people's emotions. This was formed by the King, the Government, and the nationalist party, a new and noisy incarnation of the upper middle class. The King's lukewarm religious sentiments were well known. Was the participation in the war an attempt on the part of the country's anticlerical forces to regain the control they had been losing in recent years through the advance of popular classes and the closer relations between Church and State? Was it meaningless that the King and his Government, when accepting the Pact of London, by which they committed the nation to enter the war, had stipulated that the Holy See should be kept out of future peace negotiations?

The months between August, 1914, and May, 1915, were the period of Italy's neutrality. By now it was clear that the conflict would be a long one, and that to enter it would cost the country more than it could afford both in man-power and finance. In the encyclical *Ad Beatitudinem* the Pope declared that the war was being fought under the influence of principles to which the Church had always been opposed. No Italian Catholic could, then, understand how any of the war issues could appeal to his conscience.

But things changed in 1915, after Italy declared war. Patriotism outweighed all other matters, and even the firmest believers felt that their country's interests held first priority. Chaplains were assigned to fighting units and the whole country underwent a revival of religious sentiment. By succouring the wounded, by giving spiritual support to the fighting men and courage to their families at home, the clergy was serving the country and contributing to victory. Some priests also became active propagandists of the war and helped in raising the people's morale. When Premier Boselli formed his war Cabinet of national unity he invited Filippo Meda, a Catholic deputy, to join it. Meda accepted the post of Minister of Finance, showing that in time of danger the country could count on Catholic loyalty and co-operation. This loyalty was also proved by the increasing number of Catholics who were sacrificing their lives for their country.

In spite of the tragedy and sorrow caused by World War I, its conclusion in 1918 led to one great event: the end of the conflict between Church and State. The way was paved for the formation of the Partito Popolare (Popular Party), which represented and defended the rights, interests, and programmes of that part of the population to whom religion was the basic issue of life. Founded in 1919, it was destined to become one of Italy's leading forces. Pope Benedict XV favoured it, although he stressed that it should in no way be regarded as the Vatican's mouthpiece.

The setting up of the movement was chiefly due to Luigi Sturzo (b. 1871). A great statesman and a Sicilian by birth, he belonged to one of those middle-class families which consider priesthood a sign of prestige and dignity. His Sicilian environment afforded him the opportunity of studying the political and social questions in which he was most interested. Italy and France offer several such examples of priests who play a leading part in politics. For several years, as Deputy Mayor of Caltagirone, his native town, Sturzo had shown ability in dealing with public affairs.

The party soon became the only movement in which Catholics had faith and for which they voted, and this explains its immediate electoral success. In the 1919 elections, after only a few months' existence, it won 100 seats in Parliament, increasing them to 108 in the elections of 1921. The party's programme appealed, in fact, to several strata of the population, for it advocated agrarian reform and the partition of large estates among landless peasants. Other points were fiscal reform, social insurance, and the moral and economic defence of the family group.

It was a major disaster for Italy that Fascism prevented the Popular Party from putting its policies into effect. From the beginning Catholics made the mistake of under-estimating the fact that Fascism was led by a man of considerable talent who knew how to deal with men and how to employ his unscrupulous cynicism. They insisted on regarding Fascism as an adventure which would not last. When they eventually realised their mistake it was too late. The existence of the Popular Party came to an abrupt end under Fascist aggression. Its short life, however, had been sufficient to prove how important a Catholic movement could be, and that, under normal conditions, it could easily attain power.

Was Mussolini a religious man? No dictator of his kind can be a believer. His first experiences had been inspired by anti-clericalism and atheism. He had belonged to the most advanced faction of the Socialist Party, for which no compromise with religion was possible. When, in 1919, he founded Fascism (the same year in which the Popular Party came into being), he still remained a man with an anti-clerical past who did not refuse to run for Parliament on the same list as Guido Podrecca, the editor of the most anti-clerical journal ever printed in Italy. Mussolini was, however, far too shrewd a politician not to realise how invaluable the Church's support would be and that the clergy's favour would be a deciding factor for victory. At a certain period, therefore, Fascism adopted a more friendly attitude towards Catholicism and it became a party rule that religion was never to be attacked. When the march on Rome took place in 1922, although Fascists did not spare their adversaries any violence, priests were respected and protected.

After gaining power, Mussolini decided to attempt a formal reconciliation with the Church. This he intended doing not for the purpose of giving Italy the religious peace she had lost in 1870, but of keeping Catholics closely linked to his regime. In the beginning the Church's attitude towards Fascism was one of suspicion and doubt. What especially worried her were its nationalistic tendencies. Nationalism, she believed, was the development of the theories she had constantly opposed, which intended making of religion an instrument of the State. She was against Fascism also because she had seen so much of her economic and social work destroyed by it. Not only the Popular Party but also the entire network of Catholic co-operatives, banks, and trade unions had in fact been dissolved. Besides, it was not sufficient to respect parish priests or leave processions undisturbed. It was the general philosophy of Fascism which the Church could not accept.

Nevertheless, other factors were capable of bringing her closer to the State. The accusation that the Fascist Government was not a legal one did not concern her. Experience had taught her that the foundation of power is often an act of revolt and that legality is at times the respect of certain rules originally enforced through the rebellion against a pre-existent system. When Christ said: 'Render unto Caesar the things that are Caesar's', he did not query if Caesar's power was legal or not. For instance, an Italian Jesuit, Father Taparelli D'Azeglio, has been quoted as saying that the sceptre of a monarch must be respected, even if it has been picked out of the gutter. Was this not an acknowledgment that the Government must be obeyed and that all the Church can do is to inspire its actions? But Fascism also meant the end of the laical mentality, which the Church had fought against for so long. Anti-clericalism was officially ended.

This was the background which led to the conciliation. The State wanted the support of religion, and the Church wished to destroy all vestiges of an unhappy past. The first approaches were made immediately after the march on Rome. They were facilitated by the new Pope, Pius XI (1922–39), a practical man who throughout his ecclesiastical career had always advocated realistic solutions. The foundation of an agreement was ably prepared by Mussolini. He began by enforcing certain provisions that were bound to impress the Vatican favourably. The Crucifix, which Liberal Governments had banned from schools and hospitals, quickly reappeared and religion was again taught in the schools. The salary of the clergy paid by the State was raised. How could the Church ignore these advances? After several decades of open conflict, it was time for a settlement. This was at last reached on February 11, 1929. Church and State put an end to their feud through a treaty and a concordat, generally known as the Lateran Pacts. Their meaning and provisions are examined in another chapter of this book.

Soon they were ratified by Parliament, both branches of which were subordinate to Fascism but in a different degree. In the Chamber of Deputies there was no opposition and the vote was unanimous. Matters went differently in the Senate, the members of which, having been appointed by the King at various epochs, still included a few anti-Fascists. Six of them had the courage to vote openly against the Pacts, and one of them in particular, Benedetto Croce, the philosopher, delivered a speech in which he explained the reasons for his vote. He said that he was not against the conciliation in principle, but that he was opposed to the manner in which it had been prepared. If Croce had been speaking in a free parliament, not dominated by fear, the Lateran Pacts would probably also have received his approval, but under the existing conditions, to vote against them was equivalent to confirming one's attachment to liberty.

Although the agreements were enforced immediately, the friendly atmosphere of understanding was not destined to last. For a dictator the Pope is in fact not the head of an independent body, but the head chaplain of the State. Co-existence is, therefore, always difficult. Barely three months elapsed after the signing of the Lateran Pacts before Mussolini delivered a speech in which he stated that Catholicism had become the most powerful religion on earth only because it had been transplanted in the structure of the Roman Empire. This opinion could hardly be considered that of a believer, as it reflected doctrines constantly opposed by the Church. His approach was very similar when he spoke of politics. The following are some of his phrases: 'We have not resuscitated the temporal power of the Popes. We have buried it.' (An extremely undiplomatic statement at a moment when the Holy See was probably considering the sacrifices it had made in order to reach an agreement.) 'Education belongs to us. Our children must be raised in our religious Faith, but we must integrate their education. We must give youth the sense of virility, of power, of conquest.' And again: 'Fascism is vigilant and nothing escapes its control. Nobody must think that even the most insignificant paper edited by the smallest parish will escape the eye of Mussolini.' (An odd way of reassuring the Church as to the kind of liberty she was destined to enjoy.) A few days later Pope Pius XI delivered in his turn a speech condemning war and imperialism, and sent a letter to Cardinal Gasparri stressing the Church's opinions as to the primacy she is entitled to in several fields.

These were the first indications that Mussolini had in reality no intention of remaining on good terms with the Church. His controlled Press began to attack the Catholic Action—an organisation of Catholic laity—accusing it of competing with Fascist trade unions and of offering refuge to former leaders of the Popular Party. The campaign was accompanied by violence. It is difficult to understand the reasons for these tactics. Mussolini's mood was that of a man who would never admit he was wrong. In fighting the Catholic Action, he probably wanted to penetrate certain recesses of the people's conscience which he knew had remained untouched by his propaganda. Catholic reaction was expressed in an encyclical published in 1931. The strife ended in a compromise by which the Church promised to issue a new statute for the Catholic Action and to keep its activity on a strictly non-political basis. The State in turn promised to put an end to all persecution. From then on the two powers, although formally at peace, kept aloof from each other. Contacts could hardly be described as friendly. No fervent Catholic ever really advanced in the Fascist hierarchy. The same may be said regarding Fascists in the Catholic Action. Catholics were preparing themselves for the political inheritance which they were bound to take over after the fall of Fascism. In the latent struggle between the two forces the Church was the stronger and better prepared. She had in fact the tradition, the experience, and, above all, men capable of carrying on the task.

Anti-Fascists have often accused the clergy of having backed Fascist wars in Ethiopia and Spain, as if, by giving moral support to fighting troops, she had been sharing the responsibilities of war. If this theory were true, one might say that the Church was responsible for the conquest of India because some Irish units, fighting under the British flag, had Catholic chaplains. Certain features of the Ethiopian and Spanish campaigns interested the Church. Ethiopia was already a Christian nation where she could expand her influence, as she had already done in French North Africa. In Spain a Communist victory would have been the death-knell of Catholicism in one of its strongholds. Looking at the situation from this point of view, it is quite comprehensible that the Church should favour Franco's victory.

But when the racial campaign began, the Church was adamant in her approach. Nothing could be more opposed to her doctrine than the idea of superior and inferior races. It is said that when Pius XI died in 1939 he was preparing a speech condemning racial discrimination. Had it been delivered, it would certainly have provoked a major conflict with the State. This was probably why Fascists, aware that something of the sort was afoot, and with the usual lack of tact and diplomacy, again attacked Catholic organisations, together with anyone who showed too much friendliness towards the Church. During 1939, in Rome and other Italian cities, it was dangerous to read the *Osservatore Romano*, the official Vatican daily paper, which was openly opposing some of Fascism's more absurd policies. Fascist squads were on guard near news-stands, and beat unmercifully anyone who tried to buy the paper. One may well visualise what would have happened if the Church had intensified her hostile attitude.

Subsequent events prevented an open conflict from breaking out. The nation was soon plunged in a war for which she felt no enthusiasm. Fascists had no time to open hostilities against the Church. In fact the agonising years of World War II were those of religious revival. Suffering and pain have always brought man nearer to God. When Pius XII, during the bombing of Rome on August 13, 1943, toured the area where the greatest devastation had taken place and blessed the wounded and the dead, he was responsible for rallying a great many people to the Church.

The end of the war marked the beginning of real progress in the political movement which draws its inspiration and programme from the Church. Christian Democracy, the heir to the Popular Party, has since 1945 been at the centre of Italy's public life. Its men have constantly led all Cabinets and held key positions in them. Policies inspired by the Catholic doctrine have been enforced. The Church to-day holds such a position of prestige that it seems impossible that only a few years ago relations with the State could have been so tense.

In 1947 the Constituent Assembly introduced into the constitution the following article: 'The State and the Catholic Church are, each within its own orbit, independent and sovereign. Their relations are regulated by the Lateran Pacts. Such amendments to these Pacts as are accepted by both parties do not require any procedure of Constitutional revision.' Another victory had been scored by the Church which wanted these agreements not only confirmed but also embodied in the constitutional charter. It was no coincidence that the Communist deputies approved that article. It was the acknowledgment of the Church's power and of the fact that in Italy nobody can oppose Catholicism beyond a certain point if he desires to retain the people's favour.

Time has brought about many things. The electoral victory of 1948, by giving Christian Democracy an absolute majority in the Chamber of Deputies, has enabled the Catholic social programme to be enforced in many fields. This programme is founded on liberty and on respect for individual rights. Catholics are to-day the defenders of democratic and parliamentary methods and are consequently concerned with the solution of Italy's material and moral problems. In the middle of the nineteenth century Niccolò Tommaseo wrote that 'there can be no liberty without Christ'. This statement seemed out of place at a time when the Church was opposing Italian unity. To-day it is a reality. The country's future is linked not only to the people's intuition and intelligence, but also to the Church's venerable wisdom, her moral guidance, and her determination not to cede her spiritual domains to the encroachments of totalitarian slavery.

Chapter 12

Italy's Economy

ITALY'S economy was always influenced by the shape and geographical position of the peninsula, which spreads into the Mediterranean, is surrounded by the sea and the Alps, and crossed by the Apennines. While the sea is beneficial in keeping the climate temperate, the mountains are, in a certain sense, the cause of the people's low standard of living. When looking on a map at the long line of the Apennines, one often wonders how different this country's economy might be if they were replaced by plains—less interesting, perhaps, from the panoramic standpoint, but certainly more advantageous to general prosperity.

With the exception of the Po Valley and a few other plains of limited extent, the larger part of the country is mountainous and difficult to cultivate. Some soil on which peasants succeed through hard work in making a living, though a poor one, would not be worth tilling were it not for the existence of a surplus population and the scarcity of good land.

The variations of climate are yet another hindrance to agriculture. Though Italy is small, it would be difficult to find another country with such varying weather conditions. The climate of the Alpine districts is similar in many respects to that of Central Europe, but in the South and in Sicily it is thoroughly Mediterranean and characterised by a scarcity of rain.

Despite these drawbacks, the nation's agricultural production has increased during the last half-century because of extensive land reclamation and the use of fertilisers and better equipment. At present the agrarian reform is resulting in the reclamation of more land, but there are certain natural limitations which cannot be overcome and which restrict the possibilities of expansion.

The variety of farm products is great, ranging from wheat to hemp, from rice to fruit trees, from the vine to the olive. Wheat is the principal product and is the basic food in the people's diet, the chief constituents of which are carbohydrates. The wheat area is generally believed to cover a third of the arable land. The 1953 crop reached 90 million quintals, the highest record ever registered. Governments have all tried to increase the output of wheat through greater productivity and better working methods, but results achieved so far, though outstanding, have not made the country self-supporting. The yearly deficit is made up by purchases on the international market.

Among other cereals we must mention maize and rice, the production of which in 1953 was 32,073,000 and 9,262,000 quintals, respectively. Rice, of which Italy is one of the greatest world exporters, is chiefly cultivated in certain marshy areas of the North.

The olive, which grows especially in the South, enables the farmer to make use of certain hilly and stony lands that would otherwise be useless. Olive oil is one of the basic elements of the diet of southerners.

Wine production is high, although consumption is not as large as in other countries. Wines are generally produced on farms, and there is little tendency to standardise the product. Because of the many existing qualities, Italian wines are not well known abroad, with the notable exceptions of chianti, barolo, vermouth, and marsala. If a greater effort were made on the part of farmers to co-ordinate production, Italian wine would be much better known and command a larger market.

Fruit and vegetables are exported abroad in large quantities. Especially important are limes, lemons, oranges, and tangerines, which are grown in the South and in Sicily, where weather conditions are favourable. Among other cultivations one should mention hemp and the mulberry tree, the leaf of which is necessary for raising the silkworm. Even forests, although deforestation has been carried on very intensively during the last decades, have a certain importance for the country's economy.

The dairy industry is developed in the North, where dairy cattle and pigs are produced in large numbers. The predominant livestock of the South, on the contrary, consists of sheep and goats. Seventy-five per cent of Italian cheeses, a number of which are exported, are produced in the North. Domestic consumption of dairy products is generally low.

The fishing industry provides employment to over 150,000 people, but it could certainly increase in importance if it were supplied with more modern equipment, and if domestic consumption were greater.

Even Italy's industry has been dominated by natural factors and by the recent achievement of national unity. When other European countries had already built their economy and could think of conquering foreign markets, Italy was still struggling for independence.

Besides, the country lacks two basic raw materials the possession of which started industrial expansion—namely, coal and iron. It also lacks cheap and easy communications, especially the fluvial ones which enable other countries—Germany, for instance—to reduce the cost of transport. Before they were tunnelled through, even the Alps were a great obstacle to the exchange of goods with Central Europe.

Despite these natural difficulties and its recent birth, industry has developed satisfactorily. While in 1870 it employed only 400,000 people, the equivalent of 1·5 per cent of the whole population, in 1952 it gave work to over 4 millions, equivalent to 9 per cent. In 1870 industry was using only domestic raw materials, a fact which hampered its possibilities of expansion and of export. Later development was made possible by increased imports of foreign materials. New factories were built, fresh activities started, and existing enterprises were enlarged. An important contribution was made by the use of electric power, which could be produced in a certain amount to replace imported coal. At the beginning of the century industry had developed in several fields. An inquiry made in 1903 revealed that 117,341 firms, employing 1,275,109 workers, were already in existence.

The upward trend continued regularly. An indication of this is provided by the increased consumption of coal, the importation of which rose from 5 million tons in 1901 to nearly 11 millions in 1913, while consumption of electric power increased from 45 million kilowatt-hours in 1895 to 2·5 billions during the years 1914–15.

New smelting establishments were built; the production of pig iron rose from 16,000 tons in 1901 to 385,000 tons in 1914, and that of steel from 129,000 to 911,000 tons. The steel-using industry also increased production of engines, agricultural machinery, railway equipment, scientific instruments, and automobiles. In this last field the country gained renown for its high-quality cars.

World War I compelled factories to switch over to war production. Some enterprises expanded, more were established.

Standardised production was widely adopted. The greatest effort was made in the mining, steel, chemical, and manufacturing fields. The few cannons the army could dispose at the beginning of the war had become over 7,500 by 1918, most of which had been produced at home. The number of machine-guns had also increased from 613 to 19,904. The automobile industry was in a position to satisfy domestic demand, and to export its products. The number of aircraft rose from 143 in 1915 to 3,335 in 1918.

After 1918 industry went through a crisis. Factories which had been working for the armed forces found themselves with their warehouses full of goods which they were unable to sell through lack of demand. Nearly all firms succeeded, however, in switching to peace production. Recovery was expedited by a better customs law, the renewal of equipment, the adoption of new technical methods, and the increased purchasing power of the consumer, the living standards of whom had slowly risen. Expansion was temporarily checked in 1927 by Mussolini's financial policy of revaluing the lira, but it got under way again very soon and continued until 1929. The index of national production increased from 100 in 1922 to 202 seven years later. The output of automobiles, for instance, jumped from 6,000 in the pre-war period to 64,000 in 1926.

When the world crisis broke out, many factories closed, while unemployment increased sharply. The index of industrial production dropped by 27 per cent between 1929 and 1932. Yet not all the consequences of the crisis were detrimental. The closing of certain firms producing at high costs and the amalgamation of others brought about a reorganisation in several branches of industry. The reduction of costs enabled national economy to improve slightly, so that by 1933 the levels of 1929 were again reached.

Foreign trade suffered from the situation. Following the example of other countries, the Government imposed restrictions on foreign exchange, which in 1934 became a State monopoly. Private brokers were prohibited from transacting in foreign currencies. The following year imports were restricted.

Preparations for the Ethiopian campaign and economic sanctions decreed by the League of Nations compelled industry to make a new effort to free production as far as possible from reliance on the import of raw materials.

This was the beginning of a rigidly protective policy which is generally known by the name of *autarchia* (autarchy) and which aimed at attaining self-sufficiency. It required a great effort of organisation, especially in certain fields where production, for lack of materials, was definitely non-remunerative, but was made possible through high custom rates and State subsidies. Nearly all branches benefited from the new trend. During this period certain activities started, such as the extraction of natural gas and the refining of imported oil, which increased still further after the war.

In 1940, when war was declared on France and Britain, the *autarchia* policy was going through a very difficult phase. A long period of peace would have been necessary to establish it. Instead, the new conflagration made much recent planning obsolete, because, just as in 1915, industry was called upon to back the war effort.

As an immediate consequence, industry was cut off from supplies of such basic materials as iron, coal, petroleum, rubber, cotton, etc. Germany became the country's principal source of supply, but as she also was badly in need of raw materials, her help became irregular and insufficient. Coal especially was short because it had to be transported by rail, a much slower and more expensive method than by sea.

On the other hand, increasing inflation, and the need of supplying the armed forces and the country were a stimulus for more production and for the expansion of mining, manufacturing, and chemical industries. This phase did not last long. After 1942 not only were raw materials and electric power lacking, but factories had to bear the heavy consequences of the Allied blockade and of air bombing. Even certain war industries were obliged to close. The situation became more serious because of military and political events following the armistice. The transport network broke down, while reserves came to an end.

By the Spring of 1945, when World War II ended in Europe, Italy's industry was exhausted by the ordeal and in a parlous condition. In certain branches (fertilisers, refined petrol, for instance) production dropped to insignificant levels.

We have already spoken of Italy's scarcity of raw materials, placing special emphasis on coal and steel. Yet scarcity does not mean complete absence. There are in fact a few lignite mines, which are intensively exploited, although the quality of their product cannot be compared with that of foreign anthracite. Coal extracted in 1953 amounted to 1,902,514 tons, while imports exceeded 9 million tons. Iron is mainly extracted from the mines of Isola d'Elba and Cogne. The total output in 1953 was 933,375 tons, which was much below the annual consumption. The country's iron and steel industry may seem small when compared to that of other countries, but if one considers that it was set up despite the insufficiency of raw materials, results may appear outstanding. In 1953 pig-iron production amounted to 1,222,300 tons and that of steel to 3,500,200 tons.

Italy's steel-using industry has ancient origins and has largely developed in modern times. Among its main branches are the automobile factories, the output of which in 1954 was 216,700 vehicles (compared to the 77,780 of 1937), most of which were destined for the domestic market. Motorisation has been expedited by the greatly increased sale of motor-scooters—light and economical vehicles, which are especially adapted to Italy's temperate climate. The output of motor-scooters and motorcycles in 1946 was 166,000 and rose to 1,335,000 in 1952.

Aircraft building, although enjoying a period of prosperity up to 1945, is now going through a crisis. There are nevertheless certain indications that production may begin again.

Shipbuilding was extremely prosperous while wood was the chief material employed in the making of ships. When steam navigation began, and steel became the principal material used, shipyards had to compete with foreign production. Despite the lack of domestic steel, which had to be bought abroad, new shipyards were set up, especially around Genoa. During World War II these were busy repairing ships damaged by enemy action. The war over, greater emphasis was placed on building new vessels. The Mercantile Marine was then in a most tragic condition, having being reduced from 3,500,000 tons in 1940 to 385,716 tons in 1945. American aid, Liberty ships, and national production enabled it to regain its lost position. By June, 1953, tonnage had already reached the 3,456,000 mark. Unfortunately, due to high costs, shipyards are unable to compete favourably with foreign firms or to sell many ships abroad.

Production of machinery has steadily developed. Italy now makes farm equipment and tractors, which, because of farm industrialisation, are in constant demand. But nearly all other types of machinery are also produced, from tools to railway equipment, from boilers to building machines, from arms to household appliances. Quite important is the output of electrical materials.

In the field of metals, we should mention the outstanding production of mercury and aluminium and the satisfactory production of lead and zinc. The output of antimony, tin, and copper, is, however, insufficient.

There is a large extraction of pyrites, generally used to obtain sulphuric acid, but from which even iron is now being extracted. In the past sulphur held an important place among mining activities, but the industry is now passing through a grave crisis caused by foreign, especially American, competition.

Mining also includes asbestos, magnesium, graphite, mica, asphaltic rocks, talc, quartz, salt, several qualities of marble, etc.

The peninsula's geological formation led experts to hope that its soil might contain much natural gas and oil. Researches were carried out by a State-controlled agency just before the last war. Natural gas was found in the Po Valley, a network of pipelines has been built, and several large industries have started using natural gas instead of coal. Total output was 2,297,891 cubic metres in 1953. Recently the situation has improved because oil has been discovered in considerable quantities both in Sicily and the Abruzzi.

Oil-refining has also become an important activity. Italy has now thirty-six refineries with a yearly production of over 12 million tons, which fulfils domestic needs and contributes to exports. The refined product is chiefly obtained from foreign crude oil, although domestic oil should soon be used in increasing quantities.

A country lacking coal was inevitably compelled to develop electric power as much as possible. The first power-producing station was built as far back as 1883. Since then the power industry has constantly expanded, production reaching 32,619,000 kilowatt hours in 1953.

Reconstruction of houses and public buildings destroyed by war was first started by private enterprise and was later assisted by the Government. Building has to-day become one of the country's basic activities. It has advanced hand in hand with the building materials industry. 346,265 living rooms were built in 1951, against 149,382 in 1938.

Although it is not the country's most important economic

activity, as was the case before World War I, even the textile industry has advanced during the last decade, contributing to exports to foreign markets. It is at present passing through a crisis, which might be solved if domestic consumption increased, and this may take place as a consequence of the improving standard of living in the South.

Natural silk, of which Italy is the greatest European producer, and artificial silk manufactured in modern factories are also exported.

Italian clothes are to-day largely appreciated for the excellence of their fabrics and of their tailoring. They are competing successfully on the international market with French clothes, traditionally considered the best in the world.

The variety of Italy's chemical products is very great, and there is a constant demand for them both at home and abroad, and the industry continues to grow.

A branch of industry which has largely developed since the war is that of films. Italy's moving pictures are greatly appreciated to-day for their human approach and their artistic formula, generally known as 'Neo-realism'.

This brief survey of the country's chief activities should also include handicrafts, such as wood and leather objects, faience, hammered iron, jewellery, blown glass, laces, etc. These crafts are based on an ancient tradition which is still very much alive.

Immediately after the country's unification foreign trade was small. Imports consisted principally of farm products and manufactured goods, exports of other farm products and of a few raw materials, such as sulphur and marble. The yearly deficit of the balance of trade was generally small.

Following the birth of industry the situation changed, because many more raw materials had to be imported. Estimating the lira at its 1938 value, Italy's foreign trade increased from the yearly average of 11 billion lire during the period 1871–80 to a yearly average of 27 billion lire during the period 1909–14 and to 34 billion lire during the period 1921–25.

Before World War I raw materials had increased their percentage of total imports from 9 to 36, while their percentage of total exports had declined from 15 to 11. Imports of finished goods had decreased from 28 to 17 per cent, while exports increased from 14 to 40 per cent of the total.

These figures show the radical changes undergone by the

country's economy, caused especially by industrial development.

Following the great world crisis and the preferential policies adopted by other Powers, Italy restricted her imports. The trend was, of course, carried on during the Ethiopian campaign at the time of the economic sanctions. When these measures were cancelled trade improved again, but it never reached the level of the immediate post-war period. A further reduction of trade followed the country's entry into World War II. As the conflict went on, the situation worsened, so that during the years 1944–45 the country had practically no foreign trade at all.

At the end of the war the picture was a most critical one because traditional trade relations had been destroyed and it was extremely difficult to make a prompt recovery. This was clearly shown by the very serious deficit in Italy's international accounts, caused chiefly by the large imports of food supplies and raw materials and by the poor recovery of exports.

At this point the Marshall Plan began to operate, the chief purpose of which was to reduce the dollar deficit by supplying raw materials and manufactured goods. The effects of this aid were immediately felt, for a trade deficit of 661 million dollars in 1947 dropped to 320 million in 1948, to 306 million in 1949, and to 157 million in 1950.

If foreign trade is an aspect of a country's economic condition, the increase in that of Italy is an encouraging factor, even if a deficit still exists in her balance of trade. In 1953 imports amounted to 1,497 billion lire, an increase of 2·6 per cent on 1952, while exports amounted to 930 billion lire, an increase of 7 per cent on 1952. The deficit of 567 billion lire was caused chiefly by the still existing need to import certain foodstuffs, such as wheat, fats, meat, and raw materials for industry. It is nevertheless believed that the situation will improve in the near future. New farming methods are especially important. Food items amount to a third of total imports, and an increase in farm production will certain have a major influence in balancing foreign trade.

Invisible exports, generally favourable to Italy's economy, contributed to reducing the deficit in international accounts, which amounted to 361 billion lire in 1952, as against 293 billion in 1953.

This deficit was reduced still further by American aid (granted by the Mutual Security Act), which amounted to 150 and

155 billion lire respectively in the years 1952 and 1953. The total deficit of international accounts was, therefore, 211 billion lire in 1952 and 138 billion in 1953.

Economic data on agriculture, industry, and foreign trade should be critically examined and compared with those of other countries. But this would exceed the purposes of our book. We will therefore limit our study to the most serious problem of Italy's economy: unemployment. If we consider that the Western world is now enjoying a period of prosperity, and that several nations are successfully enforcing a policy of full employment, it seems impossible that a nation should still be afflicted by such a serious handicap.

Information gathered on the subject up to a short time ago was far from reliable. For this reason Parliament decided in 1952 that a special commission of experts should investigate the problem thoroughly. The commission decided to follow two different ways to ascertain the total number of unemployed. It analysed figures registered at the Provincial Labour Exchange Offices, and it also conducted a special inquiry on a nation-wide basis, through the Central Institute of Statistics.

Although the two inquiries were made on the same day (September 30, 1952), the answers were not identical. The first registered 1,715,710 people out of work and the second 1,286,000. Neither of these figures is to be relied upon. One of the peculiarities of Italy's economy which makes researches of the kind difficult is that, added to the number of unemployed, there are many under-employed, who work only a few days in the month, and whose position is very uncertain.

The number of people out of work is somewhere between the above two figures, probably around the 1,600,000 mark. This figure, however, does not include the seasonally unemployed, which are estimated at 600,000. Researches were, in fact, made at the time of year when there is the greatest number of people working in agriculture. Five months later (February, 1953) registrations at the Labour Exchange Offices amounted to 2,301,765. In October, 1954, they were 2,085,565.

At the time of the inquiry the unemployed included 1,115,887 men and 599,823 women. They were generally unskilled and had followed no course of professional specialisation. Only 4 per cent of them drew unemployment benefit.

The main cause of this state of things is excess population.

Italy's inhabitants, according to the first census, taken on December 31, 1871, were 27,436,806. On December 31, 1953, their number had grown to 48,256,608. As a consequence of increased population, the offer of labour rose heavily, greatly exceeding demand. The problem became more serious because of the switching of land workers over to industrial employment and of the increased competition of women in search of paid work.

Among other causes is Italy's low production level. According to statistics published by the Department of Economic Affairs of the United Nations, the net yearly amount of agricultural and industrial products in Italy in 1948 was 58 dollars a head—a much lower amount than in many other countries.

Scarcity of capital, another cause of unemployment, was and is a result of low incomes, which do not enable the population to save as much as it would like to do.

Foreign capital has been discouraged from investing, at first by the economic policy of Fascism and then by other political factors. Before World War I, although economic problems were more serious than now and industry was less developed, unemployment found an outlet in emigration. Large numbers of Italians left the country. Between 1901 and 1914 emigrants amounted to over 8,000,000. After World War I the American Congress adopted the first restrictive measures, soon followed by other countries, especially after the 1929 crisis. Emigration consequently dropped to extremely low figures, a fact which naturally increased unemployment. In recent years some countries, such as Argentina, Venezuela, Canada, and Australia, have adopted a more liberal attitude towards Italian emigration. This, however, is still low, and can bring only a small reduction in excess labour.

Italian authorities have studied several schemes in order to solve the problem, but up to now these have given only temporary help. In December, 1954, budget Minister Vanoni presented a ten-year development plan which deals with the question of surplus man-power and will endeavour to solve it within the span of ten years by creating 4,000,000 new jobs.

The plan has been submitted to O.E.E.C., and has been fully discussed by public opinion. The document considers it possible to reach a satisfactory employment level, provided that the rate of expansion of the country's economy is at least 5 per cent a year, to be invested chiefly in productive activities, and not in consumer goods. It also intends to increase public investments in agriculture, public works, public utilities, communications, and housing, to develop the industrial set-up, and to promote private enterprise. The gross investment needed is estimated at about 34,000 billion lire, of which 16,000 will be required for new industrial equipment. Success is linked to the increase of savings, to the strengthening of currency, and to the balancing of international accounts. It is assumed that this last goal can be reached by raising exports, including the invisible ones, to 60 per cent above the current level, while the increase in imports should be only 44 per cent.

This scheme is regarded by some as exceedingly optimistic. Yet we believe that, at least partly, it can be put into practice. Every plan of the kind must have a certain degree of flexibility and must take changing situations into account. This one, however, shows that Italians intend to face their main economic problem with determination and are trying to find the right solution.

Chapter 13

Post-war Reconstruction

War in Europe was brought to an end in 1945. This meant that after the Peace Treaty Italy was no longer to be an occupied country and that foreign troops would at last be withdrawn, leaving her to sort out her economic troubles. For nearly two years the country had been the jostling point of two armies, and for nearly five the people had been submitted to a terrific strain. The amount of damage and devastation caused was now to be catalogued.

It is believed that a third of the nation's wealth was lost by war operations, shipping losses, bomb damage, arrears of replacement and maintenance, and reduction in producing capacity. This was the equivalent, according to present-day values, of 10,000 billion lire.[1] Public works destroyed, for instance, including highways, buildings, ports, and aqueducts, totalled 500 billion lire in value. 3·2 million rooms had either been demolished or made uninhabitable, thus worsening the already acute housing problem. Railways had been destroyed either by air-raids or by the Germans during their retreat. One-fourth of the tracks, one-third of the bridges, 47 per cent of railway buildings, 60 per cent of locomotives, 60 per cent of freight cars, and 80 per cent of passenger trains had been put out of service. Travelling in those days was far from easy. At times it would take several days to cover the smallest distances, especially as priority over the few available means was given to military requirements. The Mercantile Marine had been reduced to a tenth of its former tonnage—a striking loss in a field where Italy had always held an outstanding position for the efficiency and good service of her lines.

Total damages suffered in the three fields of agriculture, industry, and trade are difficult to estimate, because too often no figures are available. It is, however, believed that agriculture underwent a loss of 550 billion lire. The country's industrial set-up had suffered a reduction of 20 per cent of its total value.

[1] The approximate present exchange is at 1,700 lire to the pound.

Practically all sectors had been affected, from power production to metal industry, from shipbuilding to chemical and textile industries. Trade damages amounted to approximately 400 billion lire.

Apart from the actual destruction of plants, production had decreased owing to social unrest. Workers, especially in the North, had often been in the middle of armed conflicts. Many episodes of violence had taken place in factories. Partisan activity had been influenced by Communism. Many had been led to believe that a revolution was imminent and that it was not a case of going back to work as usual. This sort of mental outlook could not possibly fit in with the peaceful approach so necessary to industrial recovery. When war ended in April, 1945, nothing was really accomplished in factories except lengthy political discussions. A few months were necessary for workers to regain their sense of proportion, so as to face the task with which they were confronted.

Plants and equipment were now out-of-date. During the last ten years there had been no technical progress and nothing had been done to renew or modernise old equipment. After 1943 the Germans in the North and the Allies in the South had called for a maximum effort, without stopping to consider whether or not machinery and equipment were in a position to support it. Stocks of raw materials had been consumed and nothing had been done to replace them.

As Italy even in normal times relies on foreign materials, the lack of stocks was creating a very serious situation, especially since other nations, equally in need of supplies, were competing with her to get them on foreign markets. For lack of coal, heavy industry was reduced to very low margins. As compared with 1938, the 1945 output of steel and metal industries was down to a sixth, that of the textiles, chemical, and building industries was down to a tenth, while mining was down to a third. Difficulties had become even greater because there were more people to feed. At the end of 1945 the nation's total population amounted to 45·7 million and everything indicated that it was steadily increasing. By the end of 1954 it had in fact grown to over 48 millions.

Other factors made the situation critical. The war being over, many soldiers had been demobilised, and this had worsened the labour problem. These men were generally unskilled, and after several years of service in the armed forces had acquired a mentality of unrest and dissatisfaction, which defeat had heightened. Some of them had been serving in the army since the days of the Ethiopian campaign (1935–36), and were now anxious to find an occupation. Refugees were flocking into the country from the colonies and from territories occupied by Yugoslavia. The authorities were confronted with the difficult task of providing them with employment, food, and accommodation.

War production had also caused changes in the economic structure. Factories had sprung up to meet new requirements and had provided work for people who until then had been satisfied to toil on the land. Peasants thus changed into industrial workers had no intention of returning to the farms: they wanted to be employed in factories and were easily influenced by Communist propaganda. The labour situation in 1945 was therefore very serious.

As a direct consequence of inflation, State assets fell to a very low level. Money to meet Government expenses was derived from taxation, but taxes could not keep up with the increase in prices, and although public revenue rose yearly on paper, its real value steadily decreased with the fall in the currency's purchasing power. In the fiscal year 1938–39 the State's revenues amounted to 27·6 billion lire, in 1944–45 they became 64·6, and in 1945–46, 160·2, but the devaluation of currency had outpaced them.

Italian economy had suffered from Fascist autarchy. This highly protective policy had created a lack of balance in the country's industrial organisation. Certain sectors had been excessively developed because their production was necessary to the nation's military preparation, others had been restricted. War had done the rest by compelling industry to produce more and more goods for which there was no market in ordinary times. Industrial change-over to peace production had become the problem of the moment, but it could not be solved immediately.

The standard of living had deteriorated alarmingly. The quantity of available calories per person was grossly insufficient, dropping from 2,652 per day in the 1936–40 period to 1,737 in 1945. Meat and fats had become so scarce that serious concern over the health of the population was fully justified. During 1944 and 1945 the food situation reached such a low level that it was the worst Italy has suffered in recent history. Her people were compelled to rely on local resources, which were meagre, as the nation had never been self-supporting. Scarcity of food meant a flourishing black market, which, although prohibited by law, was tolerated, as it was the only way people could get enough to eat.

Consequences brought about by the war were so serious that Italy's recovery seemed impossible. People felt she would be unable to regain her feet and that the future would only show a passing from bad to worse down a hill of progressive poverty and starvation. If this did not happen, the credit goes to the initiative of the people and to the democratic governments that took over the sad heritage. Although they were confronted with grave foreign and domestic problems, together with the necessity of resisting Communist violence at home and of negotiating tolerable peace conditions, they tackled the country's reconstruction competently.

Tasks confronting the Italians were not only the outcome of the war, but also of several economic deficiencies. The following were, and still are, the most striking:

(1) Lack of resources as compared with the number of inhabitants. Anyone who speaks of Italian fertility has probably restricted his visits to the richer areas, which form but a small percentage of the territory. The amount of fertile land is in fact little more than half. The rest is either pasture land (17·3 per cent), or covered by forests (18·6 per cent), or formed by mountainous waste land, unsuitable for farming (13 per cent).

(2) Lack of raw materials. Italy's self-sufficiency is limited to a few raw materials. She imports 90 per cent of her petrol, coal, copper, tin, nickel, cotton, and rubber, and depends on foreign supplies for cellulose, wool, and steel. When the importation of these commodities proves difficult their shortage is acutely felt.

(3) Differences between economic and industrial development in the North and in the South. This is a centuries-old problem for which the nation is only now trying to find a remedy.

The most urgent necessity was to provide the people with consumer goods, and as far as possible industries started supplying the market with merchandise they were still in a position to produce. This helped to get commerce going again.

But the market needed raw materials in especially large quantities, which could only be imported from the United States. Imports rose rapidly, and food supplies, which in 1938 had made up barely 15 per cent of total imports, increased in

1945 and 1946 to more than 33 per cent. Imports of coal also increased—an encouraging sign, as this proved that industry was at last on the move.

Production of electricity regained in a short time much lost ground. Factories had suffered so much damage through the war that their output had fallen to a dangerously low level. Companies started rebuilding their plants as soon as possible. The 1947 output was already 6,489,000 kilowatts—more than in 1942. All branches of industry were on the upgrade, from mining to car manufacturing, from civil engineering to shipbuilding, from textiles to mineral-oil refining. Especially important was the progress made by State railways. By the end of 1947, 78 per cent of the double-tracked and 62 per cent of the single-tracked railway lines were already in working condition.

During the first two post-war years a successful effort was made to keep the wheels of industry turning. But this task had still to face the danger of a steadily increasing inflation. Financial weakness had undermined all trust in the currency's stability. People could see their salaries and savings sinking in the quicksands of higher living costs. Prices, which in 1944 were already ten times higher than during the pre-war period, rocketed in 1945 to twenty times, in 1946 to twenty-eight times, and in 1947 to fifty-two times. Increases were irregular, varying with the type of goods. While, for example, the price of an automobile tyre in 1938 was equivalent to that of 17·5 kilos of olive oil, in 1946 one tyre was equivalent to 26·7 kilos of olive oil. The explanation of this lies in the fact that tyres were made from imported materials, whereas olive oil was a domestic product. The situation was critical. Something had to be done immediately to stop the continuing devaluation of the lira.

Until 1947 this perilous trend continued unchecked. Among the reasons for the Government's apparent inertia was the necessity for resuscitating, with first priority, the country's production machinery, even if this implied an inflationary movement. Besides, up to May, 1947, Communists and Socialists were members of De Gasperi's Cabinet, and their constant effort was to increase public expenditure so as to cause more inflation and social unrest. It is not without significance that Communists generally wanted one of their men as Minister of Finance to enable them to control the nation's economy in accordance with their party's interest. The De Gasperi Cabinet of May 31, 1947, was the first in which the two leftist parties took no part. It is hardly a coincidence that it was the first to check public expenditure and to follow a policy of economy which aimed at halting inflation. American assistance was also bound to influence public opinion favourably and to encourage activities based on a stable currency. The election of April 18, 1948, in which the electorate gave an absolute majority to Christian Democracy, added an element of stability to the Government's financial policy. This was now based on the necessity of curbing public expenditure, of increasing revenues, and of gradually putting an end to the deficit.

An effort was made to check the circulation of paper money, and although inflation was not halted immediately, its effects became less dangerous. Banking accounts and post-office savings accounts (the latter is a traditional way of saving among farmers) increased respectively from 165 and 698 billion lire in 1946 to 855 and 2,271 billion lire by April, 1951. Only under these conditions of improved confidence could industry expand. The Government's policies were also favouring free commerce. Controls on domestic trade were abolished and foreign imports were authorised, so as to provide industry with more raw materials and stimulate private enterprise. This policy proved successful, as total production in 1948 was nearly equal to that of 1938 and continued to increase during the following years. It was 5 per cent higher in 1949, 21 per cent higher in 1950, and 37 per cent higher in 1951.

Italy again began to trade with foreign countries. Her industries were given substantial help under the form of fiscal exemptions. Exports steadily increased.

But economic recovery would have been much slower had it not been for the great assistance given by the United States. Ever since the Allied landing in 1943, the country had been given economic aid. At the beginning this was distributed by the armed forces, and amounted to 490 million dollars, of which 363 million came from the United States. Later specialised agencies sent further aid, not only to meet the people's immediate needs, but also to assist economic and industrial recovery. The Federal Economic Administration (FEA), financed by the United States, aided the nation with such basic materials as cereals, fats, coal, mineral oils, metals, and cotton, to an amount of 144 million dollars. Soon the United Nations Relief and Rehabilitation Administration (UNRRA) stepped in and provided assistance from 1945 to 1947 to a total amount of 589 million dollars, of which 75 per cent (440 million dollars) were paid by the United States. During 1947 (before the European Recovery Programme came into existence) aid was provided through two special organisations (Aid United States of America—AUSA—and Interior Aid) to a total amount of 116 and 176 million dollars, respectively. Between 1946 and 1947 special loans were granted at favourable rates. They amounted to 375 million dollars. After the signing of the Peace Treaty, Italy was also exempted from paying 339 million dollars which she owed the United States.

In 1947 the American Government decided to help European economies in a more effective way. In his famous speech delivered at Harvard University, General Marshall informed Europe that his Government was going to promote the recovery of the West. The amount of aid granted was to be determined by the millions of dollars required yearly to cover the trade deficit. This figure could be considered the barometer of each country's necessities, as it showed how many goods had been imported over and above its spending capacity. It was a new way of summing up a nation's economic condition, and reflected the practical nature of the Americans, who like to get the essential point of any question. Aid was therefore granted to Europe in the form of dollar allotments to be used for the purchase of goods on the American market. These purchases were to take place in accordance with a yearly plan prepared by the Italian authorities and approved by the Americans.

The amount of dollars allotted was indeed a generous one. From April 3, 1948, until June 30, 1951, Italy in fact received 1,308 million dollars of Marshall Aid. In this way a large quantity of goods reached her without any payment being required. Preference was given to raw materials, such as wheat, coal, oil, cotton, and copper. These were not simply handed to consumers, but sold to them. The sums thus obtained were deposited in a special account of the Bank of Italy, called the 'Lire Fund', and were invested according to plans approved by both Governments.

Through the aid of these funds the third phase of the recovery programme started, which aimed at modernising the country's economic set-up and developing industrial sectors and depressed areas. This phase is at present in full swing. Since then big problems have been faced which had hitherto lain dormant, always awaiting a solution. Industry, having emerged from the state of frustration through which it had passed, was now to receive capital investments capable of increasing production, reducing prices, and encouraging trade. Agriculture was among the first to see some of its problems solved. In the following chapters we will examine the two major schemes now being enforced: the land reform and the Fund for the South.

All fields of industry received substantial benefits. Plants were modernised and working methods brought up to date. Goods improved in quantity and quality. Several sectors developed, and their structure and equipment were renewed. Power plants were built or improved so as to keep pace with the country's needs. Marshall Aid was used to increase the already existing hydro-electric plants, while greater emphasis than in the past was placed on steam plants, some of which ran on natural gas.

Despite Italy's well-known deficiency in coal and iron, good results were attained by the steel industry. After the war the steel output was down to a sixth compared with pre-war levels. New planning aimed at increasing production and reducing costs, thereby enabling the industry to regain its former position.

When Marshall Aid came to an end, American assistance was carried on under a new scheme known as the Mutual Security Act, which enabled the country to reduce its deficit to reasonable levels. Aid, in the form of dollar credits, enabling the Government to purchase goods on the American market, amounted in 1953 to 133 million dollars, and in 1954 to 104 million dollars. The Government's present programme, as laid down in the Vanoni Plan, is of increasing exports to a point at which it will be possible to balance international accounts without external aid. This should be possible by 1964.

The general outlook is one of optimism, and Government circles believe the present trend will be carried on successfully. As recently as December, 1954, economic changes were in full swing. All over the country funds were being invested in works of public utility, while private enterprise was trying to increase production at lower costs.

Chapter 14

Land Reform

BEFORE speaking of the agrarian reform, one of Italy's most important problems, we should like to explode the myth that Italy is a fertile country, resembling California, that only needs to be tilled to provide a bountiful crop. Italians are responsible for this legend, which the Romans were the first to spread. Vergilius spoke of Italy as 'the great producer of wheat'. Quintino Sella, one of the nineteenth-century ministers of finance, said that Italy was 'especially rich', while Depretis stated that she was 'the most beautiful and fertile land in Europe'.

It is often said that Italians are poor workers. The phrase *Dolce far niente* (sweet idleness) has been coined for them. Those who are still of this opinion should visit some southern district where peasants have practically created the land on which they work. At times they have been compelled to build little terraces and plateaux, carrying baskets of earth up from the valleys, or crushing by hand the rocky soil. With the sweat of generations they have finally cleared the stony ground. Hard work, not idleness, has always been the motto of these people, who have courageously faced the difficulties caused by the poverty of their land.

Despite the poor geological nature of some districts which are often quite unsuited to farming, agriculture accounts for about one-third of the nation's production. It is therefore Italy's main industry and provides work for millions. Rural workers can be divided into the following three groups: small proprietors who work the land together with their families and generally live on it; share-croppers who work the soil and keep a portion (53 per cent) of what they produce, surrendering the rest to the owner; labourers who are hired by proprietors and receive a salary.

Small proprietors are generally untouched by Communist propaganda. They are organised in a strong association which constitutes an element of stability in the nation's life. Share-croppers, on the contrary, are influenced by extremist ideas, especially in Tuscany and Emilia, where a preponderance of the Communist electorate resides. The reason for this is easy to understand. The share-cropper is a proprietor in the making. He does not own the land, but gets the fruits of it. Yet, in spite of this, he does not consider his condition satisfactory, as he does not enjoy the moral prestige of ownership, which is perhaps the most important element. Communists exploit this sentiment to the full, making him believe that by backing their party he will soon attain full ownership. Rural labourers are a most serious problem. Generally unskilled, and living a hard life in the country's less advanced areas, they easily become the victims of Communist ideas. Having no consolidated interests to defend, their desire for improvement only fosters discontent. Communist propaganda towards them is based mainly on the slogan 'Come with us. After all, what have you to lose?' The Government's policy is to turn them, as far as possible, into small landowners.

It is estimated that the destruction caused by the war to Italian agriculture amounted to approximately 550 billion lire. This figure included only the actual destruction, not indirect damages, such as reduced fertility, caused by lack of fertilisers or parasites. There were great losses also through insufficient maintenance of the irrigation systems, increased deforestation, and the abandonment of proper rotation. As compared to 1938, total production in 1945 dropped to 60 per cent, that of wheat to 50 per cent, that of sugar to 8 per cent. Livestock was down to 75 per cent, and available calories per head were down to 63 per cent.

Private enterprise soon started to repair war damage. It was a favourable period because the prices of farm products were high. Inflation, caused by military occupation, increased Government expenses and lack of trust in the lira's purchasing power caused grave alarm. Capitalists were ready to invest in agriculture all the money they had, so that capital was often transferred from industrial to agricultural investments. This largely accounts for prompt rebirth and for the building up of livestock. After 1947, when the price of farm products started to fall, the necessity for Government financial aid was felt. Prices of some commodities had fallen (olive oil, for instance, was down to 50 per cent of the previous price), and there was much less enthusiasm on the part of the public to invest money in the development of farms. During this second phase Government investments, including those financed through

American aid, aimed at improving the nation's agricultural structure. Nearly 100 billion lire were assigned for this purpose between 1947 and 1949, special attention being paid to land reclamation. The third period of structural changes started in 1949. This was undoubtedly the most important, and was centred chiefly on what is generally known as Italy's land reform.

Of 27,826,000 hectares [1] forming the cultivated portion of the nation's territory, 6,253,000 belong to the State, to the communes, or other public institutions. The rest (21,573,000 hectares) are privately owned. Public property consists largely of mountainous areas, and is therefore less fertile and poorer than the rest.

Landowners are numerous ($9\frac{1}{2}$ millions), but their estates are generally small. More than 5 millions possess only half a hectare a head; more than $3\frac{1}{2}$ millions possess between a half and five hectares; 500,000 between five and twenty-five hectares; 100,000 between twenty-five and 200 hectares; 8,000 between 200 and 1,000 hectares; 500 more than 1,000 hectares. The problem is therefore not only of dividing up the larger estates, but also of amalgamating the smaller ones in order the better to exploit the land. The basic fact remains, however, that the nation's territory is too small to satisfy everybody. With another 10 million hectares of fertile land for distribution, Italy would have no major agricultural problem.

The situation, however, being what it is, reform has acquired a moral and social meaning. That a few people should own and control large estates whilst there are many landless peasants is a cause for unrest; hence the necessity for a land reform which aims at distributing large farms among peasants. Its principles have been set down in Article 44 of the constitution, which reads as follows:

> 'With the object of securing a rational utilisation of the soil and of establishing equitable social relations, the Law imposes obligations and limitations to private landed ownership, fixes limits to its extent, which vary in the different parts of the country according to the agricultural areas, encourages and imposes land reclamation and transformation of large estates and the reconstitution of productive units and assists small and medium-sized holdings.'

[1] One hectare is equivalent to 2·471 acres.

In February, 1948, a first decree was issued granting exemption from taxation and low interest loans to peasants who intended purchasing small properties. This was a sort of land reform brought about individually through the effort of the workers themselves. Towards the middle of 1952 this decree had already enabled 130,000 persons to purchase plots of ground, and was therefore extended by Parliament for a further three years. Unfortunately it only favoured people who had already laid down certain sums which enabled them to purchase the land they aspired to. People who benefited from it were those who perhaps even without Government aid would have succeeded in bettering their condition. Yet a solution was to be found for those lacking financial means but who were also capable, under guidance, of aiding the country's agriculture. After the 1948 elections the problem was strongly felt. Public opinion, excited mainly by Communist propaganda, was pushed to demand a reform which it believed had been too long delayed.

The project, affecting the whole country, was introduced in Parliament, and has yet to be approved. But, for the purpose of expediting reform where it was most urgently needed, Parliament passed another law enforcing it in certain regions. These were the mouth of the River Po, a part of Tuscany and Latium, and several areas of the South. Special laws were approved for the Sila region in Calabria and for Sicily. The reform was therefore applied to eight million hectares, of which 700,000 became available for distribution among peasants.

The principles on which the plan was based have been partially those of expropriating owners of excess land and distributing the surplus among peasants who have a knowledge of farming and a desire to become small landowners. In order to determine which property is too large, certain standards of production and equipment have been fixed. Farms falling short of these standards (because they do not produce sufficient, are under-equipped, or do not employ enough manual labour) must undergo expropriation. Land thus obtained is administered by special organisations known as Enti di Riforma (reform bodies), which are responsible for its reclamation and distribution.

The assignment of land to peasants is provisional during the first two years, and becomes final only when the new proprietor has proved his ability. A contract is then signed. The new owner is given the assistance he requires in the difficult process —which is psychological as well as technical—of changing from a landless peasant into a small landholder. By July, 1954, 225,000 hectares had already changed hands and over 45,000 peasant families had benefited from distribution, the average size of each new farm being approximately 5 hectares.

The Government has also provided new landowners with certain amenities which are more difficult to find in the country than in the city. Anyone arriving in Rome from the North along the ancient Aurelian Way will see the rural homes built on the border zone between Tuscany and Latium which is generally known as Maremma. More than 10,000 of these houses are being built all over the country, and possession has already been taken of many of them. Villages with public buildings, churches, schools, theatres, communications, and all that goes to serve the requirements of a modern rural community have been set up. Communists at home and observers abroad have often criticised this experiment, claiming that it has proved ineffective. The contrary is probably nearer the truth, for Italy's land reform is an important achievement which is bound to develop in the future, and the first results of which are most encouraging. Difficulties have, of course, arisen, but have been overcome by technicians and executives.

Distribution of expropriated land will soon be completed. The second phase will then begin, and the reform will be enforced in new regions. Results of the previous phase will be taken into account and defects will be corrected. Every effort will also be made to facilitate the purchase of land by peasants, this practice being favourable to social and moral improvement.

These achievements would certainly be less outstanding were they not accompanied by an increase in production. In general, the output of Italian farming is satisfactory, considering the poverty and scarcity of available land. Yet, it must still reach higher levels if social conditions are to improve. More goods are to be thrown on to the market both for home consumption and for export. Efforts along these lines have evidently been successful. Since 1951 the total production of agriculture has exceeded that of pre-war years.

These results are being reached by using machinery, improving methods of cultivation, and investing more capital. This is why in 1952 a new plan was approved by Parliament known as the 'Twelve Years Scheme for the Development of Italian Agriculture', its purpose being to stimulate farmers into buying machinery, building irrigation plants and rural homes. Capital, amounting to a total of 125 billion lire, was made available up to 1957. Loans are granted at the low interest of 3 per cent. In December, 1952, the first thirty-seven tractors bought through these loans were delivered to a group of farmers in the province of Brescia.

Mountainous areas have always been a major concern, although little was ever done in the past to improve such a large portion of national territory. Parliament approved in 1952 a new scheme which places the sum of 67 billion lire at the disposal of farmers who wish to improve mountain farms.

Another scheme which will certainly increase production is 'The National Competition of Productivity', which is held every year. Prizes awarded for the best crops amount to a total of 100 million lire. In 1953 over 21,000 farms participated, 2,000 of which were small-holdings formed through the land reform.

Chapter 15

The Southern Problem

SOUTHERN ITALY acquired fame among the English-speaking nations through a book, written by Carlo Levi, entitled *Christ Stopped at Eboli.* The author, an anti-Fascist and political internee in a small village south of Salerno, had spent his period of confinement studying the misery and unhappiness of a southern village. The title of the book has a meaning. It was inspired by a phrase, common among the peasants living in the region of Basilicata, who, comparing their conditions with those existing in other villages and cities (among which is Eboli), came to the conclusion that Christ kept away from their land owing to its depressed and poverty-stricken condition.

Undoubtedly the first and foremost of Italy's problems needing attention is the economic situation of the South, a region which includes roughly all the peninsula from Rome southwards, together with the islands of Sicily and Sardinia. This land, for centuries dormant, is now awakening and becoming conscious of its need for better living conditions. The reason for its poverty lies chiefly in the scarcity of land and in the lack of raw materials, and consequently of industries capable of providing employment.

Southern Italy is generally referred to as a land of sunshine. This may favourably impress tourists, but not farmers, who know that heat can be the worst enemy of agriculture. Very little rain falls, in fact, during summer, and the green fields and meadows which catch the eye of the traveller in spring become arid and yellow as the year progresses. Irrigation is difficult. Rivers and streams do not run smoothly. In winter they overflow and flood the countryside, whereas in summer the intense heat and shortage of water are likely to cause them to dry up completely. Hot winds blowing from Africa may also increase these difficulties.

Yet if the South could be properly irrigated it could become a most fertile land. The richness of certain parts proves this.

Areas around Naples, Salerno, and Catania, for instance, where there is no shortage of water, are more like gardens than farms. Land in general is too mountainous; in addition, it contains too much clay and is subject to erosion. Farmers who till the ground reap very little reward from the harvests.

Deforestation has been carried out in order to get immediate revenue from the sale of timber and acquire more land fit for tillage; consequently wide tree-covered areas have become barren. On soil so acquired production is in general poor. The average wheat crop is much lower than in the North. Vegetables need water, and their cultivation is possible only where weather conditions are favourable. Tomatoes, for instance—one of the main southern products—can at certain periods be produced more cheaply in the Emilia region, where water is more abundant. Calabria and Sicily are famous for their oranges, lemons, and tangerines, which, nevertheless, cannot be raised everywhere.

The only cultivation possible in certain mountain areas is that of Mediterranean plants such as olive, almond, and vine-trees. These could provide southern peasants with a steady income if the market for wine, almonds, and olive oil were a regular one. Unfortunately this is not the case. Foreign consumption of these commodities is greatly influenced by political and economic factors. Competition has also increased. Algerian oil can be produced at a lower price, while Israeli oranges are successfully competing with the Sicilian. As for wine, it is a known fact that too much of it is already flooding the world market and that several governments—France in particular—are gravely concerned and are trying to find a solution to the problem.

Deficiencies in the agricultural economy have increased during the years, owing to centuries of neglect. Despite these drawbacks, this land is over-populated and has a high birth-rate. The South and the islands have, in fact, over 17 million inhabitants. During 1953 the natural increase of population reached its highest peak in Sardinia and Calabria, where it was 1·65 per cent.

Wage-earners in the South form 35 per cent of the total population, while in other regions they constitute 50 per cent. The burden of supporting a large number of people falls therefore on a smaller group of workers than in the North. On the other hand, although southern agriculture is less prosperous, more people work on the land. Figures show that 56 per cent of workers are employed in agriculture against 42 per cent in the rest of Italy. 22 per cent of people are employed in industrial activities, against 33 per cent in the North.

When Italy attained unity, both North and South were in a position to develop an industry, because there was a mass of potential consumers in the country and few commodities were as yet available. Northerners, however, were more capable of taking advantage of the situation, and proved to be more practical. Even the Austrian Government in the provinces of Lombardo-Venetia, although tyrannical and always ready to crush a rebellion, had helped to prepare the ground for industrial growth. Agriculture, for instance, benefited in Lombardy from Government initiative during the reign of the Empress Maria Theresia, when the marshes of the Po Valley were reclaimed and turned into rich farmland. Piedmont and Tuscany profited from their enlightened Governments, which favoured local initiative.

The North had also been the land where at the beginning of the millennium communal liberties had come into being, from which trade and industry, as well as art and literature, had developed. Although several centuries had passed, a competitive mentality and a natural aptitude for private enterprise were still widely spread among people. This was not the case in the South, where even if industry and trade had at one time flourished, they had soon been crushed by despotic Governments.

Northerners took advantage of their superior knowledge and their industries benefited from the wider market with which unity had provided them. Success increased their self-confidence and urged them to seek new outlets. With its amateurish and half-hearted approach, the South stood little chance against an aggressive and experienced North, where an industrial class, consisting of executives, white-collar and skilled workers, was already being formed.

The coming of the last war made the situation worse. Conditions in 1944, after months of front-line fighting in Abruzzi and Campania, were pitiful. Anyone who fought in the hills surrounding Cassino will never forget the sight of that devastated area when at last the Allies pushed on in May, 1944. Life had become almost impossible and the people's attitude was one of utter despair. Investments were practically non-existent. If before the war the South had lacked industrial initiative, matters were now at breaking point, and an immediate solution was imperative if Italy was to rebuild her economic edifice.

What was primarily to be done? Was industry to be set up in the South through private or public enterprise? Had it not already been proved that the State is rarely an efficient industrialist? Or was the South to be placed in a condition in which private initiative might develop?

This last approach appeared the most appropriate, for industry will generally expand when conditions lend themselves to making it profitable. Where there are good roads, water, power, labour facilities, a market for the sale of goods, local and foreign firms will expand their businesses and new ones will come into being. Experts concluded that the only way in which the existing state of affairs could be changed was by bringing up-to-date the people and the land. For a task of such magnitude State intervention was imperative. A new organisation was therefore set up for the purpose of investing vast capital, so as to change the region's entire framework and stimulate further development. This organisation was called Cassa del Mezzogiorno (Fund for the South) and was allocated a capital of 1,280 billion lire, the equivalent of two billion dollars, to be distributed over a twelve-year period.

This new scheme was planned and carried out in a modern and efficient manner. The control of public expenditure in Italy by Government officials has often proved to be a hindrance rather than a help. Complicated systems and red-tape prevent the spending of a single lira without the necessary authorisation. This hampers the transaction of important business, when decisions have to be made at a moment's notice. To overcome this difficulty the Cassa was given great free-trading facilities which enable it to invest large sums in a short time, without passing through controls. Expenditures are checked only by a special committee of ministers. Its executive body consists of a chairman, a director-general, a board of directors, and an accountancy committee.

The following is a tentative estimate of how the allotted sums are to be spent. For land reclamation and irrigation, 415 billion lire (32·4 per cent of the total); for land reform, 280 billions (21·8 per cent); for reafforestation and the reclaiming of mountain areas, 225 billions (17·6 per cent); for aqueducts, 145 billions (11·4 per cent); for roads, 115 billions (9 per cent); for railways, 70 billions (5·5 per cent); for tourism, 30 billions (2·3 per cent).

Whether or not these funds will be enough to modify conditions created by centuries of neglect preoccupies the minds of many Italians. Yet results may be greater than one can foresee at the moment, for the investments are considerable, even judging them according to standards of richer countries. Besides, they do not replace normal public expenditure, but must be added to it. Changes in the way of living will certainly take place.

Our optimism regarding the future is by no means exaggerated, for such substantial investments in a country where so little had previously been done are bound to bear fruit. If an additional road is built in a region where others exist, it will scarcely contribute to the changing of living standards, but the building of such a road in an area which lacks other means of communication and was previously isolated is bound to bring good results all round. In the South many such roads are to be built under the supervision of the Cassa del Mezzogiorno.

The Cassa's investments in agriculture are destined to be the largest, for, no matter how much industry develops, land cultivation will always hold priority as the basic source of income. The greatest efforts are therefore being concentrated on the improvement of farming. The most urgent necessity is a reliable irrigation system. Old irrigation schemes which had remained on paper have been revised and newer and more modern ones have been studied. Mountain dams and reservoirs are being constructed, which will also be used as power-producing plants.

One of the most important irrigation schemes is that of the Flumendosa River in Sardinia, a project which will affect a territory of 40,000 hectares. The dam will also produce 125 million kilowatts of electric power annually and supply water to a new aqueduct. There is not one region in the South which is not included in some irrigation scheme, for other major dams are being built in Apulia, Campania, Basilicata, Calabria, Sicily, and Abruzzi.

Large sums of money will be spent on agrarian reform. As we have examined this question in the previous chapter, we will limit ourselves to saying that such a vast scheme as the Government is now carrying out would have no chance of succeeding were it not for the large financial issues involved. Rural homes and roads are to be rebuilt and the basic necessities of life are to be guaranteed to a population which in a sense is pioneering a virgin soil.

Reafforestation and reclamation of mountainous areas are other urgent tasks. Timber-felling has been endless since the unification of Italy, and, due to lack of knowledge as to the importance of forests, much of this national wealth has disappeared. During the last hundred years Government forces set fire to entire woods in which they thought outlaws might be hiding. This vandalism has practically changed the character, climate, and whole aspect of the South. In certain areas it was carried out on such a large scale that erosion has washed away the humus and destroyed fertility. In Basilicata, for instance, there are mountain regions where erosion has made the landscape look like a lunar panorama.

Small villages are often to be found in these districts. Malaria, enemy invasion, and feudal conflicts caused the inhabitants to flee from the valleys and coastal districts to seek refuge in the mountains, and although of late there has been a tendency among peasants of hilltop villages to descend to the plains, freed at long last from the incubus of malaria, many of them still remain there.

When in 1951–52 great floods caused so much damage in the Po Valley and in Calabria it was realised that an immediate solution of the problem was imperative. Strangely enough, although 39 per cent of Italy's territory is formed by mountains (while 40 per cent is hills and 21 per cent plains), previous Governments had done little to solve the problem.

The Cassa has therefore allocated a large part of its budget to this purpose. The task is enormous, and it would be absurd to expect immediate results. Any plan of land reclamation and reafforestation must also take into account the fact that, poor as some grounds may be, they nonetheless provide the means of livelihood to many persons. Complete reclamation would call for an allocation of funds which even richer countries than Italy would find it impossible to face. The Cassa has therefore undertaken only the most urgent works and has allotted 225 billion lire for mountain areas covering a territory of 1,600,000 hectares. This sum is over and above those already assigned in the normal budget of the Ministry of Agriculture, which grants loans and partially reimburses expenses to farmers who wish to improve their properties, if these are located in the mountains.

As a result of these investments, several streams and rivers will benefit from necessary embankments, the lack of which was the cause of many floods. Erosion will be curbed where it is most dangerous and reafforestation will be carried out as quickly and efficiently as possible. Land is being reclaimed with enthusiasm and zeal, and results up to now have been encouraging. Even the reclamation of the Pontine Marshes, carried out by Fascism, and to which so much publicity was given, seems today a minor scheme in comparison with those now in progress. The spirit in which the Cassa is breaking the ancient crust of southern agriculture is such as to justify the greatest confidence in its success. Hope is also placed in private enterprise, which is bound to complete the Government's efforts.

The increase in production which will eventually follow will also bring with it new problems. Where will the South find new markets if the demand for her products does not increase? How will foreign buyers react to an increased supply of goods from southern Italy at a time when custom barriers still have a tendency to remain high and free trade is more an aspiration than a reality? A solution must be found. The selling methods of Italian farm products will have to be modernised and more emphasis will have to be placed on advertising. The home market will have to expand because, strangely enough, the southerner is not a heavy consumer of his own products, especially of fruit and vegetables.

Because of neglect, the water system of many centres was in a very bad condition. Figures concerning this problem make one wonder why Fascists spent so much money in creating an empire when capital might more usefully have been employed at home. To-day roughly 1,000 communities in southern Italy are without aqueducts, and water is supplied in the most primitive fashion. In some villages it has to be obtained from the public fountain, as there is no running-water system in private homes. Apulia, Campania, Sicily, Abruzzi, and Molise are the regions where the largest amounts are being spent and where aqueducts are being erected as speedily as possible. One hundred and fifty communities will benefit from that now under construction in Campania.

The conveying of water from spring to consumer will be accompanied by a widespread plan of road construction. Even this question had never been given proper attention, although probably few regions in Europe needed roads as badly as the

South. The fact that in ancient times certain localities were chosen for defence purposes may explain why building proper roads may to-day be a major difficulty. A Sicilian village of 2,500 inhabitants called Castel di Lucio has still no connecting roads other than a mule-track. This, of course, is an exceptional case, yet even other centres possess inadequate communications.

Highways that run along the coastlines have all been repaired since the war, and, although they need widening to cope with increasing traffic, they suffice for present-day needs. What is absolutely inadequate is the network of 'off-the-beaten-track' roads. For the improvement of these the Cassa del Mezzogiorno is allocating considerable sums.

All this will help to raise the standard of living. When travelling on a newly opened or recently macadamised road, one may sometimes wonder if the money spent on its construction has been wholly justified in view of the small amount of traffic which passes over it. We believe it has, because, apart from making travelling easier, improvement of communications contributes to the people's social welfare. Some thoroughfares now under construction are being built to attract tourists. This will be the case of the 'Highway of the Two Seas' in Calabria, which will link the Ionian with the Tyrrhenian Sea.

Roads and tourism go hand in hand. The Cassa has allocated 2·3 per cent of its funds to the improvement of accommodation, so that the natural beauties for which Italy is famed may attract more foreign visitors, and thus increase this already important source of revenue. Until now, apart from Naples and a few other places such as Capri, Sorrento, and Taormina, the South has been practically unexplored by tourism and is little known. It is up to the Cassa to develop other centres, equally outstanding for their beauty and historic interest, some of which have been known since earliest times.

Tourism will also benefit from better railways. A special agreement between the Cassa and the State Railways includes extensive improvement of several lines. One of the first works will be the doubling of tracks running along the Adriatic and Tyrrhenian coasts.

Plans to provide people with housing, education, and public buildings are outside the Cassa's jurisdiction. The housing problem is most urgent, because the homes of many southerners are not only inadequate, but destined to become more and more so as time passes and progress reaches the most isolated centres.

The lack of houses was already serious before World War II, and Fascism did little to remedy it. War devastation made the necessity of immediate action more urgent than ever. The average number of rooms available for every southerner was 0·62 in 1933 and this meant extensive overcrowding. Besides, this figure did not indicate the bad state of maintenance of several old buildings. The situation worsened during the war. If the problem is acute in countries like Canada and the Argentine, which were untouched by war, it was bound to be more serious in war-damaged Italy, where also the birthrate has been steadily increasing.

Although democratic governments have been concerned with this problem ever since the fall of Fascism, a complete solution does not appear imminent. The needs are, in fact, too great to be dealt with all at once.

As builders have found it profitable to concentrate on the erection of houses for the wealthier classes, who have the money to pay for them, most of the lodgings destined for the working class have been built with Government aid. This situation will probably change when private initiative has exploited to the full the higher-income market and is compelled to turn to the lower one. Private enterprise has also concentrated, sometimes with and sometimes without Government assistance, on the rebuilding of war-damaged properties. In Naples alone over 100,000 living rooms have been either completely rebuilt or repaired.

Unfair judgments on the housing problem have often been made. At times people, homeless owing to the war, have been compelled to live in places which normally would be considered unfit for human habitation. Even caves have been used as temporary dwellings. These have been visited by foreign journalists, who have taken them as proof that American aid is being misused and that reconstruction is practically non-existent. This is not true, even if the Government has not sufficiently publicised its efforts and achievements. Some of the worst cases have in fact already been remedied. The famous 'Sassi' (Stones) of Matera, in Basilicata, where people lived as cave-dwellers, have been sealed up and the inhabitants have been given rural and urban homes of their own. One housing scheme which has provided the South with many new homes is the Piano Fanfani (Fanfani Plan), so called from the name of the Minister of Labour who studied the way to finance it.

When the structural changes effected by the Cassa del Mezzogiorno and other specialised agencies are completed, conditions will exist for industrial development. Indications are already promising. In 1952 the Cassa was entrusted with the task of promoting and assisting the birth of enterprises. Once the wheels of industry start moving, progress is bound to follow in their wake. Recent experience has also shown that the legend of the southerners lack of initiative is greatly exaggerated, for they have proved themselves to be industrialists, executives, and skilled workers who can stand comparison with anybody.

It is therefore an encouraging symptom that many applications to build new industrial plants are coming from the South, and that they concern regions which are almost devoid of factories. Over 14 per cent of the total financing done by the Cassa is concentrated in the Basilicata region, which accounts for only 4 per cent of the population of the South and where plants up to now were practically non-existent. The Abruzzi and Molise also stand out clearly in the picture, as regions where progress is making way.

The South is undoubtedly taking its first steps in this field, but if present conditions remain and the Government's assistance continues, it will soon gain valuable ground. Skilled labour will be obtained sooner than expected, as the people's alertness will make up for lack of experience. Highly specialised goods are already being produced. Dietetic foods, motor-scooters, typewriters, radar equipment, electronic tubes, and farm implements are being made by workers who until a few years ago were completely unskilled. In this field the most important thing is to make a start. The rest will follow in a chain-like fashion.

As to the people's economic conditions, figures are now available to prove their upward trend. Until February 28, 1954, projects financed by the Cassa del Mezzogiorno (excluding land improvement and land-reform operations) had already required over 42 million working days, which obviously had provided employment to many workers. This has brought about an increase in the consumption of basic commodities. By comparing the figures of October, 1950—when the Cassa operations started—with those of June, 1953, the improvement in the average standard of living is apparent. In less than three years southern expenditure for meat has risen 452 per cent, for milk 235 per cent, for sugar 121 per cent, for clothing and fabrics 211 per cent, for linen and underwear 166 per cent, for soap 45 per cent, for fuel and power 135 per cent, and for medicines and doctors' services 70 per cent. In fact there have been signs of improvement in practically all fields. One may certainly conclude that people are living in better conditions than they were a few years ago.

Chapter 16

Italy's Future and Democracy

FUTURE historians will remember the present age as one of advancement towards political maturity. We have witnessed great events during our time, many of which prove that, after all, things are not as bad as pessimists would like to have us believe. The gradual disappearance of colonialism is, for instance, such an achievement that it is difficult to foresee that any other event will have such far-reaching consequences. It is often said that moral progress has not kept up with material or scientific development. We, on the contrary, believe that the spiritual conquests of our era compare favourably with those of the past and in some cases are even greater. As to Italy, we wish to emphasise again how recently she attained her unity and began to develop domestic and external policies of her own.

Democracy in the modern parliamentary form was imported into Italy. More than three centuries of political servitude had prevented the people from forming a liberal system of their own, although in different circumstances this would probably have taken place. The first communal liberties originated as far back as the eleventh century. Forty years before the granting of the Magna Charta, Italians were fighting at Legnano (1176) against the German emperor in a successful attempt to defend those liberties. The 'Garden of the Empire'—as Italy was called—would not have been the chosen battlefield for clashing European ambitions had unity been achieved at the same time as the national States of France and Spain were being formed. If this had been the case, her people would probably have developed their own autonomous liberal institutions. When, instead, under the impact of the French Revolution and of Napoleon's conquest, they felt the urge to unite, they took from Great Britain the idea of a representative government and from Montesquieu that of the division of powers. Since the dawn of the Risorgimento patriots had been asking—and it was a seditious request—to be granted a constitution resembling that of Spain, in which those two principles appeared to be embodied. Had they only looked back a little farther into their own history, they might have found in the communal statutes of the eleventh and twelfth centuries equally inspiring documents.

It made no difference, however, whence democratic and liberal institutions originated: the most important thing was that they should be consonant with the nation's temperament. Had it not been so, Italians would have found it most difficult to adapt themselves to a system which, although appealing to their sense of responsibility, was so different from the one previously experienced.

Less than a century has passed since the fulfilment of the ideals of the Risorgimento, and one cannot say that these years have been wasted. Certain principles which seemed so distant from the nation's character have been accepted, and unity has given Italians something which at times they had lacked: national pride. Until 1870 culture and economy had developed on a regional background of limited interests and means. Technique and science had evolved slowly, for knowledge and intelligence had been applied to theoretical matters which, although important, were likely to become futile issues in a world that was asking for practice rather than for theory. But unity had given the Italians a wider outlook and inclination to action. The strengthening of their international position and the newly acquired importance found a response in the minds of the people, creating in them the determination which goes towards the making of a great nation.

Democracy must be given credit for these achievements and for the building up of a national personality. Italians were regenerated by its practice and their future was planned in an atmosphere of alertness. This should be emphasised, as many critics, both at home and abroad, believe that everything done in the peninsula during the past ninety years was either obsolete or pernicious and that no attempt was ever made to keep up with the times.

Democracy has consolidated itself in the people's mind, becoming an essential part of their way of life. It is enough to attend a political meeting to realise that it is not an artificial matter but a genuine sentiment felt by all. Political discussions are vehement and ideologies are vigorously analysed before acceptance. A Latin love for abstractions and general principles makes discussions extremely interesting. It is amazing to see how in small villages, where the amenities of life are few, there is nevertheless a direct and constant participation in political debates. This is a proof of maturity, and denotes that democracy is a living factor. When the great issues of our time—materialism or idealism, capitalism or socialism, religion or atheism—succeed in interesting even the smallest communities, one may conclude that the nation is progressing, and there is no reason to despair of the future.

Democracy is so rooted in individual minds and so much a part of the nation that no party would achieve success were it to advocate the re-establishing of dictatorship. This is proved by the attitude of the extreme right and left, neither of which has any love for democracy and each of which would abolish all liberties were they in a position to do so. Yet they seldom make any statement revealing their true attitude or anti-democratic tendencies, but they continually emphasise their devotion to liberty. So great was the contrast between Fascism and the people's minds and hearts that to be called a 'Fascist' is still considered an insult. Noboby wishes to be linked to a regime the ideals of which were so foreign to those of the nation.

In spite of the so-called emotional nature of Italy's people, changes have taken place gradually. If one considers, for instance, how electoral suffrage and political rights were enlarged by degrees over a period of half a century, one cannot say that structural changes were sudden or abruptly enforced. They resulted from a careful and calculated study of the nation's necessities and aspirations.

The way of democracy was never easy in any country. In Great Britain it passed through the tragic tests of Cromwell's era, of the execution of Charles I, and of the Stuarts' expulsion. In France it caused much bloodshed with the great revolution and the trial of Louis XVI. In the United States it had to face the ordeal of civil war, when the nation's unity was on the verge of collapse. It is little wonder, therefore, that Italy was compelled to pass through a period of unrest. There was, however, much more stability in her political life than is generally admitted. Since the beginning of parliamentary government certain names have been constantly and conspicuously to the fore. After Cavour came Depretis, then Crispi, followed by Giolitti, whose last Cabinet, in 1921, was formed thirty years after his first. With the fall of Fascism, De Gasperi took over office, and was Premier for eight years, while since 1945 his

Christian Democratic Party has continuously carried the burden of leading the nation.

The democratic method evolved at a time when people had become aware of their national entity. The search for liberty was therefore accompanied by the movement for independence. We read to-day with emotion letters and articles wherein patriots expressed their certainty that only through the practice of liberty could the country overcome completely the evils besetting her. With the passing of time their love for abstract formulas faded away without impairing their genuine enthusiasm and idealistic approach. They remained firm believers in what was called 'the religion of liberty'.

Despite appearances, Italy is a tolerant country, especially in religious matters. Although Rome is the See of the Papacy and Catholicism is the official religion, other faiths are permitted and respected, and a man would never be persecuted on account of his beliefs. To this day missionaries of all religions, including the Jewish, are trying to make Italian converts. That their efforts are nearly always fruitless is beside the point. Their liberty to preach has been limited only by a few provisions of law, the equal of which are to be found in all countries. If one remembers that little more than a century ago the founder of the Mormon faith was murdered in the United States by a mob and that there are still in America forms of religious and racial discrimination—despite the fact that the first emigrants went there in search of religious freedom—one must conclude that Italy's general approach is, to-day as a century ago, one of acknowledgment of all rights and opinions and of freedom from bigotry.

Through the exaltation of liberty the Risorgimento provided the Italians with the philosophy and inspiration they needed. This is possibly the reason why Fascism has left so few traces. More than twenty years of propaganda should have at least influenced the opinions of a minority and should have left in many the memory and the desire for things and ideas which had been so widely propagated. Nothing of the kind happened. Comparisons between pre-Fascist elections and the latest ones have proved that the number of extreme nationalists has, if anything, diminished, remaining always the smaller portion of the country's electorate.

This short but stable tradition has resulted in the rise of an administrative class which, despite occasional faults, has proved itself reliable and shown its devotion to service. The forming of such a class in a new State is not an easy task, nor is it always successful. With the exception of Piedmont, where a tradition of service already existed, the other regions in general had nothing of the kind. For, indeed, servitude is not the best system under which intelligence and public abilities may reveal themselves. Yet when the nation was engaged in the fight for freedom new energies developed and later gave birth to an efficient Civil Service. Its members emerged chiefly from the legal profession.

The political class that formed Parliament has also provided the nation with leadership and service. It included industrialists in the North and farmers in the South, but it was chiefly made up of lawyers. After the birth of industry and the granting of universal suffrage, trade-union leaders became part of it. Devotion to duty among these people has been much stronger than is generally admitted. Political activity in Italy is no sinecure. Before voting for a candidate, electors must make sure that their ideas and interests will be protected. When a man is elected to Parliament his main activity is that of assisting and guiding his supporters. All actions of deputies or senators are carefully scrutinised. If something is not quite clear and doubts arise concerning their moral behaviour, a scandal may easily ensue. Political activity is, therefore, not easy, and keeps the people concerned in constant fear of the consequences which might arise from the most innocuous act. Vocation, enthusiasm, and ambition are qualities required in a man who wishes to undertake this perilous career. Despite these drawbacks, however, some of Italy's best men have sacrificed to their country's political life much time and energy, which they might have employed in more lucrative activities.

Similar to that of politicians is the position of industrialists, constantly accused of being incapable of handling their country's economy and of being miserly and brutal towards workers, without any understanding that higher wages would increase production and be more profitable all round. Although some factory owners may, of course, justify this conception, generally speaking they comply with their obligations and try to combine the needs of their businesses with a better standard of living for their workers. Yet Communists and other such extremists are constantly complaining of the harshness of management. These grievances are voiced by the foreign Press, and create the opinion abroad that the industrialist is a monster who prospers on the sweat and blood of his labourers.

What explanation can be given for the Italians' strong inclination towards self-criticism? First, there is on their part a certain amount of natural iconoclasm, so that they instinctively challenge cherished beliefs. The average citizen does not automatically accept acknowledged values. This is a useful approach so long as it does not prevent people who are in charge of the nation's future from carrying out their responsibilities.

There are other factors behind this mental attitude. Italians tend to be reformers or, at least, to appear as such. Idealism is often the chief inspirer of their actions. There is a widespread opinion that dishonesty is bound to be present wherever money matters are concerned. Against such a background does political life revolve. The soundness of the Italians' attitude may be questioned and it may at times give unsatisfactory results, but no one can argue against its moral merits. In countries where less importance is attached to ideas and principles, the leading activities of Government are left in the hands of competent administrators, without much regard to their ideological background. In Italy and France, on the other hand, questions of principle have priority over all others.

Another characteristic of the Italians is their extreme interest in legal problems, the origin of which goes back to ancient times. It is enough to remember how much the nation contributed to the forming of Roman and Canon Law to understand why juridical matters have so much influence over the people's minds.

In Italy the legal profession is one of the most difficult, for clients usually consider their version of the case so important that they seldom, if ever, accept the lawyer's view of the question at once. The fact that many people have a certain knowledge of juridical matters can often prove very trying, and may account for so much preliminary work being done between lawyer and client before the case comes before the judge. This attitude of mind can partly be blamed on the Latin mentality. The nation's legal system is founded on the precision of its rules, which the judge has only to interpret and enforce. A dividing line exists between legislator and magistrate, and the system is complete in the sense that through analogy it is always possible to determine the provision governing a given case. Full evidence of the Italian's observance of juridical forms was provided in

1946 with the changing of regime. Seldom has the passing from a monarchy to a republic taken place in a more legal manner and with such respect for the people's choice.

We have endeavoured to stress that the nation's history during the past 150 years has been a conflict constantly fought in the interest of democratic principles. Fascism was a parenthesis and, although it took twenty years of political servitude, a lost war, and a civil conflict to destroy it, it is no longer a danger. If danger exists at present, it comes from Communists and their Socialist allies. There is, indeed, a widespread fear that these two forces may combine to gain power and give birth to a new form of dictatorship, more brutal and dangerous than the previous one. The United States, which has done its best to give military, economic, and diplomatic assistance to Italy, is afraid of this possibility, and so are Catholics all over the world, who see in such an event one of the greatest evils which could befall Christianity.

Strange as it may seem, many of those who vote for the extreme left would view with concern the advent of a Communist regime. People who basically have nothing in common with this idea vote for its candidates simply because they see in it the Government's most formidable adversary and because Marxist proselytism skilfully presents its programme to suit all voters. The best example of this is provided by the deceptive methods used among peasants who are promised the ownership of the land. An absurd promise, if only one considers recent events in Communist-governed countries.

The rural South, recently brought into contact with modern and industrial techniques and undergoing new experiences, may be more attracted to Communist propaganda, especially as it is active and well organised. But despite these and other facts, it is improbable that the Communists and their allies will ever rally sufficient support to attain power.

A distinction must be made between Communists and fellow-travelling Socialists, two parties that are considered one and the same, especially abroad. This is not the case, for left-wing Socialism is independent of foreign influence and must take into account the wishes and freely expressed opinions of its members. Communists, on the other hand, are linked to a strict discipline and must silently comply with orders. Under such conditions it is by no means certain that the alliance between the two movements will last indefinitely. At times there are indications of serious unrest among Socialists and of their desire to abandon their powerful and better-organised companions. On two occasions groups of leading Socialists have abandoned the party, giving birth to the Social Democratic movement.

Until a short while ago there was a tendency to consider Italy a second-class nation, only needing assistance and incapable of following a truly independent policy. This was partly caused by the attitude of several Italians who believed there was no future for their country and that the state of political bondage, economic crisis, and international inactivity caused by defeat would last indefinitely. The picture has now changed. The first years immediately following the war coincide with the nation's tentative efforts to advance from the condition in which the conflict had left her. From the signing of the Peace Treaty down to the present day her constant aim has been to regain lost ground. This inferiority complex has disappeared and she now enjoys a moral initiative and autonomy which a short time ago would have been unbelievable. The last few years should be a reminder that a nation's history continues in spite of military defeat, and that new realities, rather than ancient feuds, should be the gauge by which her vitality is measured. The situation caused by the cold war calls for co-operation among democratic countries. Italy now holds a very vital position in western defence, and this has brought about full recognition of her importance. In spite of all that has been said or written, defeat has in no way meant an irrevocable censure. The condemnation contained in the preamble of the Peace Treaty has already been cancelled because it was recognised as unjust.

The Italians' tone and approach are those of men and women who have gained experience through sorrow and suffering—an experience which has made them sensitive towards the opinions of others, but which has given them more confidence, together with an added awareness of their rights and duties. These qualities may only increase with the coming years, and Italy's friends and allies will have to acknowledge them. This will benefit everybody concerned and advance the cause to which Italians are to-day committed.

In the decade since World War II many serious issues have troubled the nation. First there was the problem of physical survival, of establishing a democratic system, of bringing an official end to the war, of achieving complete freedom of action and of re-establishing the country's administration. Despite all this, the people were fully aware of the part they would play in future world affairs. If ideological discussions seemed at times more important and urgent, if tempestuous arguments took place in Parliament, in the country, and in the Press, external issues were always kept in view. The Marshall Plan, the Atlantic Pact, the contribution to European integration go to prove this. Italy's statesmen have ably taken advantage of circumstances as they have skilfully handled national affairs. While Fascist diplomacy only succeeded in playing a dangerous game which ended in tragedy, democracy has proved itself able and efficient, successfully rebuilding a network of friendships and alliances. This was accomplished through complete fidelity to moral commitments and a constant effort to obtain a greater esteem among the nations. It is not without satisfaction that we read the speeches delivered in recent times by men like De Gasperi and Sforza, and we stop to consider how they placed moral values above everything else, trying to break foreign resistance by making a strong appeal to the moral, not the material issues of our times.

Democracy is not the old and inefficient regime its enemies from left and right would have us believe. It approaches problems with determination. Some examples may prove this. Illiteracy has always been one of Italy's gravest drawbacks, and much is now being done to facilitate education where it is most needed. Emphasis is being placed on the necessity of a good family atmosphere, which is the first condition for proper schooling. In this battle democracy is being invaluably assisted by technical progress. Radio, for instance, has to-day entered many homes and is helping to break down the wall of ignorance.

Yet we believe that the spread of culture and economic recovery will be effective only if they are accompanied by the disappearance of social differences among classes and individuals. Even this is becoming a reality. In the North equality has permeated all social strata; men and women are judged mainly by their stability and intelligence, for birth and family influence are of little avail. In the South this evolution has not yet been completed. There is still, what we might call, a 'feudal crust'. In certain southern villages the local squire is entitled by tradition to a formal respect, which gives him a social superiority over other mortals. Even here the situation is changing. Better housing, improved medical care, better food and, above all, the development of industry and agrarian reform are bringing about significant social changes. People who have lived for centuries under the weight of ancient habits are at last awakening. The Government's efforts favouring technical education for the peasantry have also been met with success.

Making prophecies is a difficult and ungratifying task, and we shall accordingly abstain from making them. The picture we have tried to present has nonetheless been inspired by optimism—striking as this may seem at a time when facts concerning Italy are often presented in a negative manner. This seems to us fully justified by the people's moderate approach, by their sense of judgment, and by the self-confidence which is inspiring their actions. They understand that their mission is to create a new place to live in and to carry on their moral and material rebirth. They appreciate fair criticism but resent biased opinions. These, we believe, are excellent symptoms.

On the other hand, Italians are also aware that they are being administered by a superior form of government, the only one capable of guaranteeing social progress and economic prosperity in an atmosphere of individual liberty. They also understand that democratic contrasts of ideas are not a waste of energy, as the followers of the totalitarian myth would have us believe, but a fertile soil in which new programmes may flourish and ancient aspirations materialise. All this justifies our optimistic approach.

Index

THIS BOOK IS SET
IN ELEVEN POINT BASKERVILLE TYPE
AND PRINTED IN GREAT BRITAIN BY
RICHARD CLAY & COMPANY LIMITED
AT THE CHAUCER PRESS
BUNGAY · SUFFOLK